European Currency Crises and After
Christian Bordes
Eric Girardin
Jacques Mélitz   *editors*

The speculative crises of 1992-93, which shook the EMS during Europe's worst postwar recession, left in their wake a series of important questions about the monetary future of Europe, exchange rate behaviour and exchange rate policy.

The book looks at recent theoretical models of exchange rate target zones, exchange rate crises, and central bank credibility. It also examines the empirical evidence on misalignment, the efficiency of central bank intervention by the G3, measures of exchange rate risk under wide official bands, the exchange rate crises in 1992-93 and central bank behaviour in the EMS.

The book will be of interest to lecturers in and students of international finance, international monetary economics and monetary policy.

Christian Bordes and Eric Girardin are at University Bordeaux I - LARE, and Jacques Mélitz at INSEE and CEPR. Contributors include Michael Artis (European University Institute and CEPR); Renzo Avesani (University of Brescia); Juan Ayuso (Bank of Spain); Lorenzo Bini-Smaghi (European Monetary Institute); Paul De Grauwe (Catholic University of Leuven and CEPR); Giampiero M. Gallo (University of Florence); André Icard (Bank of France); Paul Masson (International Monetary Fund); Marcus Miller (University of Warwick and CEPR); Maria Pérez-Jurado (Bank of Spain); Fernando Restoy (Bank of Spain); Mark Salmon (European University Institute and CEPR); Alan Sutherland (University of York and CEPR); Mark Taylor (University of Liverpool and CEPR); Oreste Tristani (Bank of Italy); Axel Weber (University of Bonn and CEPR); and Lei Zang (University of Warwick).

European Currency
Crises and After

Christian Bordes, Eric Girardin
and Jacques Mélitz   *editors*

Manchester University Press
Manchester and New York

Distributed exclusively in the USA and Canada by St. Martin's Press

Copyright © Manchester University Press 1995

While copyright in the volume as a whole is vested in Manchester University Press, copyright in individual chapters belongs to their respective authors, and no chapter may be reproduced wholly or in part without the express permission in writing of both author and publisher.

Published by Manchester University Press
Oxford Road, Manchester M13 9NR, UK
and Room 400, 175 Fifth Avenue,
New York, NY 10010, USA

Distributed exclusively in the USA and Canada
by St. Martin's Press Inc.,
175 Fifth Avenue, New York, NY 10010, USA

British Library Cataloguing-in-Publication Data
A catalogue record for this book is available from the British Library

Library of Congress Cataloging-in-Publication Data applied for

ISBN 0 7190 4706 4 *hardback*
ISBN 0 7190 4707 2 *paperback*

First published in 1995

99 98 97 96 95   10 9 8 7 6 5 4 3 2 1

Printed in Great Britain
by Biddles Ltd, Guildford and King's Lynn

Contents

List of figures

List of tables

Contributors

Michael Artis	European University Institute and CEPR
Renzo Avesani	University of Brescia
Juan Ayuso	Bank of Spain
Agnès Bénassy	University of Cergy-Pontoise
Lorenzo Bini-Smaghi	European Monetary Institute
Christian Bordes	University Bordeaux I - LARE
Benoît Cœuré	INSEE
Paul De Grauwe	Catholic University of Leuven and CEPR
Giampiero M. Gallo	University of Florence
Eric Girardin	University Bordeaux I - LARE
André Icard	Bank of France
Jean-Pierre Laffargue	University Paris I and CEPREMAP
Daniel Laskar	CEPREMAP
Paul Masson	International Monetary Fund
Jacques Mélitz	INSEE and CEPR
Marcus Miller	University of Warwick and CEPR
Jean-Sébastien Pentecôte	University Bordeaux I - LARE
Maria Pérez-Jurado	Bank of Spain
Jean Pisani-Ferry	CEPII
Fernando Restoy	Bank of Spain
Mark Salmon	European University Institute and CEPR
Marc-Alexandre Sénégas	University Bordeaux I - LARE
Alan Sutherland	University of York and CEPR
Mark Taylor	University of Liverpool and CEPR
Oreste Tristani	Bank of Italy
Axel Weber	University of Bonn and CEPR
Lei Zang	University of Warwick

Preface

This book is the outcome of a conference held in July 1994 at the University Bordeaux I, one year after the last stage of the speculative attacks which led to the abandonment of the narrow-margin ERM.

The conference was organized by the Laboratoire d'Analyse et de Recherche Economique (LARE), a research center in international economics and finance attached to the Centre National de la Recherche Scientifique.

We would like to thank the Commissariat Général du Plan, the Ministère de l'Enseignement Supérieur et de la Recherche and the University Bordeaux I for providing financial support for this conference.

The editors
December 1994

1 *Christian Bordes, Eric Girardin & Jacques Mélitz*

Introduction

The speculative crises which shook the European Monetary System (EMS) in 1992 led to the exit of the United Kingdom and Italy from the exchange rate mechanism. Thereafter, various efforts to explain events took place. But more trouble was still to come. A speculative attack of greater fury than any of the preceding occurred at the end of July 1993. On this occasion, the margins were widened from 2.25 to 15 percent. Now, a year later, the EMS seems to have entered a calmer phase. Exchange rates in the system are back approximately to where they were prior to the most recent speculative attack. Exchange markets are quiet. The recession of 1991-93 is also over while a vigorous recovery has entered. Perhaps the time has come to attempt a new assessment.

In order to understand the recent troubles of the EMS, we must clearly go back at least to German unification in 1990. As a result of the huge increase in public spending that took place in the country as a whole, a large current account surplus turned into a deficit and inflation rose. Under the pressure of booming demand, German monetary policy relaxed only moderately, and domestic interest rates rose as well. The country requested an appreciation of the mark in the EMS and was refused by the other members. When the Bundesbank subsequently moved toward increasingly tight monetary policy, the others in the EMS continued to follow the mark. They did so despite the onset of the most severe recession that Europe had experienced since the Second World War. Paul De Grauwe records in clear and very telling terms the full extent of the tightness of monetary policy that resulted in the rest of the EMS from 1991 to 1993. As he explains, the very expansion of economic activity in

Germany at a time when the rest of the EMS slid into a recession (which eventually caught up with Germany) translated into tighter monetary policy for the rest than for Germany itself.

The next chapter, by Lorenzo Bini Smaghi and Oreste Tristani, raises an important and intriguing question: How large an output and employment loss in the EMS can be attributed to the speculative crises of 1992 and 1993? The focus of these authors is on the three EMS members which kept the central parity of their currency constant relative to the mark throughout the period: Belgium, France, and the Netherlands. As Bini Smaghi and Tristani observe, an astronaut who had returned to earth in 1994 after a three-year voyage would not have guessed that the currencies of any of these three countries had been subject to pressure in his absence. He would have found their prices the same relative to the mark than when he had begun his journey and the short term interest rates in all three countries to be standing in about the same relationship to German interest rates as when he left. Therefore, the problem of the impact of the speculative attacks appears in a particularly clear light in the case of these three countries: with policy unaltered, we can focus better on the disturbances resulting from the speculative flurries themselves, or what would have happened had there been no increase in interest rate differentials in the intervening time. Interestingly enough, the authors' econometric simulations make clear that the shortfall in output and employment in all three countries - but principally Belgium and France[1] - is not yet over but will continue over the next few years.

The speculative attacks themselves call for explanation. We know that fixed exchange rates generally offer speculators one-way bets, since markets can always be sure that the movements of some of the pegged exchange rates will be in one particular direction. As regards the EMS, speculators never needed have worried about the possibility of a devaluation of the mark. This alone will explain speculation on a continuous basis but not a speculative attack. Why do concentrated sales of some currencies take place on specific dates? We have two sorts of explanations, one of which depends on inconsistent monetary policy and the other on speculators' perception of a profit opportunity. According to the former explanation, the market sees that the authorities will eventually shift the exchange rate independently of speculative action. In the usual formulation, the authorities would run out of reserves. The speculators then pick an optimal date (on the basis of profits, and in view of officials' reserves) which merely hastens the arrival of an inevitable outcome.

According to the latter sort of explanation, everything would have stayed fine if only the speculators had not attacked. However, they do in the knowledge that their action will induce the authorities to depreciate and will earn them profits. In this case, the speculators' behavior as such makes the present parity too costly to defend.

Alan Sutherland has shown us in earlier writings with Gulcin Ozcan (1994a, b) how to avoid one embarrassing implication of the former explanation - the one which rests the blame on the authorities : namely, its exclusive reliance on reserves. We know reserves not to have been the principal issue in many cases in the EMS. On a formal plane, reserves may always be possible to borrow in a cooperative arrangement since they consist of liabilities of other central banks. Ozcan and Sutherland have developed models where a speculative attack comes about as a result of inconsistent monetary policy, apart from any lack of reserves : for example, because of an official concern with unemployment. The official welfare function always plays a capital role in these models. The inconsistency in the policy-maker's position must be explained on the basis of an unforeseeable shock since his last announcement of a particular parity. In this volume, Sutherland takes a wide look at the whole variety of ways to model either of the usual sorts of speculative attacks in a stochastic environment with an official welfare function. Except as a special case, never do the attacks require a drop in reserves to any minimum.

When the bands were widened to 15 percent around the central parity in August 1993, many observers declared the EMS to be dead. The survival of the system had become a mere pretense and flexible exchange rates had arrived. Subsequent events contradict these early verdicts. The monetary authorities in the EMS have exploited little of the wider bands. Indeed the exchange rates in the system have progressively moved back into the old bands. Thus, the true bands are now implicit, and the system operates like a target zone which requires markets to infer the width of the bands. Alternatively, the system can now be likened to the Williamson proposal of target zones with "soft buffers", the "soft buffers" referring to the fact that the authorities may go outside the limits whenever the market pushes exchange rates to those limits. Standard arguments exist for and against implicit bands as opposed to official ones. The implicit variety have the advantage of giving the authorities more latitude and the market less of a target to shoot at. On the other hand, implicit bands also offer the authorities fewer benefits of stabilizing speculation. When declared bands are highly credible, private speculators enter the market in support of the bands whenever the exchange rate nears the edges. (This advantage of explicit bands is known as the "honeymoon effect" in the target zone literature).

The tension between the two preceding views is nicely reflected in this volume in the contributions of Marcus Miller and Lei Zhang, on the one side, and Renzo Avesani, Giampiero Gallo and Mark Salmon, on the other. Miller and Zhang show why declaring bands rather than letting markets guess them can yield benefits. Moreover, these two authors handle a tricky problem that has evaded most of the target zone literature : the optimal size bands. Avesani, Gallo and Salmon, by contrast, argue for implicit bands. They treat credibility as a variable. This makes an important difference. When credibility drops, it may be optimal to widen the bands in order to avoid destabilizing speculation or a speculative attack. The issue of credibility is clearly central. These two chapters, together, provide a basic key to the latent issue, which could burst out into the open at any time, whether the EMS should return to narrow bands or stick to the current wide ones.

The dismal record of the EMS in 1992-93, as described by De Grauwe and discussed in these comments, raised a lot of other questions about credibility besides that of the width of the bands. Did the various members of the EMS which resisted the depreciation of their currencies really enhance their credibility? Evidently, some of their decisions to raise interest rates during the 1991-93 recession failed to convince the markets that monetary policy would stay unchanged. Indeed, we know from general principles that a central bank with a strong anti-inflationary reputation may lower its short-term interest rates in the face of a very adverse demand shock without damaging its credibility, whereas another one with a weaker reputation may not be able to do the same. A decision to fight inflation during a recession could thus be interpreted as a sign of a frail reputation. Allan Drazen and Paul Masson (1993) have recently produced a model which captures this argument and rigorously shows that tight monetary policy under adverse circumstances can also damage the credibility of the central bank. Their essay additionally provides an empirical test of the possible adverse influence of tight monetary policy on credibility.[2] In his contribution to this volume, Masson applies the test to the United Kingdom during the critical period of the country's membership in the EMS between October 1990 and September 1992. He finds, strikingly, that while entry in the EMS raised the United Kingdom's credibility at first, the adverse effect of its tight monetary policy became increasingly felt once the recession set in.

The EMS experience of recent years also raises questions about the measure of exchange risk. We often measure this risk on the basis of the observed volatility of exchange rates. But such a measure must be flawed in the case of a fixed exchange rate system with narrow bands, since any application of the measure in between realignments will necessarily yield the conclusion of low exchange risk, while the interest rate may clearly signal that the market expects a realignment. The probability and size of the expected realignment should be taken into account in measuring exchange risk. Juan Ayuso, Maria Pérez-Jurado and Fernando Restoy tackle this problem and resolve it neatly. Having done so, they show that following the widening of the bands in the EMS in 1993, the exchange risk on the Spanish peseta (whose total band in both directions grew from 12 to 30 percent) diminished. Therefore, we learn from them that exchange risk, as properly measured, may have fallen in the EMS since adoption of the wider bands.

The next chapter in the book, by Michael Artis and Mark Taylor, concerns the possible role of misalignment in currency crises. The issue of misalignment was clearly present recently in the EMS. German unification created some disequilibria in the system with short run manifestations. Quite independently, the Italian lira was plainly overvalued at the time of the speculative attacks of 1992. Even though the likelihood of misalignment may now have receded since the exchange rate adjustments of the last couple of years and the widening of the margins in the system, we still cannot exclude the problem for the foreseeable future. The issue that Artis and Taylor examine is one that we generally recognize in theory but typically neglect in practice: the impact of trade adjustment on the real equilibrium exchange rate and therefore misalignment. Theoretically, the real equilibrium exchange rate will change in the course of adjustment because of movements in the accumulated foreign debt, as these movements affect the permanent cost of servicing the debt (in the steady state). Artis and Taylor study this endogenous evolution in the real equilibrium exchange rate. One important result of their effort is to show that we should probably worry about the impact of adjustment on the real equilibrium exchange rate in instances of prolonged misalignment in one direction, such as that of the overvalued dollar in the middle of the eighties.

The chapter by Axel Weber concerns the matter of sterilization. Exchange rate agreements lead to foreign exchange interventions in some situations. These interventions, in turn, may affect the domestic money supply and will do so unless sterilized (or offset through strictly domestic operations). Past efforts to assess the extent of sterilization have neglected the fact that the changes in exchange rates that are associated with movements in reserves could either result from exchange intervention or themselves be the source of the interventions. Thus, simultaneous-equation methods of estimation are required. Based on such methods (and much more sophisticated techniques than classical two-stage least-squares), Weber confirms the earlier findings that foreign exchange interventions tend to be sterilized and that sterilized interventions are ineffective in the long run. He studies interventions in the EMS as well as by the G3 since the Louvre accords of 1985. It follows that little can be expected from sterilized interventions in the EMS. Whenever significant market pressures occur, interest rate differentials must be adjusted in order to lean againt the wind in an effective way.

Students of exchange rate management and speculation obviously have much to learn from central bankers. In the last chapter, André Icard of the Banque de France provides readers the views of the French monetary authorities on a good many of the issues that are covered in this book. Icard regards the recent calm in foreign exchange markets as testimony to the market's recognition of the tenability of the current exchange rates in the EMS. The widening of the bands is itself a significant disincentive to speculation, since the operators must now weigh some additional risk in case they take large, uncovered positions. Contrary to some interpretations of the recent speculative attacks as self-fullfilling prophecies, the monetary authorities did not relax their stance after August 1993. Exchange rate volatility went down following the switch to wider bands. Progress has also been made recently toward the convergence of inflation rates. Thus, the current arrangements in the EMS seem to be robust enough. The achievement of a single money remains more a matter of political will than practical feasibility.

Notes

[1] The authors consider reciprocal influences on Germany as well.

[2] It may be noted that Avesani, Gallo and Salmon apply a different measure of credibility than Drazen and Masson's (though the two measures are perfectly consistent).

References

Drazen, A. and P. Masson (1993), "Credibility of Policies versus Credibility of Policymakers," *NBER Working Paper*, N° 4448, September.

Ozcan, G. and A. Sutherland (1944a), "A Currency Crisis Model with an Optimising Policy-Maker," mimeo., University of York.

Ozcan G. and A. Sutherland (1944b), "Policy Measures to Avoid a Currency Crisis," mimeo., University of York, forthcoming in the *Economic Journal*.

8 – 25

Monetary policies in the EMS during the 1990s.[1]

EU

E52

F33

F36

1 Introduction

During 1991-94, continental Europe experienced its worst recession of the post-war period. In 1993, when the recession reached its low point, output declined by 1 to 2 percent in almost all countries of the European Union.

In this paper we concentrate our attention on the monetary policies that were conducted in Europe during this recession. We first describe the nature of these policies (section 2). This will naturally lead to the issue of whether the stance of monetary policies in the European countries was the appropriate one (section 3). Finally, we analyze the role the EMS has played in determining the monetary policy stance in Europe (section 4).

2 The stance of monetary policy in the EMS during the recession: a descriptive analysis

Measuring the stance of monetary policy is not an easy task. Several indicators can be used. Quite often these indicators give an unclear, and even conflicting, view of the nature of the monetary policies. Here we use three alternative indicators:

(a) the real short term interest rate,
(b) the real growth rate of the money stock (M1),
(c) the difference between the short-term and the long-term interest rate.

The indicators (a) and (b) are widely used and do not need much introduction. Indicator (c) has only recently been recognized as providing useful information on the stance of monetary policies. In particular, the difference between the short and the long rates can give information on the degree of tightness of monetary policies. When the monetary authorities follow restrictive monetary policies this will tend to show up in a positive differential. It should be stressed, however, that according to the expectations theory of the term structure, this differential is also influenced by the expected future interest rate. It is, therefore, important that this indicator is interpreted in conjunction with the other ones.

In order to describe the stance of monetary policies in the EMS we have constructed weighted averages (GDP-weights) of national indicators. We then systematically compare these EMS-indicators with the average growth rates of GDP in the EMS. The results are shown in figures 2.1 to 2.3.

The most striking feature of figures 2.1 to 2.3 is that all three indicators point in the same direction of monetary tightness in the EMS during the recession of 1991-93. From figure 2.1 we note that the real short-term interest rate reached its highest level since 1979 precisely during the worst recession of that period. From figure 2.2 we observe that the real growth rate of M1 became negative during the recession of 1991-93 (as it also did during the recession of 1980-82). Finally, during 1991-93 the differential between the short and long term interest rates remained positive all the time. This is the longest consecutive period of positive differential since the inception of the EMS.

The figures 2.1 to 2.3 also highlight some differences in the conduct of monetary policy during the recessions of 1991-93 and of 1980-82. In the latter case we find conflicting signals from the three indicators. The money growth figures seem to indicate that considerable monetary tightness was exerted at that time. The other two indicators, however, suggest that monetary policy was not particularly tight in the EMS. This contrasts with the more recent experience where the three indicators all point towards considerable monetary tightness.

It is also useful to compare the experience of the EMS with that of the US during the same period. We, therefore, constructed the same indicators for the US and present them in figures 2.4 to 2.6. The contrast with the EMS is strong. At the start of the US recession in 1989-90, which occurred two years before the EMS-recession, the real short term interest rate and the differential between the short and the long term

interest rates started a steep decline, whereas the real growth rate of the
money stock started to increase significantly. All this point to a US policy
of considerable monetary ease.

The comparison between the EMS and the US is interesting for
another reason. It appears that the conduct of monetary policies in the
EMS during the 1991-93 recession was very much comparable to the US
monetary policies during the worst US recession of the postwar period, in
1980-82. During that period the real short-term US interest rate and the
interest differential reached record high levels, whereas the growth rate of
the US money stock was strongly negative. We observe precisely the
same phenomena in the EMS during 1991-93.

Figure 2.1: Real short-term interest rates and growth rate of GDP in the
EMS-countries.

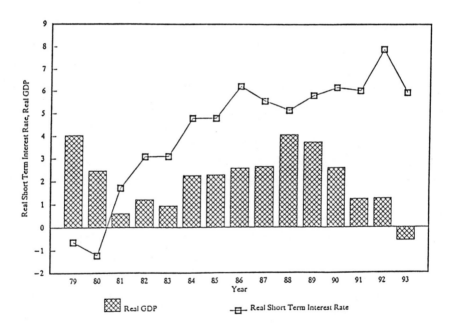

Source: IMF, International Financial Statistics.

Figure 2.2: Growth rate of M1 and real growth of GDP in EMS-countries.

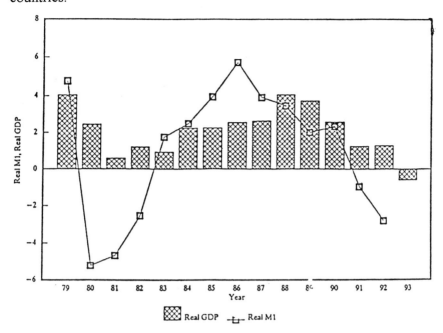

Source: IMF, International Financial Statistics.

Figure 2.3: Real GDP and difference of short and long term interest rates.

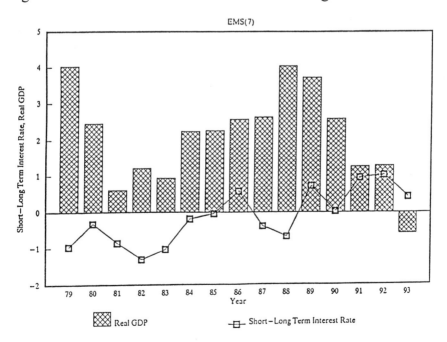

Source: IMF, International Financial Statistics.

It is now generally recognized that the Fed's monetary policies in the early 1980s contributed to the severity of the US recession of 1980-82. It is also well known that the reason why the US Federal Reserve engaged in this policy of monetary tightness was to reduce inflation which in 1980 reached 13.5%. (As will be argued later, the monetary tightness in the EMS was similarly motivated by a desire of one country, Germany, to reduce its inflation rate which in 1992 had reached 4% ...).

The descriptive nature of the monetary indicators presented in this section does not yet allow us to make a definitive judgment about the stance of monetary policy and about its appropriateness. In order to do so, the actual values of the indicators must be compared against the hypothetical values given some policy objective pursued by the monetary authorities. We perform such an exercise in policy evaluation in the next section.

Figure 2.4: Real short term interest rate and real GDP.

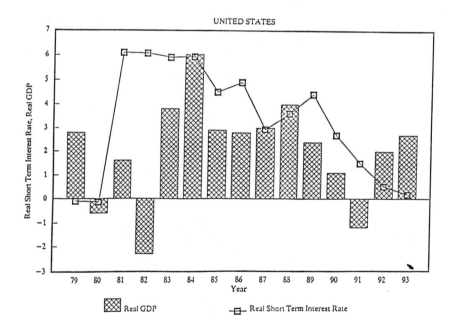

Figure 2.5: Real M1 and real GDP.

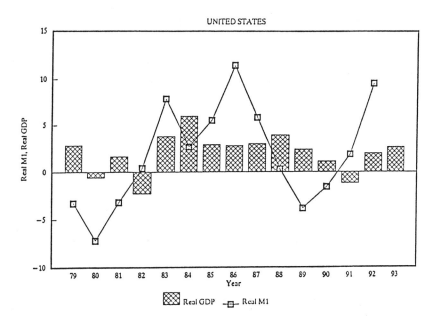

Figure 2.6: Real GDP and difference of short and long term interest rates.

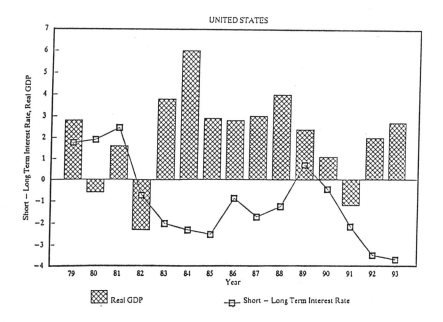

3 The stance of monetary policy in the EMS during the recession: an evaluation

In order to evaluate the monetary policy stance we propose the following simple procedure. We compare the observed growth rates of M1 of the EMS countries with a constant money growth rate. Thus we ask the question of how much the actual money growth rates have diverged from the hypothetical money growth rate if the European authorities had followed a (Friedman-type) constant money growth policy. We set this constant money growth rate at 5%, assuming that the long term growth rate of real GDP is 3% and the inflation target is 2%.[2] We do this exercise for Germany and for the rest of the EMS separately. The results are shown in figures 2.7 and 2.8. The sample period only extends to 1992 (there were insufficient data to do the calculation for 1993).

We observe the following. First, the German monetary authorities, who are known to follow explicit money targeting policies, were not really very successful in stabilizing the growth rate of M1. The overshooting during 1990 and 1991 is especially noteworthy. This overshooting certainly is related to the problems of monetary control encountered during the process of German monetary unification. Second, when analyzing the EMS data, one finds that during the first half of the 1980s the money growth figures in the EMS outside Germany were consistently above the constant money growth norm. Put differently monetary policies during that period were too expansionary compared to a (hypothetical) policy objective aiming at stabilizing nominal GDP growth at 5%. From 1986 to 1990, however, actual money growth came much closer to this constant growth norm. Finally, in 1991-92 when the European recession started, the observed money growth in the EMS declined below the constant growth norm. In 1992, this decline was substantial, i.e. close to -5%. Put differently, if the EMS-authorities had followed a Friedman type rule, aimed at a 3% real growth rate and 2% inflation rate they should have expanded the money stock in 1992 by 5% more than they actually did. The EMS mechanism, however, forced them to follow a monetary policy which was much too restrictive measured against the Friedman rule. In this sense it can be said that the ERM led the EMS-countries to follow excessively deflationary monetary policies.

Why did the EMS countries pursue such deflationary monetary policies during the worst recession of the postwar period? The answer must be found in the way the EMS functioned during the 1990s.

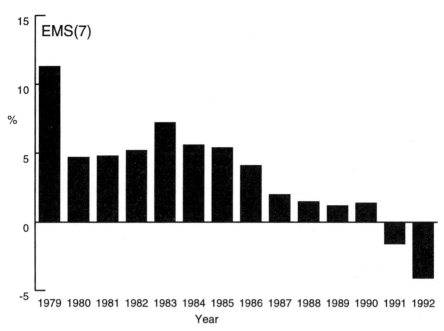

Figure 2.7: Nominal M1 growth: deviation from 5% growth benchmark

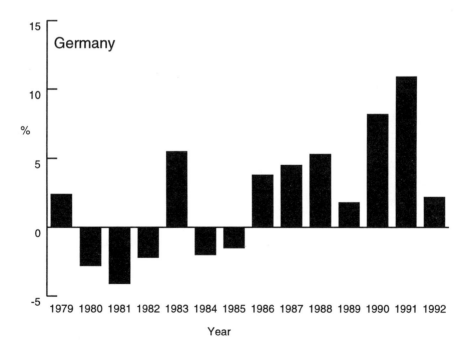

Figure 2.8: Nominal M1 growth: deviation from 5% growth benchmark

4 The EMS during the 1990s

At the end of the 1980s it became the ambition of the major EMS countries to move to a truly fixed exchange rate system. This changed the essence of the EMS which up to that time had been a system with the limited ambition of providing an organizational structure for changing exchange rates in an orderly fashion.

This movement towards a rigidly fixed exchange rate regime also revealed the basic flaws of the system. As is well-known, every fixed exchange rate regime must find some collective decision process that will determine how the system-wide monetary policy is conducted. Typically, this problem has been solved by delegating this job to one country. In the EMS this has been Germany. As a result, the money supply process evolved into an asymmetric system.[3]

One can analyze such an asymmetric money supply process in the context of a simple two-country model of the money markets.[4] The model can be described as follows.

The money demand equation in country A is specified as follows:

$$M_D^A = P_A + aY_A - br_A$$

where P_A is the price level in country A, Y_A is the output level in country A, and r_A is the interest rate in country A.

Money market equilibrium is obtained when demand equals supply:

(1) $M_S^A = P_A + aY_A - br_A$

For country B we have a similar money market equilibrium condition, i.e.

(2) $M_S^B = P_B + aY_B - br_B$

For the sake of simplicity we assume identical money demand equations in both countries.

Adding the assumption of perfect capital market integration in the two countries allows us to use the interest parity condition, which we specify as follows :

(3) $r_B = r_A + \mu$

where μ is the expected rate of depreciation of the currency of country B. Note that we assume that there are no risk premia.

Now suppose countries A and B decide to fix their exchange rate. Let us also assume that economic agents do not expect that the exchange rate will be adjusted in the future. This means that $\mu = 0$. The interest rates in the two countries will be identical.

We can now represent the equilibrium of this system graphically as follows (see figure 2.9). The downward sloping curve is the money demand curve. The money supply is represented by the vertical lines MA_1 and MB_1. Money market equilibrium in both countries is obtained where demand and supply intersect (points E and F). In addition, given the interest parity condition, the interest rates must be equal.

It is clear from figure 2.9 that there are infinitely many combinations of such points that bring about equilibrium in this system. We show two such equilibria each corresponding to a differ$\llcorner$it level of the interest rate. One can say that the fixed exchange rate arrangement is compatible with any possible *level* of the interest rates and of the money stocks. There is a fundamental indeterminacy in this system.

This indeterminacy can be solved by allowing one country to take a leadership role. Suppose, for example, that country A is the leader and that it fixes its money stock independently, say at the level M_1^A (see Fig. 2.9). This then fixes the interest rate in country A, at the level r_1. Country B now has no choice any more. Its interest rate will have to be the same as in country A. Given the money demand in country B, this then uniquely determines the money supply in country B that will be needed to have equilibrium. Country B has to accept this money supply. Its money stock is determined endogenously in this system. Country B cannot follow an independent monetary policy.

We now analyze the effects of disturbances in output on the money supply process in this asymmetric system. We therefore solve the model for exogenous changes in Y_A and Y_B. We also assume that country A fixes its money stock. The asymmetric nature of the system allows us to solve the model recursively. Starting from equation (1) we obtain the effect of the output shock in country A on the interest rate (for a given price level):

(4) $dr_A = (a/b) \, dY_A$

Since $dr_A = dr_B$, we can use (4) to substitute into equation (2). This yields

(5) $dM\overset{B}{_S} = a(dY_B - dY_A)$

From (5) it follows that an increase in output in country A which exceeds
the output increase in country B leads to a decline of the money stock in
country B. Thus a more pronounced boom or a less pronounced recession
in country A (the leader) compared to B leads to a monetary contraction
in country B. Since country A keeps its money stock fixed, the total
money stock in the system also declines when such an asymmetric shock
occurs. The opposite holds when the output growth in country B exceeds
the output growth in country A. In that case the money supply process
has an expansionary bias.

Figure 2.9: Money market equilibrium in a two-country model.

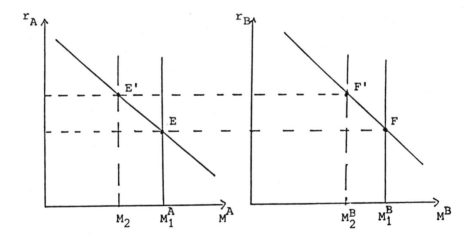

This result has a simple graphical interpretation which we present in
figure 2.10. We assume an asymmetric shock in output. To simplify the
analysis, we assume that output increases in country A while it remains
constant in country B. (Other combinations of asymmetric shocks produce
the same results qualitatively). The effect is to increase the interest rate in
country A (given that country A fixes its money stock). As a result,

country B's interest rate also increases. This forces country B to reduce its money stock. Thus, an increase in output in the leading country has a restrictive monetary effect on country B. At the same time it leads to a decline in the total money stock in the system.

Figure 2.10: Asymmetric output shock.

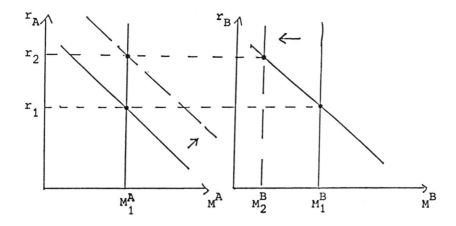

From the preceding analysis it also follows that a money supply target by country A does not stabilize the money stock in the system when asymmetric shocks occur in output. On the contrary, the money supply targeting of country A produces procyclical movements in the money stock of country B if the shocks in output are not perfectly synchronized in the two countries.

Is there evidence for such asymmetric shocks in the EMS during the early 1990s? In figure 2.11 we show the growth rates of GDP in Germany, France and the UK. It can be seen that the recession started almost two years earlier in France and the UK than in Germany. This asymmetry in the business cycle is certainly an important factor explaining the monetary restriction imposed on countries like France and the UK in the early 1990s.

Figure 2.11: Real growth of GDP.

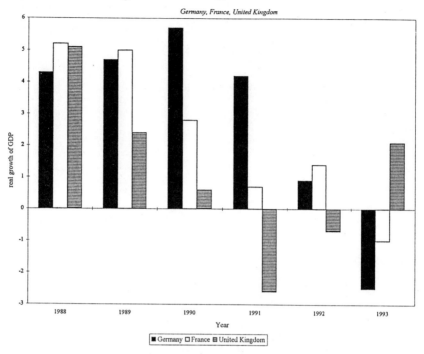

Figure 2.12: Inflation in Germany and the EMS.

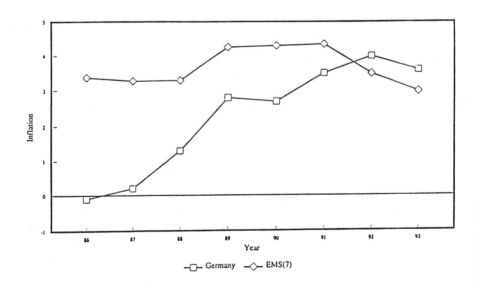

The deflationary monetary effects of the workings of the EMS during the recession was exacerbated by two other factors. First, as noted earlier, inflation accelerated significantly in Germany from 1989-90. In figure 2.12 we present the German inflation rates and compare them with the EMS inflation rates. It can be seen that whereas inflation increased in Germany (in fact prior to unification) it declined in the other EMS-countries. This acceleration of inflation in Germany led the Bundesbank to restrict the growth rate of the money stock. This German monetary restriction was then transmitted to the other countries which were forced to reduce their money stocks. Thus, the EMS forced the other countries to engage in monetary restriction so as to reduce the *German* inflation rate. This happened at a time when their own inflation rate had declined significantly and when the main policy problem was the recession.

Second, the policy conflict between Germany and the other major countries about the appropriate monetary policy reduced the credibility of the system and induced expectations of future realignments. In the context of our model this had the effect of making μ in the interest parity equation (3) a positive number. Since Germany was sticking to its monetary policy objective, the increase in μ had to be accommodated fully by an upward movement in the interest rate in the other countries. As a result, an additional monetary restriction ensued.[5] Thus, to the extent that the recession induced a loss of credibility in the fixity of the exchange rate, the money supply process in the EMS became even more deflationary.

From the preceding it can be concluded that the asymmetric monetary arrangement in the EMS amplified the monetary effects of the asymmetric shocks that occurred in the early 1990s. As a result, the EMS probably also made the recession in the countries that tied their currency to the German mark worse than it would have been in a different, more symmetrical, monetary arrangement. Let us take such a different monetary arrangement. Suppose a European central bank had existed in the early 1990s, and suppose it had targeted the money stock of the whole system, much in the same way as the German Bundesbank targets the German money stock.

We can analyze the effects of such a symmetrical monetary arrangement, confronted with the same asymmetric shocks, in the context of our monetary model as follows. We now fix the sum of the money stocks in the two countries, i.e.

$$(6) \quad M_S^A + M_S^B = \overline{M}$$

We then solve for the interest rate and the money stocks:

(7) $dr_A = (a/2b)(dY_A + dY_B)$

(8) $dM_S^B = (a/2)(dY_B - dY_A)$

(9) $dM_S^A = (a/2)(dY_B - dY_A)$

We now observe that following the same asymmetric output shock, the money stock in country B declines whereas country A's money stock increases. The latter is necessary because the European central bank aims at keeping the total money stock fixed. Note also that the decline in country B is smaller in this symmetrical system than in the asymmetric monetary arrangement (compare (8) with (5)). The reason is that the increase in the money stock of country A reduces the need to restrict the money stock in country B. Thus, although the symmetrical monetary arrangement cannot fully eliminate the monetary effects of asymmetric shocks, it does a better job than the asymmetrical EMS system which amplifies the asymmetrical monetary effects of the shock.

5 Conclusion

The EMS evolved into an asymmetric monetary arrangement in which the German Bundesbank played a dominant role in determining monetary conditions in the system. Such an asymmetric system worked well as long as the participating countries perceived their national interest to be well-served by following the leading country. This was the case during most of the 1980s when countries like France, Italy, Belgium pursued anti-inflationary strategies, and when the EMS was seen as a device making this disinflation easier. Things changed dramatically during the early 1990s when inflation dropped to historically low levels (except for Germany) and the recession became the major policy problem. It then appeared that the asymmetric monetary arrangement inherent in the EMS exerted a deflationary bias to monetary policies in the system.

This deflationary bias occurred as a result of three self-reinforcing phenomena. First, the business cycles of the EMS-countries were desynchronized. While the other EMS-countries were already turning into a recession in 1990, Germany experienced a boom. Given the money targeting strategy of Germany, this led to an (unwelcome) monetary restriction in the other EMS-countries. Second, the EMS had the effect of forcing those countries who stayed within the system to follow a restrictive monetary policy so as to help Germany in its objective of reducing its domestic inflation rate. Thus the EMS was an arrangement in which the total money stock was geared towards the exclusive objective of reducing the inflation rate in Germany (which stood at 4% at its peak). Third, the loss of credibility of the system which was induced by the policy conflict between the major EMS-countries forced the EMS-countries outside Germany to raise their interest rates.

The asymmetric feature of the EMS in which one country is allowed to follow its own national interest without taking into account the interests of the others, tended to amplify the negative monetary effects of the recession which hit the EMS-countries during the early part of the 1990s.

A monetary arrangement between nations should serve the interests of all participating members. The EMS performed this role during most of the 1980s. It did not during the 1990s, when it contributed to intensifying the deflationary forces of the recession. A monetary union in which one central bank would have targeted a European money stock would have been better equipped in avoiding the excessive monetary restriction of the early 1990s.

The recent European experience with monetary policies is reminiscent of what happened in the US during the 1930s. As is well-know Friedman and Schwartz (1963) have claimed that by following too restrictive monetary policies, the Federal Reserve intensified the severity of the Great Depression. Although there is still dispute about the importance of the Fed's monetary stance in explaining the Depression in the 1930s, few will contest that the restrictive nature of these policies contributed to its severity.[6] In a similar way it can be argued that the restrictive nature of the monetary policies in Europe has contributed to the severity of the European recession of 1991-93.

Notes

[1] I am grateful to participants at the conference "European Currency Crises and After," for comments and suggestions.

[2] These numbers are in accordance with the nominal growth rate of GDP used by the drafters of the Maastricht Treaty when they fixed the fiscal convergence criteria (3% deficit and 60% government debt). The rule we apply here is crude. We are in the process of applying other policy

rules, in particular the nominal income targeting proposed by McCallum (1987). Sea also Dueker (1993).

[3] There is a lively literature on the nature and the intensity of the asymmetry in the EMS. See e.g. De Grauwe (1988), Fratianni and von Hagen (1990), Weber (1990). These studies suggest that during the 1980s other countries also influenced monetary conditions despite the fact that Germany was the dominant partner.

[4] See P. De Grauwe (1992) for an exposition.

[5] It can be seen from figure 2.10 that an increase in μ increases the interest rate in country B (given that country A keeps its own interest rate fixed). This then necessitates an additional decline in the money stock of country B.

[6] For a recent survey see Wheelock (1992). A recent restatement of the argument is Bordo, Choudri and Schwartz (1994).

References

Bordo, M., M. Choudri, and A. Schwartz (1993), "Could Stable Money have averted the Great Contraction?" Paper presented at the *Konstanz Seminar on Monetary Theory and Policy*, May.

De Grauwe, P. (1988), "Is the European Monetary System a DM-zone?" *CEPR Discussion Paper*, N° 297.

De Grauwe, P. (1992), "The Economics of Monetary Integration," *Oxford University Press.*

Dueker, M. (1993), "Can Nominal GDP Targeting Rules Stabilize the Economy?" *Review, Federal Reserve Bank of St Louis*, May/June.

Fratianni, M., and J. Von Hagen (1990), "German Dominance in the EMS: the Empirical Evidence," *Open Economies Review*, January, pp. 86-87.

Friedman, M., and A. Schwartz (1963), *A Monetary History of the United States*, Princeton University Press.

McCallum, B. (1987), "The Case for Rules in the Conduct of Monetary Policy: A Concrete Example," *Economic Review, Federal Reserve Bank of Richmond*, Sept./Oct.

Weber, A. (1990), "Asymmetric and Adjustment Problems in the European Monetary System: some Empirical Evidence," *University of Siegen Discussion Paper.*

Wheelock, D. (1992), "Monetary Policy in the Great Depression: What the Fed did and Why," *Review, Federal Reserve Bank of St Louis,* March/April.

25-27 EU
ES2
F33
F36

p 8 : **Discussion**

JACQUES MELITZ

Paul De Grauwe shows convincingly that the non-German members of the European Monetary System (EMS) suffered from German leadership during the 1991-93 recession. As he argues, even a European Monetary Union pursuing the same rate of monetary growth as the Bundesbank would have benefited the rest during this episode since this rate of growth would then have pertained to the money stock in the union as a whole and therefore monetary policy would have been easier outside of Germany. I would add one qualification. Since German inflation accelerated in 1990-91 and the German boom still proceeded at the time, it is not really clear that German leadership amplified the recession right from the start. Early on in the recession, the expansion of German demand associated with unification increased exports in the rest of Europe, and the monetary discipline imposed by Germany was not plainly excessive from the standpoint of many of the other EMS members. On the other hand, as the recession continued, the impact of German leadership in the EMS became even more punitive than De Grauwe suggests. Once the Danish referendum on the Maastricht Treaty was over and the French one approached, expected devaluations of many currencies in the EMS required a general rise in interest rates *relative to* German levels. Thus, German leadership caused much tighter monetary policy than De Grauwe implies in assuming that the others simply needed to match German interest rates. This last remark serves to underline his basic message.

But if the Germans led, the others followed. Why did they? The question is less troubling in the case of those who decided to cease following mid-way and either dropped out of the EMS, like the British and Italians, or devalued several times, like the Spanish and Portuguese. But it is very troubling as regards the rest: those who stuck to the same parity relative to the mark through thick and thin. The French example is the most important - all the more so because the markets mistook French official intentions. The first two speculative attacks on the franc, in September and November 1992, yielded speculators no profits. The most recent one, at the end of July of 1993, was only a qualified success. The speculators who got out soon enough (or who bought back francs quickly) benefited from a 2 to 3 percent devaluation (4 to 5 percent if they were unusually lucky). But those who decided to wait for the French authorities to exploit their new margins of 15 percent around parity got essentially nothing. Contrary to their hopes, the franc went back up to the July levels within months.

The rest of my remarks about De Grauwe's fine paper - more specifically, his subject-matter - concentrate on France.

Reputational issues probably cannot explain French official behavior in 1992-93. French inflation was two percent below German levels at the time, the French current account looked stronger than the German one, and French unemployment rates rose steadily by two percentage points to attain a level above 12 percent. Under these conditions, the French authorities need not have feared that markets would question their monetary discipline if they devalued the franc. The French official behavior can best be explained on the basis of long run political goals. By maintaining the policy of the *franc fort,* the French authorities wished to promote the aim of monetary union and, in addition, assure themselves an important place, along Germany's side, in future European monetary control. On this view, French behavior should be seen in the context of a larger political game in which the country wished to keep Germany under constant pressure to give up its monetary independence while the latter had no interest in doing so (except in return for concessions outside the monetary sphere).[1]

As for market behavior, it seems to me that we need to think harder about models of speculative attacks under uncertainty about official intentions. Our current models of speculative attacks on currencies under fixed exchange rates either deal with cases where the market knows that the authorities will switch regimes independently of their behavior (for lack of reserves or purely political reasons) or else where the market knows that it can induce the authorities to devalue or switch regimes by making any other decisions too costly. But in the case of the recent speculative attacks on the franc, the French authorities did not switch regimes and neither sort of explanation will do.

Two ingredients are probably essential in modeling the speculative attacks on the franc. One is ambiguity of official intentions (not ambiguity of the kind that the authorities foment themselves in order to widen their discretion but of the sort that they cannot dispel despite their attempts to do so).[2] The other ingredient is the theory of options. Individuals do not buy options when they know that something will happen - would they know they would act differently - but when they accord a sufficient probability to the event taking place. The value of options rises with the underlying uncertainty against which the instruments buy protection. The recent speculative attacks on the franc can be viewed as the outcome of decisions to purchase options allowing the owners to benefit from a fall in the price of the franc. Shocks in the environment must serve to explain the timing. As a result of these shocks (whatever they be),[3] the probability of a depreciation of the franc rose sufficiently to warrant moving to a negative position in francs given the current cost of doing so. With enough people acting this way in a concentrated period of time - despite uncertainty about French official intentions and awareness of the probability of making a mistake - a speculative attack took place.

Notes

[1] I have developed this view more fully in Mélitz, J. (1994) "French Monetary Policy and the Recent Speculative Attacks on the Franc," in David Cobham, ed., *European Monetary Upheavals,* Manchester University Press, chapter 4.

[2] The ambiguity also cannot be modeled, as we often try to do, by supposing that the market does not know whether the government is "hard" or "soft." Monetary policy has been the same in France with several changes of government since 1987.

[3] Of course, we know them, but this is not the place.

The 1992-93 EMS Crisis: Assessing the Macroeconomic Costs[1]

28-52

EU
F33
F36
F41
F31

1 Introduction

If an astronaut had come back to earth early in 1994 after a two-year long flight in space (without a Reuter's screen in his shuttle!) and looked at the FT as soon as he landed to check the situation of his diversified portfolio, he would probably not have been very surprised. He would have found the exchange rates of the DM and the other ERM currencies participating in the "original narrow band" practically unchanged and likewise for interest rate differentials at both the short and the long end of the market (although at a lower level of interest rates). Even the DM-dollar rate, at around 1.65-1.70, was close to the rate prevailing two years earlier.

However, he would undoubtedly have noticed that a group of currencies - the lira, the pound sterling, the peseta and the escudo - had substantially depreciated with respect to the DM, something which had certainly not been expected before his departure in early 1992. On second thoughts, however, he would probably have concluded that he had been too optimistic two years earlier about the value of these currencies and the ability of the countries in question to adjust their imbalances. Another interesting aspect that he would have noticed is that the interest rate differentials of these countries with respect to Germany, both short and long, were at levels close to those prevailing two years earlier. He might therefore have reasonably imagined that during his absence the EC monetary authorities had decided to realign a few currencies in order to adjust previous imbalances and prepare for the "run to EMU" (he had not yet read the other news about the fate of European integration!) and that markets had adjusted smoothly to this "last realignment".

Our astronaut would, of course, have to be told that, unfortunately, he was wrong. The early 1994 picture of broad stability in EC monetary relations came after two years of tensions, crisis at times, as those who remained on earth well know. One of the peculiarities that would have to be explained to the astronaut is that the crisis had affected not only countries with internal or external imbalances, where a realignment was more or less justified on the basis of fundamentals, but also countries whose fundamentals were highly convergent with respect to Germany.

After giving the astronaut a full account of events and attempting to provide a coherent explanation of the crisis one might wonder what the world would have been like if the scenario first imagined by the astronaut had been true, i.e. if the realignment of the diverging countries' currencies had taken place in an orderly fashion, without affecting the overall stability of the system. In this paper we examine what could have happened in that scenario in terms of macroeconic performance. The aim is to assess the macroeconomic costs of the crisis, without questioning whether and how the crisis could have been avoided. We simply make the assumption that the exchange rates between the formerly narrow band currencies remain unchanged and that interest rate differentials converge further. The objective is to throw light on the impact of monetary and exchange rate policies during the transition phase of EMU.

We attempt to address the question through the use of a macroeconometric model, the main features of which are described in the next section. In section three the results of a "no-crisis scenario" for some currencies are compared with the baseline. In section four alternative exercises are conducted, mainly for the purpose of sensitivity analysis. The last section presents some concluding comments.

2 Methodology

The analysis is carried out using the framework provided by the Global Econometric Model (GEM) developed at the NIESR. GEM contains a description of the 7 major industrial countries, plus Spain, the Netherlands and Belgium, with detailed equations for the balance of payments, national income and employment, wages and prices, the financial sector and the public sector. For the other OECD countries, output, prices and international trade are aggregated into broad areas, such as the rest of the EC (including Denmark, Ireland, Greece and Portugal).[2]

The model is characterized by short-term nominal rigidities in the goods and labor markets; government bonds are considered net wealth (Ricardian equivalence does not hold). Expectations are formed rationally: in particular, long-run interest rates and wages are forward-looking. Terminal conditions are imposed to ensure that current account imbalances and stocks of government debt do not follow explosive paths in the long run.

We used the version of the model released in February 1994 and estimated, on quarterly data, over the sample period from 1984-I to 1993-III. This includes the 1992-1993 financial crisis, when interest rate differentials with respect to the Deutsche mark increased in defense of the ERM bands, by 3 percentage points in France in the first quarter of 1993 and by 2 points in Belgium in the third quarter of 1993, and the French and Belgian francs depreciated by respectively 2.5 and 3.5 per cent after the bands were widened in August 1993.

In January 1994 the French and Belgian currencies returned inside their previous ERM (narrow) bands with respect to the Deutsche mark, and their respective interest rate differentials dropped back to levels very close to those prevailing before the crisis. In the baseline, French and Belgian interest rates are assumed to converge on the German levels (6.0 and 6.5 per cent in the short and long-term respectively) between 1994 and 1995.

The exercise consists in simulating a "no-crisis" scenario in which the French franc and the Belgian franc are not affected by the ERM crisis, and their respective interest rate differentials and exchange rates continue to converge on their long-run baseline equilibrium levels. The simulation exercise is performed by assuming that French interest rates are equal to the German rates from the second half of 1992 on (see Figure 3.1). The short-term interest rate differential between the Belgian franc and the Deutsche mark is assumed to fall to zero in 1993; the long-term interest rate differential is maintained at 40 basis points until 1994, and at the equilibrium level (20 basis points) afterwards (see Figure 3.2). The French franc and the Belgian franc are assumed to attain their equilibrium levels at the end of 1992 and in the third quarter of 1993, respectively .

For other small ERM countries, such as Ireland and Denmark, which were also affected by the crisis, the GEM does not provide separate equations. Consequently, the baseline for these countries cannot be

Figure 3.1: French franc-Deutsche mark interest differentials and exchange rate.

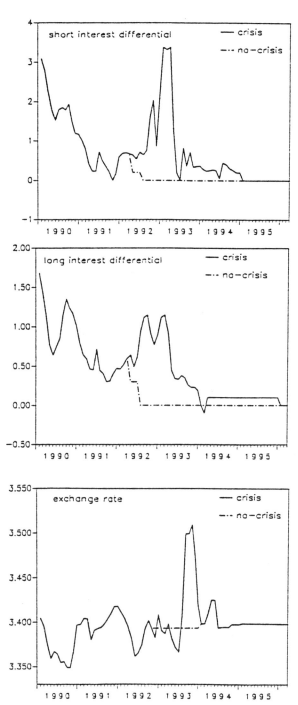

Figure 3.2: Belgian franc-Deutsche mark interest differentials and exchange rate.

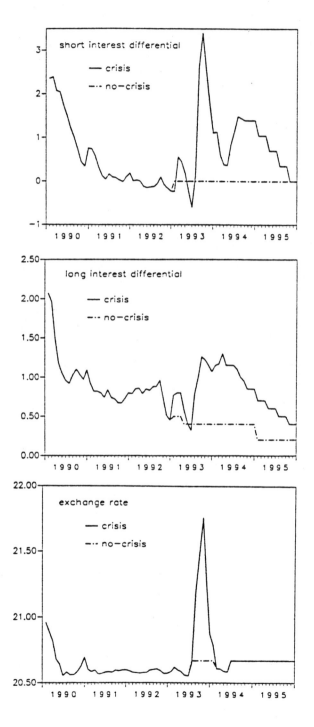

modified. For all other countries inside and outside the ERM no changes are made to the baseline.

3 Main results

The results of the simulation are presented in Table 3.1, expressed in terms of differences between the "no-crisis scenario" and the GEM May 1994 baseline, which instead incorporates the "crisis scenario".

With respect to the exogenous variables, exchange and interest rates, which are shown in the right-hand columns of Table 3.1, the "no-crisis scenario" implies : i) a short-term interest rate in France lower by 77, 118 and 23 basis points on yearly average from 1992 to 1994 (105, 132 and 52 basis points in Belgium); ii) a long-term rate lower by 55 and 49 basis points in 1992 and 1993 in France (41 and 65 basis points in Belgium); iii) a more appreciated effective exchange rate, by .87 per cent in France on a yearly average in 1993 and by 1.08 per cent in Belgium, and DM and guilder exchange rates that depreciated more, by .3 per cent (Table 3.1).

In the no-crisis scenario French GDP is higher in 1993-96, by about 1 per cent cumulatively. The lower level of interest rates increases real net wealth, and hence private consumption, and stimulates investment. Domestic demand rises by over 1.6 per cent cumulatively over the four-year period. The appreciation of the exchange rate partly offsets this effect: the current account balance deteriorates by about 0.3 per cent of GDP in the 1993-96 period. Import volumes rise, by about 2.5 percent over 1993-96, while export volumes initially fall, with respect to the baseline "crisis scenario", recovering only in 1995. French employment increases on average by 8 thousand units in 1993 and by 25 thousand yearly in 1994-96. Inflation is virtually unchanged. Public sector saving improves with respect to GDP by around .30 per cent. For Belgium the results are very similar. GDP and employment increase slightly, while the current balance deteriorates. The model for this country is more simple and the results are provided only for a few variables. An important factor is the improvement in public sector saving following the impact of lower short and long-term interest rates on debt service.

The better growth performance in France and Belgium contributes marginally to an improvement in the growth and employment performances of Germany and the Netherlands. Their current account balances also improve.

Lorenzo Bini Smaghi & Oreste Tristani

Table 3.1: Exercice 1: "No-crisis scenario" with 1994 model. [1]

	GDP (2)	Domestic Demand (2)	Employ-ment (1000s)	Inflation (3)	Current Account (mill.$)	Export Volume (2)	Import Volume (2)	Long-Term Rate (3)	Short-Term Rate (3)	Effective exch.rate (2)
France										
1992	0.03	0.08	0.17	–	-410	–	0.18	-0.55	-0.77	0.03
1993	0.23	0.49	8.04	-0.04	-1417	-0.02	0.92	-0.49	-1.18	0.87
1994	0.22	0.48	19.44	-0.09	-2513	-0.07	0.91	-0.07	-0.23	–
1995	0.26	0.38	27.65	-0.06	-1240	0.11	0.50	-0.10	–	–
1996	0.22	0.28	27.97	0.03	-668	0.08	0.25	-0.02	–	–
1997	0.15	0.18	22.08	0.04	-314	0.04	0.09	–	–	–
Belgium										
1992	0.02	n.a.	0.01	n.a.	27	0.03	–	-0.41	-1.045	–
1993	0.05	n.a.	0.34	n.a.	-114	0.06	0.17	-0.65	-1.325	1.08
1994	0.13	n.a.	0.9	n.a.	-340	0.22	0.58	-0.35	-0.525	–
1995	0.19	n.a.	2.1	n.a.	-605	0.19	0.40	-0.02	–	–
1996	0.11	n.a.	2.17	n.a.	-451	0.08	0.26	–	–	–
1997	0.05	n.a.	1.82	n.a.	-240	0.03	0.15	–	–	–
Germany										
1992	–	–	0.2	–	54.9	0.01	0.01	–	–	–
1993	0.04	0.03	3.4	–	162.8	0.12	0.06	–	–	-0.25
1994	0.04	0.03	7.72	0.02	521.8	0.19	0.09	–	–	–
1995	0.02	0.02	7.3	0.02	385.2	0.12	0.08	–	–	–
1996	0.02	0.02	4.89	0.01	212.8	0.07	0.06	–	–	–
1997	0.01	0.01	2.07	0.01	67.6	0.02	0.04	–	–	–
Netherlands										
1992	0.01	n.a.	–	n.a.	23	0.02	–	–	–	–
1993	0.03	n.a.	0.27	n.a.	107	0.16	0.01	–	–	-0.3
1994	0.06	n.a.	0.66	n.a.	172	0.21	0.10	–	–	–
1995	0.05	n.a.	1.09	n.a.	112	0.14	0.09	–	–	–
1996	0.04	n.a.	1.23	n.a.	43	0.09	0.07	–	–	–
1997	0.03	n.a.	1.19	n.a.	-7	0.04	0.05	–	–	–

(1) Difference from the baseline ("crisis scenario");
(2) Percentage difference;
(3) Difference in percentage points.

In summary, the results of the simulation conducted with the GEM model suggest that the crisis of 1992-93 and the policies aimed at counteracting it led to a reduction in French and Belgian GDP of about .25 per cent, on a yearly average over the period 1993-96.

4 Extensions

The analysis conducted in section 3 suffers from several limitations.

The first is that the EMS crisis may have had an impact on macroeconomic fundamentals through channels other than those related to the interest and exchange rate developments, which are the only ones considered in the analysis. In particular, the uncertainty in the foreign exchange markets may have generated a change in agents' expectations, eventually leading to a crisis of confidence with strong repercussions on households' and firms' behaviour. There is some evidence that this factor played an important role in France, but it can hardly be captured by an analysis based on a relatively simple macroeconometric model.

A related problem is that the structural equations may have been affected by the crisis. The differences between a crisis and a no-crisis scenario may therefore not be fully appreciated either with a model estimated in a no-crisis environment or with a model in which the crisis has induced a change in behaviour. In any case, there is evidence that the performance of certain equations of the GEM model has deteriorated in the 1992-93 period. In particular, for France the model makes a large over-prediction of consumption in the first quarter of 1993 and of investment in the first two quarters of 1993. Constant negative add-factors have been included in these equations in order to make the forecasts, which suggests that the behavioural equations may have been subject to structural changes. Section 4.1 addresses the issue by conducting an exercise similar to that of section 3 but with an earlier version of the GEM model. However, too few post-crisis observations are available to assess the extent to which behavioural parameters have changed.

Another limitation of the exercise conducted in section 3 is that it is restricted to the formerly narrow-band countries, ignoring what happened to other EMS currencies and to currencies not participating in the EMS. Section 4.2 examines the impact of the devaluation of the lira. The analysis could also be extended to the pound sterling and the Iberian currencies. Section 4.3 analyses the impact of dollar exchange rate changes that may have resulted from the tensions within the ERM. Some strong assumptions are made as a benchmark case. Other minor currencies are not considered in the model. However, the foreign exchange tensions that developed in the Nordic countries in parallel with those in the EMS had a strong impact on these countries, which are the major trading partners of the EC. The repercussions on the EC could not be examined with the available model.

4.1 *Using the ex-ante GEM model*

The exercise conducted in section 3 is based on the February 1994 version of the GEM model, which was estimated on the basis of data collected up until the second half of 1993. The sample period used for the estimation thus encompasses the observations regarding the 1992-93 crisis period. Simulating a no-crisis scenario with a model estimated over a period in which the crisis occurred might lead to biased results. This bias could be particularly important if the crisis produced substantial changes in the behavioral equations and in the structural parameters.

To take account of this problem, we conducted an exercise with the May 1992 version of the GEM model, estimated on the basis of the information available up until early 1992. It is interesting to notice that the baseline scenario of the May 1992 version is very similar to the "no-crisis scenario": it is based on the assumption of unchanged exchange rates within the ERM and further convergence of interest rates; in early 1992 the NIESR, like financial markets, was not expecting the foreign exchange crisis of 1992-93.

The exercise is symmetric to the one conducted in the previous section because in the present case the baseline is equivalent to the "no-crisis scenario", while in the former simulation, based on actual exchange rates and interest rates rather than on the baseline forecast of May 1992, the baseline corresponds to the "crisis scenario". In sum, the exercise now consists in simulating the effect of the crisis with a model that did not forecast it.

Table 3.2 reports the difference between the "crisis scenario" and the "no-crisis scenario". The results, which are of the opposite sign to those presented in Table 3.1, are very similar to those of the previous section. In France, the impact of the crisis appears to be slightly smaller, compared with the 1994 model, for GDP and larger for employment. This suggests that the more recent data referring to the 1992-93 crisis may have affected some of the behavioural relationships. It will have to be seen whether

Table 3.2: Exercice 2: "Crisis scenario" with 1992 model[1]

	GDP (2)	Domestic Demand (2)	Employ-ment (1000s)	Inflation (3)	Current Account (mill. $)	Export volume (2)	Imports volume (2)	Long-Term Rate (3)	Short-Term Rate (3)	Effective exch.rate (2)
France										
1992	-0.03	-0.07	-0.01	-	388.8	-0.01	-0.19	0.55	0.77	-0.03
1993	-0.23	-0.44	-8.02	-0.01	1165.8	0.01	-0.94	0.49	1.18	-0.95
1994	-0.17	-0.41	-20.64	0.09	2946.2	0.06	-0.68	0.07	0.23	-
1995	-0.20	-0.33	-29.10	-0.04	1539.8	-0.04	-0.46	0.10	-	-
1996	-0.15	-0.21	-31.20	-0.02	837.9	0.01	-0.18	0.02	-	-
1997	-0.09	-0.11	-30.50	-0.06	427.1	-	-0.01	-	-	-
Belgium										
1992	n.a.	n.a.	n.a.	n.a.	-139.6	-0.04	-0.01	n.a.	n.a.	-
1993	n.a.	n.a.	n.a.	n.a.	-171.7	-0.27	-0.07	n.a.	n.a.	-1.07
1994	n.a.	n.a.	n.a.	n.a.	-173.1	-0.22	-0.09	n.a.	n.a.	-
1995	n.a.	n.a.	n.a.	n.a.	-47.0	-0.11	-0.07	n.a.	n.a.	-
1996	n.a.	n.a.	n.a.	n.a.	91.1	-0.02	-0.03	n.a.	n.a.	-
1997	n.a.	n.a.	n.a.	n.a.	149.9	-0.04	-0.03	-	-	-
Germany										
1992	-0.01	-0.01	-0.57	-	-72.2	-0.03	-0.03	-	-	-
1993	-0.07	-0.05	-7.58	-0.01	-22.0	-0.19	-0.16	-	-	0.29
1994	-0.06	-0.04	-12.24	-0.02	-373.0	-0.19	-0.13	-	-	-
1995	-0.03	-0.02	-10.22	-0.02	-98.1	-0.09	-0.07	-	-	-
1996	-0.01	-0.01	-7.50	-	165.9	-0.02	-0.03	-	-	-
1997	-	-	-4.64	-	323.8	-	-	-	-	-
Netherlands										
1992	n.a.	n.a.	n.a.	n.a.	-121.4	-0.02	-0.01	n.a.	n.a.	-
1993	n.a.	n.a.	n.a.	n.a.	-118.5	-0.15	-0.07	n.a.	n.a.	0.29
1994	n.a.	n.a.	n.a.	n.a.	-135.1	-0.16	-0.09	n.a.	n.a.	-
1995	n.a.	n.a.	n.a.	n.a.	-32.1	-0.09	-0.06	n.a.	n.a.	-
1996	n.a.	n.a.	n.a.	n.a.	64.4	-0.03	-0.02	n.a.	n.a.	-
1997	n.a.	n.a.	n.a.	n.a.	117.3	0.01	-	n.a.	n.a.	-

(1) Difference from the baseline ("no-crisis scenario");
(2) Percentage difference;
(3) Difference in percentage points.

these changes are of a temporary or permanent nature. In the latter case the negative effects of the "crisis scenario" might be larger than those reported in section 3.

In the case of Germany, on the contrary, the impact of the ERM crisis appears slightly larger in the 1992 version, especially for employment; it remains in any case relatively modest.

In the early version of the GEM, the equations for Belgium and the Netherlands were extremely simple: they only included equations for trade and the current balance.

4.2 *"No crisis" for other ERM currencies*

The exercise conducted in section 3 is based on the hypothesis that in the "no-crisis scenario" the exchange and interest rate differentials of the countries that did not devalue between 1992 and 1993 remain unchanged, but those of the other countries are instead affected by the crisis and behave as historically experienced. However, the exchange rate of the lira and the pound sterling, although floating since 17 September 1992, were subsequently affected by the ERM turbulence from October 1992 to end 1993.

It is, of course, difficult to make an assumption regarding the behavior of currencies outside the ERM on the hypothesis that after their devaluation the ERM would have become calm again. As a benchmark hypothesis we assume that after the devaluation the exchange rate of the lira remains until end-1993 at the level corresponding to the lower margin of the narrow band adopted after the September 12 devaluation, which is the level reached at around end-September 1992, i.e. 900 lire per DM. Short and long-term interest rate differentials with respect to the DM are assumed to come down immediately after the devaluation to the level prevailing before the crisis. This implies an appreciation of the lira in effective terms, with respect to historical levels, by 5.5 per cent in 1993 and by 0.7 per cent in 1994. Italian short-term interest rates are reduced, on a yearly average, by 78 basis points in 1992 and by 43 basis points in 1993 compared with the historical level (Figure 3.3).

In this scenario Italian income falls. Domestic demand increases by over 1 percentage point cumulatively over the 1993-95 period, but exports fall by about 1 per cent and imports rise by 3.0 per cent over the same period. The current balance deteriorates, with respect to the baseline, starting from 1994.

Figure 3.3.: Italian lira-Deutsche mark interest differentials and exchange rate.

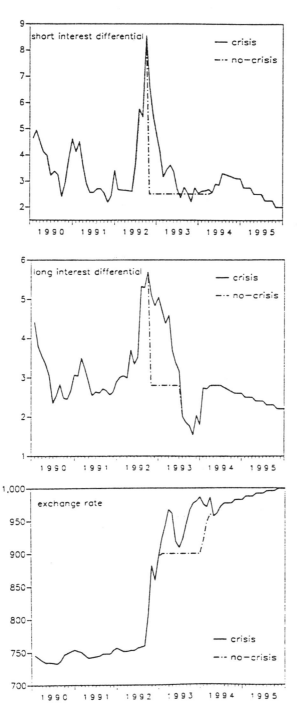

Table 3.3: Exercice 3: "No-crisis scenario" with stable lira/DM exchange rate.

	GDP (2)	Domestic Demand (2)	Employment (1000s)	Inflation (3)	Current Account (mill.$)	Export Volume (2)	Import Volume (2)	Long-Term Rate (3)	Short-Term Rate (3)	Effective exch.rate (2)
France										
1992	-	-	-	-	-1	-	-	-	-	-
1993	0.02	0.01	0.5	0.04	-437	-0.02	-0.06	-	-	-0.82
1994	0.07	0.01	2.6	0.03	801	0.27	0.04	-	-	-0.10
1995	0.04	-	4.2	-0.01	379	0.15	0.03	-	-	-
1996	0.02	-	3.4	-0.01	163	0.04	-0.02	-	-	-
1997	0.01	-	1.3	0.01	76	0.01	-0.01	-	-	-
Belgium										
1992	-	n.a.	-	n.a.	-2	-	-	-	-	-
1993	0.05	n.a.	0.1	n.a.	53	0.16	0.05	-	-	-0.35
1994	0.05	n.a.	0.5	n.a.	128	0.08	0.03	-	-	-0.04
1995	0.02	n.a.	0.4	n.a.	77	0.02	0.01	-	-	-
1996	-	n.a.	0.3	n.a.	56	0.01	-0.01	-	-	-
1997	-	-	1.2	-	28	-	-	-	-	-
Germany										
1992	-	-	-	-	-3	-	-	-	-	-
1993	0.04	0.01	2.2	0.01	-506	0.02	0.08	-	-	-0.62
1994	0.11	0.05	12.1	0.04	1044	0.29	0.07	-	-	-0.07
1995	0.04	0.02	10.3	0.03	423	0.10	0.02	-	-	-
1996	-	-	3.8	0.01	47	0.01	0.01	-	-	-
1997	-0.01	-	-0.3	-	-71	-0.01	0.01	-	-	-
Netherlands										
1992	-	n.a.	-	n.a.	-1	-	-	-	-	-
1993	0.04	n.a.	0.1	n.a.	193	-0.02	-0.07	-	-	-0.31
1994	0.05	n.a.	0.7	n.a.	141	0.07	0.11	-	-	-0.04
1995	0.03	n.a.	0.9	n.a.	32	0.01	0.05	-	-	-
1996	0.01	n.a.	0.8	-	-30	0.01	0.02	-	-	-
1997	0.01	-	0.7	-	-32	-0.01	0.01	-	-	-
Italy										
1992	-	-	-	-	-2	-	-	-	-	-
1993	-0.26	0.21	-13.0	-0.59	708	-0.48	0.46	-0.53	-0.78	5.52
1994	-0.20	0.49	-36.1	-0.05	-5122	-0.41	2.51	-0.58	-0.43	0.64
1995	0.11	0.29	-14.5	0.27	-1226	-0.02	0.65	-	-0.04	-
1996	0.11	0.12	3.5	0.05	55	0.04	0.04	-	-	-
1997	0.14	0.12	10.3	0.02	188	0.06	0.03	-	-	-

(1) Difference from the baseline ("crisis scenario");
(2) Percentage difference;
(3) Difference in percentage points.

The changes in the Italian economy also affect the other countries, as their growth performance is marginally improved, by between 0.1 and 0.2 per cent cumulatively, over 1993-95 both in France and Germany. Net exports improve in both countries as a result of the improvement in competitiveness resulting from the stronger exchange rate of the lira.

The size of these effects appears particularly small, especially in view of the huge turnaround of the Italian trade balance that took place after the devaluation (about 16 per cent in effective terms between 1992 and 1993) and contributed by more than 3 per cent to GDP growth in 1993 (with an 8.5 per cent increase in exports and a 10 per cent decrease in imports). A likely explanation is that the model underestimates the response of trade flows to sharp exchange rate changes.[3] Indeed, the GEM model systematically underpredicts Italian export volumes in 1993.

4.3 *"No crisis" for the ERM-dollar exchange rate*
In the exercise conducted in section 3 it was assumed that the crisis affecting the ERM did not influence the exchange rate of ERM currencies with respect to the rest of the world, in particular the dollar. It is difficult to establish a clear-cut relationship between the DM-dollar exchange rate and the exchange rate of the DM with the other European currencies. During the EMS period the correlation seems to have gone both ways, a strong dollar at times contributing to exchange rate stability in the ERM, at times putting pressure on the weaker currencies. During the 1992 summer crisis the weakness of the dollar has been held responsible to have helped fuel tensions in the EMS as investors getting out of dollar-denominated assets tended to privilege DM-denominated ones. However, the emergence of tensions in the EMS in itself encouraged disinvestments from dollar assets to finance "divergence plays" between EC currencies. The analysis of market participants' behaviour during the summer of 1992, conducted in particular by the G-10 central banks, tends to confirm that a large number of US-based institutional investors participated in the speculative run on some European currencies using dollar funds.

For the purpose of the analysis we make the benchmark assumption that in the absence of the EMS crisis the DM-dollar exchange rate would have remained at the rate of 1.68 prevailing in early 1992 until the end of 1993, when it again reached this level (Figure 3.4). Assuming that other intra-ERM exchange rates remained unchanged, this implies a depreciation of the DM in effective terms by 2.7 per cent in 1992, on a

Figure 3.4: Deutsche mark-US dollar exchange rate.

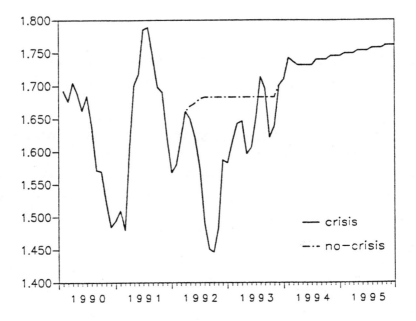

yearly average, and by .65 per cent in 1993 (1.64 and .39 per cent for the French franc).

The results of this exercise are shown in Table 3.4. GDP is higher in France and Germany in 1992-93, largely as a result of higher exports. The improvement is reversed in the following years. Inflation is higher in Germany by .1 percentage points in 1992 and by .4 points in 1993.

In this scenario the interest rate policy of the Bundesbank is assumed unchanged. It is interesting to note that the improvement of GDP growth in 1992-93 is larger in Germany than in France. In sum, in the absence of the crisis and on the assumption of a more depreciated DM with respect to the dollar, the divergence in cyclical positions between Germany and France widens and inflationary pressures in the former country increase. This could have led, paradoxically, to a more restrictive policy stance in Germany than historically experienced. Such a policy would have been less sustainable from the point of view of France and might have led to a critical situation in the ERM.

5 Concluding remarks

During the time we have taken to reach the conclusions of the paper our astronaut has been able to glance at the previous two years' newspapers and catch up with the news about the "monetary earthquake" that shook Europe from mid-1992 to mid-1993. If he now looks back at the results of our simulations, he may be disappointed. The earthquake did some damage, but not as much as might have been expected. Indeed, our simulations show that in the no-crisis scenario French and Belgian GDP would have been higher by about .25 per cent, on a yearly average, between 1993 and 1996. German and Dutch GDP would have increased only marginally. Taking account of other secondary factors, the real effects of the turbulence increase only slightly. Does this mean that financial turbulence had no major impact on the real economy and should therefore be ignored?

Further research is required before daring to hazard an answer. This paper simply starts to address the issue using a rather simple methodology. The limitations of the analysis have been underlined. Macroeconomic models are a biased instrument with which to examine the effect of wide-ranging disturbances such as the ERM crisis, as they tend not to be very sensitive to major policy changes. In the case of the GEM model, in particular, income is not very sensitive to interest rate

Table 3.4: Exercice 4: "No-crisis scenario" with stable DM/dollar exchange rate[1]

	GDP (2)	Domestic Demand (2)	Employ-ment (1000s)	Inflation (3)	Current Account (mill.$)	Export volume (2)	Import volume (2)	Long-Term Rate (3)	Short-Term Rate (3)	Effective exch.rate (2)
France										
1992	0.24	0.03	7.4	0.22	842	1.02	0.66	-	-	-1.64
1993	0.25	-0.04	25.0	0.24	2412	0.48	-0.56	-	-	-0.39
1994	0.07	0.01	16.9	-0.08	447	-0.01	-0.38	-	-	-
1995	0.02	0.04	6.8	-0.01	-211	-0.15	-0.07	-	-	-
1996	-0.03	-	-1.1	-	-263	-0.22	-0.09	-	-	-
1997	-0.07	-0.03	-7.8	-	-330	-0.24	-0.09	-	-	-
Belgium										
1992	0.44	n.a.	1.4	n.a.	-303	0.98	0.16	-	-	-1.35
1993	-0.04	n.a.	2.1	n.a.	-322	0.18	-0.40	-	-	-0.33
1994	0.13	n.a.	2.1	n.a.	599	-0.05	-0.12	-	-	-
1995	-0.08	n.a.	1.4	n.a.	-53	-0.07	-0.05	-	-	-
1996	-0.07	n.a.	0.4	n.a.	-134	-0.12	-0.14	-	-	-
1997	-0.06	n.a.	-	n.a.	-107	-0.14	-0.13	-	-	-
Germany										
1992	0.61	0.28	39.2	0.11	125	1.25	0.65	-	-	-2.74
1993	0.50	0.25	94.6	0.39	5543	1.43	0.18	-	-	-0.65
1994	-0.14	-0.08	29.0	0.14	1159	-0.09	-0.22	-	-	-
1995	-0.18	-0.06	-11.1	-0.05	-121	-0.38	-0.11	-	-	-
1996	-0.17	-0.08	-24.7	-0.07	-35	-0.40	-0.08	-	-	-
1997	-0.17	-0.11	-29.8	-0.08	226	-0.35	-0.12	-	-	-
Netherlands										
1992	0.64	n.a.	3.2	n.a.	1617	0.98	-0.29	-	-	-1.49
1993	-0.11	n.a.	6.7	n.a.	-649	0.09	0.36	-	-	-0.35
1994	0.04	n.a.	3.5	n.a.	-504	-0.05	0.13	-	-	-
1995	0.01	n.a.	2.4	n.a.	-474	-0.09	0.06	-	-	-
1996	-0.04	n.a.	1.6	n.a.	-424	-0.15	-0.04	-	-	-
1997	-0.06	n.a.	0.8	n.a.	-362	-0.17	-0.10	-	-	-

(1) Difference from the baseline ("crisis scenario");
(2) Percentage difference;
(3) Difference in percentage points.

changes in countries that have followed an exchange rate target for a long time. Accordingly, the results of the simulation exercise have to be taken as the lower bound for further analysis.

A further consideration to bear in mind in addressing the issue is that although the crisis was of major proportions, the response by the policy authorities was in many respects without precedent, in particular through measures that had never been adopted in the past, such as joint public statements in defence of currencies, huge foreign exchange interventions and special financing between central banks. Looking at the interest rate effect of the crisis in France and Belgium, one can only be surprised by the small increases in these countries during the crisis. Interest rate differentials with the DM never exceed 4 percentage points on a monthly average. As the tables show, on a yearly average the interest rate increase was relatively small, around 100 basis points in 1992 and 1993. In other countries the crisis led to much larger interest rate increases. For instance, the short-term interest rate differential increased, on a yearly basis, by 160 and 320 basis points in 1992 and 1993 respectively in Denmark, by 200 and 110 points in Ireland, and by 100 and 200 points in Spain. Against this background, the impact on the real economy for France and Belgium cannot be considered as being small. On the other hand, this suggests that the policy strategy adopted, in particular for France, with the aim of reducing the impact of the crisis on domestic interest rates helped to limit the repercussions on the real economy.

This paper is only a first attempt to assess the risks of an exchange rate system exposed to serious tensions that are not always justified by underlying fundamentals and of the costs involved in counteracting these tensions. These preliminary results are presented in order to stimulate further research in this field.

Notes

[1] We wish to thank the participants in the Conference "European Currency Crises and After," in particular J. Pisani-Ferry, for their useful comments on a preliminary version of the paper. We are the only responsible for the opinions expressed.

[2] GEM is used by the NIESR to make quarterly forecasts for the world economy and to run simulation exercises. It has been used to examine possible regimes of international policy coordination (Currie and

Wren-Lewis, 1989), to assess the implications of EMU (Barrell, 1990; Barrell, Surney and in't Veld, 1991) and of a wider use of a European currency (Barrel, Britton and Mayes, 1990), and to assess the need for inflation convergence (Bini Smaghi and Del Giovane, 1995). On the structure of GEM, see Appendix 3.

[3] A similar assessment is made by Whitley (1991).

Appendix 3
The structure of GEM

We provide here a brief description of the structure of the GEM which has been used for the exercises. The version used is that of May 1994, with one modification to the equation for the stock of foreign assets, which did not perform consistently with the others in the simulations, as indicated below. The main equations for the major countries can be grouped into 8 blocks: a) trade and the balance of payments; b) national income, output and employment; c) wages, prices and costs; d) personal income; e) financial sector; f) public sector; g) wealth and debt; h) exchange rates and competitiveness.[1]

a) Trade and the balance of payments

The current account balance identity, with variables expressed in dollars, is given by:

$$CBV = XGV - MGV + XSER - MSER + IPDC - IPDD + BPT$$

where

CBV	: current account balance
XGV	: exports of goods
MGV	: imports of goods
XSER	: exports of non-factor services
MSER	: imports of non-factor services
IPDC	: property income credits
IPDD	: property income debits
BTP	: unrequited transfers

(1) Trade volumes

The volumes of exports and imports are determined by foreign and domestic demands and by competitiveness as measured by relative prices or relative costs. The equations have the following general forms:

$$XGI = f(S, RPX, RULT)$$
$$MGI = g(TFE, RPM, RULT)$$

where
  XGI : exports of goods (volumes)
  MGI : imports of goods (volumes)
  S   : import demand in the country's export markets
  TFE : domestic total final expenditure
  RPX : relative export prices
  RPM : relative import prices
  RULT : relative unit labour costs

(2) Trade prices

Each economy has equations for export and import prices of manufactured goods and of all goods. Manufactured export prices depend on domestic wholesale prices, world price of manufactured exports and the dollar exchange rate. Manufactured import prices depend on the export prices in all the other countries. Overall (import and export) prices depend on manufactured goods' trade prices and on the importance of oil and commodity prices in each country's trade.

(3) Invisibles

Invisibles are disaggregated into non-factor services, returns on foreign assets and on domestic assets held by foreign residents and unrequited transfers. Exports and imports of services are determined by foreign and domestic income and by relative prices. The stocks of assets and liabilities are posited to grow in line with each other and with nominal GDP, as a constant foreign assets to income ratio is assumed in equilibrium.

b) National Income, Output and Employment

(1) National Income

The national income identity at constant prices is written as follows:

$$Y = C + IB + IH + G + DS + XGI - MGI$$

where
Y	: national income
C	: consumers'expenditure
IB	: business investment
IH	: residential construction
G	: government spending
DS	: stockbuilding

The determination of the volumes of exports and imports has been discussed above. The remaining components of national income are determined as follows:

$$C = f\,(RPDI, R3M, CED, RW)$$
$$IB = h\,(Y, LR, CED)$$
$$IH = k\,(Y, R3M, CED)$$
$$DS = l\,(Y, R3M, CED)$$

where
RPDI	: real personal disposable income
R3M	: 3-month interest rate
LR	: long-term rate
CED	: consumer prices
RW	: real wealth

Government expenditure is determined by policy.

(2) Output and Employment

Industrial production depends on GDP and a time trend. Total employment is assumed to grow with output, but there are a negative real wage effect and a positive time trend reflecting neutral technical progress. Manufacturing employment depends on industrial production.

(c) Wages, Prices and Costs

(1) Earnings and Costs

The model has equations for both total compensation of all employees and for an index of average earnings in manufacturing. Total compensation depends on output prices, unemployment, employees in employment, GDP, productivity, expected prices and the index of average earnings in manufacturing; the index depends on employees in employment and total compensation. Trend unit labour costs are a function of average earnings in manufacturing and an estimate of the relevant level of productivity growth.

(2) Prices

Four price indices are available for the major eight economies: wholesale prices, the GDP deflator, the consumers' expenditure deflator and the consumer price index.

(d) Personal Income

The personal income identity is

$$PDI = COMP + TRAN + OPI - TAX$$

where
  COMP : total compensation of all employees
  TRAN : transfers to the personal sector
  OPI   : other personal income
  TAX   : income tax

Transfers depend on unemployment and on prices. Other personal income is a function of wealth and short and long-term interest rates. Real personal disposable income is defined by using the consumers' expenditure deflator.

(e) Financial sector

The money demand functions have the standard form:

$$M1 = f(Y, CED, R3M)$$
$$M3 = g(Y, CPI, R3M)$$

where
  M1   : narrow money
  M3   : broad money
  CPI : consumer price index
  CED : consumers' expenditure deflator

(f) Public sector

For the major seven economies and Spain the government deficit is defined as:

$$BUD = TAX + MTAX - (GC*PY/100) - (GI*PY/100) - TRAN - GIP$$

where
  BUD   : government deficit
  MTAX   : miscellaneous taxes (including indirect taxes)
  GC   : government consumption
  PY   : GDP deflator
  GI   : government investment
  GIP   : government interest payments

(g) Wealth and debt

Net financial wealth is defined as

$$NW = MASC + DEBTP + (NA/100) - LIABS$$

where
  NW   : net financial wealth
  MASC   : miscellaneous assets of the personal sector
  DEBTP : public debt held by the personal sector
  NA   : net foreign assets
  LIABS : personal sector liabilities

The existing stock of government bonds is revalued each period in line with changes in the long interest rates.

Foreign assets change either because the current account is not in balance or because of changes in the valuation of foreign assets and liabilities. The second effect is captured through an ad hoc structure: gross foreign assets are revalued by a weighted average of the changes in equity prices in the other major economies and foreign liabilities are revalued by the change in domestic equity prices; the fact that not all foreign assets have to be revalued (e.g. government debt held by foreign residents) is also taken into account. However, this structure often leads to an inconsistency in our simulations. More precisely, net foreign assets (depending on gross assets) were decreasing at times when high current account surpluses occurred. We have therefore simplified the equation for net foreign assets in the relevant countries and constructed a new series by assuming the net acquisition of foreign assets to equal the current account balance. The new variable has then been exogenised in the simulation.

The miscellaneous assets category contains mainly equities and is therefore revalued in line with equity prices.

(h) Exchange rates and competitiveness

The model contains the dollar exchange rates of each major country. Each country also has a nominal effective exchange rate and a real exchange rate adjusted for consumer prices.

Note

[1] Users can conduct simulations by making assumptions about exogeneous variables or by modifying the residuals of the equations for endogenous variables in order to determine new paths for them.

References

Barrell, R.J. (1990), "European Currency Union and the EMS," *NIESR Discussion paper,* N° 132, May.

Barrell, R.J., A. Britton, and D. Mayes (1990), "Macroeconomic Obstacles to the Wider Use of the ECU," *NIESR Discussion paper,* N° 180.

Barrell, R.J., S. Surney, and J. in't Veld (1991), "Real Exchange Rates, Fiscal Policy and the Role of Wealth," *Paper presented at the SPES Workshop,* Paris, 27-28 June.

Bini Smaghi, L., and P. Del Giovane (1995), "Convergence of Inflation and Interest Rates as a Prerequisite for EMU: an Empirical Analysis," *Journal of Policy Modelling,* Forthcoming.

Currie, D., and S. Wren-Lewis (1989), "A Comparison of Alternative Regimes for International Policy Coordination," *Blueprints for Exchange Rate Management,* edited by M. Miller et al., New York, Academic Press.

Whitley, I. (1991), "Modelling the Interdependence between European Economies: Trade Equation," *Paper presented at the SPES Workshop,* Paris, 27-28 June.

EU   52-5b

F33

p28 **Discussion**   F36

JEAN PISANI-FERRY   F41

P31

The paper by Lorenzo Bini-Smaghi and Oreste Tristiani is a very stimulating one. It addresses an important and topical issue: in the authors' words, to evaluate "what would have happened if the realignment of the diverging countries' currencies had happened *in a somewhat more orderly fashion* (emphasis added), without affecting the overall stability of the system and in particular the countries of the convergent group". This is surely a question many central bankers and treasury officials asked themselves after the battle was over. It is also clear that they could have managed "in a somewhat more orderly fashion" the de facto ERM mega-realignement of 1992-93. Yet this is a very difficult question to answer, if only because it requires determining when and to what extent the markets were right (in provoking a realignment) and wrong (in their attacks against the core ERM currencies), and correspondingly when and to what extent policymakers were both wrong or right in resisting the markets' pressures.

In fact, what the paper aims at evaluating is only part of the overall macroeconomic cost of the crisis. As everybody now recognises, this crisis raises many questions about the management of the ERM between 1987 and 1992. Was it correct to rule out realignments for countries whose inflation convergence was still far from complete? Was it wise to resist the demands for a realignment after German unification? Assuming that a maxi-realignment was needed, how costly has it been to wait until the fall of 1992 to proceed with it? Should core ERM countries have decoupled their monetary policy from that of Germany in 1992-93? These are questions the paper does not address. In other words, it does not aim at evaluating the costs of the mismanagement of the ERM in the early 1990s, but only those that arose from the fact that a general and significant realignment was not decided by the ministers of Finance at their famous Bath meeting of early September 1992. What the paper evaluates can therefore be termed the economic cost of the Bath meeting. The counterfactual simulation exercise undertaken by the authors requires making assumptions on the behaviour of interest rates and exchange rates in the absence of a crisis. Technically and conceptually, the difficulty is that neither perfect foresight nor perfect myopia provide adequate hypotheses for determining interest rates. Perfect foresight cannot be applied to the countries that have devalued. Perfect myopia cannot be assumed for those which have not.

The authors' solution is quite straightforward as regards the core ERM countries, because the natural assumption is that in the absence of an exchange crisis, the interest rate differential vis-à-vis Germany would have been zero or very close to zero (this is equivalent to perfect foresight). What is less clear is what policy would have avoided attacks on these currencies. It is disputable that a maxi-realignment of the weaker currencies taking place in September 1992 would have avoided attacks on the stronger ones. It may well be that devaluing the pound Sterling and the lira would have made the French franc stronger, for example, because it would have deprived market participants from learning that Bundesbank's commitment to "unlimited" intervention was only valid for one day, but this is by no means certain. In fact, what would have happened to the core ERM currencies depends on the model of currency crises one considers valid. For example, a maxi-realignment would have made no difference with Alan Sutherland's model of exchange crises, in which attacks arise from the macroeconomic cost of sticking to a fixed rate regime.

Making assumptions for the other currencies is even more heroic, because it implies determining the size of the realignment that could have been decided. For the currencies which are floating, their market value obviously provides a benchmark, but not a very precise one. For example, the pound Sterling initially depreciated by some 20% in early 1993, but appreciated thereafter by some 5-10%. The authors' assumption as regards the lira, which implies that the market exchange rate overshot its long-term value by some 5% in 1993, is a reasonable one (what is not clear is what they do for the other currencies, especially the Pound Sterling), yet it is obviously open to criticism.

Turning to the results, the main conclusion of the authors is that the cost of the crisis was limited because its effect on the interest rates was small. It is hard to challenge this last point, and I would even say that in the French case the simulations probably overestimate the effect of the interest rate changes, because of the rigidity of lending rates with respect to money market rates. In a recent paper, Cottarelli and Kourelis (1994) have estimated the short- and long-term elasticity of lending rates with respect to money market rates, and they have shown that the short-term elasticity is typically very low in most European countries (Britain being a significant exception). Therefore, the demand impact of a short-lived increase in the market interest rates can be considered minor.[1]

Table 3.5: France: Interest Rates

		3 months	Prime rate	Mortgage rate
1992	Q2	10.0	9.9	11.7
	Q3	10.5	9.9	11.6
	Q4	10.7	9.8	11.6
1993	Q1	11.8	10.0	11.5
	Q2	8.0	9.0	11.3
	Q3	7.8	8.4	10.2
	Q4	6.7	8.1	10.0

Source: Bank of France.

I am less confortable with the models' results as regards exchange rates. According to Table 3.3 in the paper, a 5% revaluation of the lira would have decreased Italian exports by 0.6% and increased its partners' exports by 0.2-0.3%. Yet these low figures are completely inconsistent with the actual changes in export performances observed in 1992-93, which can be considered prima facie evidence of the foreign trade and output effects of exchange rates changes. I am puzzled by the fact that this result seems to persist after reestimating the trade equations of GEM with recent data.

Table 3.6: Relative export performance
(difference with EC average)

	1991	1992	1993
Italy	-1.3	0.2	9.2
UK	-0.2	-0.8	1.8
Spain	3.6	-1.0	14.8
France	1.1	0.9	-1.3
Belgium	1.0	-2.7	-1.5
Germany	-2.5	-0.2	-6.9

Source: OECD Economic Outlook.

More generally, should we trust these results? The methodology used by the authors is a standard one, whose strengths and weaknesses are well known, and there is no need to raise once again the usual questions about policy simulations with macro-models. Yet a specific difficulty with this kind of simulations is that they do not capture a major dimension of the crisis, namely the uncertainty it created about the exchange rate and the future course of monetary policies in Europe. In 1992-93, this uncertainty may have increased the value of waiting before taking economic decisions, until a clearer picture had emerged, thereby adding to the already strong effects of the recession. Weak evidence of such a behaviour can be found in the households' saving rate, which remained at a puzzlingly high level in many countries in the end of 1992 and in 1993. The simulations ignore such effects. On the contrary, the use of a model with forward-looking expectations involves the assumption that during the crisis, private agents actually knew whether or not the currency would be in the end devalued. This is in striking contrast with reality and might be the source of a bias in the evaluation of the cost of the crisis.

Note

[1] The model's estimates obsviously take into account this elasticity. But Table 3.1 suggests that even the short-term effect taken into account in the simulations might be excessive.

Reference

Cottarelli, C., and A. Kourelis (1994), "Financial Structure, Bank Lending Rates, and the Transmission Mechanism of Monetary Policy," *IMF Working Paper*, N° 94/39, March.

Currency Crisis Models: Bridging the Gap between Old and New Approaches[1]

$57 - 82$

$F31$
$E52$

1 Introduction

The collapse of the Exchange Rate Mechanism (ERM) in 1993 has revived interest in theoretical models of currency crises. In particular it has prompted a number of authors to suggest new approaches to modelling crises which appear to differ markedly from the older literature. The traditional approach to modelling the collapse of fixed rate systems emphasises the role of limited reserves in causing a policy-maker to switch from a fixed rate to a floating rate. In Krugman (1979) the monetary policy-maker is faced with an exogenous deterministic trend in domestic credit which causes a steady loss of foreign exchange reserves. The inevitable exhaustion of reserves is foreseen by speculators so the final stage of the collapse of the fixed rate is characterised by a speculative attack.

The basic feature of the Krugman model is that the collapse of the fixed rate is the inevitable consequence of a domestic credit policy that is inconsistent with a fixed exchange rate. Obstfeld (1986) introduced the idea of "self-fulfilling" speculative attacks which can arise even when there is no inconsistency in policy. The crucial modification that is required to produce such attacks is to assume that domestic credit policy will become more expansionary after the fixed exchange rate is abandoned. This makes it possible for speculators to mount a profitable speculative attack which exhausts reserves and brings about a devaluation.

The Krugman (1979) and Obstfeld (1986) approaches have the common feature that the stock of foreign exchange reserves is the main state variable. In both models it is the exhaustion of reserves that brings about the collapse of the fixed rate system. This, however, tends not to be the emphasis in the more recent literature that has followed the collapse of the ERM. Recent authors (such as Anderson (1994), Bensaid and Jeanne (1994), Obstfeld (1994) and Ozkan and Sutherland (1994a and 1994b)) emphasise the role of an optimising policy-maker. The stock of foreign exchange reserves does not play a major role in any of these papers.

This difference in emphasis between the older and the more recent approaches to currency crises is very fundamental and very marked. It therefore seems useful to consider the differences, similarities and potential links between the old and the new approaches. It is the purpose of this paper to provide a bridge between the older approaches to modelling currency crises, which emphasise reserves, and the newer approaches, which emphasise optimising policy-makers. The paper begins by briefly reviewing the traditional Krugman (1979), Flood and Garber (1984) and Obstfeld (1986) approaches. In order to avoid confusion in the latter part of the paper, considerable care is taken in this review to draw out some of the differences and similarities between deterministic and stochastic cases and also between discrete and continuous time cases. The framework described in this review is then augmented with a simple objective function for the policy-maker. It is shown how the resulting model has close formal parallels with the Ozkan and Sutherland (1994a and 1994b) model of currency crisis. It is thus shown that the latter model (and by implication the other recent papers mentioned above) can be viewed as a natural development of the older approaches to currency crisis modelling.

2 A deterministic model of balance of payments crises

This section quickly reviews the Krugman (1979) approach to modelling a balance of payments crisis. That paper used a relatively complex framework to represent the macroeconomy. Flood and Garber (1984) showed, however, that the basic principles of the Krugman solution can be demonstrated using the simple flex-price monetary model. This is the approach adopted here. The model used is represented by the following equations:

(1) $\quad m_t^d - p_t = ky_t - \lambda i_t$

(2) $\quad s_t = p_t - p_{t}^*$

(3) $\quad E_t[s_{t+1}] - s_t = i_t - i_{t}^*$

(4) $\quad m_t^s = \gamma D_t + (1-\gamma)R_t$

where:

m^d = log of money demand
m^s = log of money supply
D = log of domestic credit
R = log of foreign exchange reserves
s = log of the exchange rate (price of foreign currency)
p = log of the price of domestically produced goods
y = log of output (fixed at its full employment level)
i = one period interest rate
E_t = expectations operator conditional on period t information
$*$ = indicates a foreign variable.

Assume domestic credit is growing at a constant exogenous rate μ as follows:

(5) $\quad D_t = D_{t-1} + \mu$

If $\overline{R}$ is the minimum level of reserves then the "shadow" exchange rate (i. e. the exchange rate that will emerge after the collapse of the fixed rate) is given by the following expression:

(6) $\quad \tilde{s}_t = \gamma D_t + (1-\gamma)\overline{R} + \lambda\gamma\mu$

where p_{t}^*, y_t and i^* have been normalised to zero. The breakdown of the fixed rate occurs on the first date at which $\tilde{s} \geq \bar{s}$ (where $\bar{s}$ is the parity at which the exchange rate is fixed while in the fixed rate system). Assume this is time T. This will necessarily require a stock shift in the level of reserves at the time of the breakdown since the switch from the fixed to the floating rate requires an increase in the rate of interest from zero to $\gamma\mu$. In fact in discrete time the rise in interest rates and the corresponding stock shift in reserves is likely to take place over two successive periods. This is because in discrete time the shadow rate changes in discrete steps (corresponding to the discrete steps in domestic credit). The shadow rate is therefore likely to step over the fixed rate in the final period rather than coincide exactly. The breakdown must therefore involve a forecastable jump in the exchange rate between time T-1 and time T. In the period before the breakdown investors must be compensated by an increase in interest rates. There must therefore be a contraction in the level of reserves in that period. The rise in the interest rate will obviously be no greater than $\gamma\mu$ since the jump in the exchange rate between T-1 and T must be less than the on-going period by period depreciation that will occur in the floating rate phase. The stock reduction in the level of reserves in period T-1 will therefore be no greater than the total amount of reserves available in that period.

3 Stochastic Shocks

Now assume that domestic credit evolves stochastically as follows:

(7) $D_t = D_{t-1} + \mu + \omega_t$

where $\omega_t \sim N(0, \sigma^2)$ and $E(\omega_t \omega_t') = 0$, $t \neq t'$. The shadow rate is again given by equation (6). It is no longer the case, however, that the breakdown of the regime is a perfectly predictable event. It is possible that in any period there will be a sufficiently large shock to reduce reserves to the minimum level and trigger collapse. In all periods there will therefore be a possibility of a step change in the exchange rate. This must generate a differential between domestic and foreign interest rates.

Assume for the moment that there is some critical level of D at which collapse takes place. Call this $\overline{D}$. If D exceeds $\overline{D}$ the exchange rate jumps onto the shadow rate schedule given by equation (6). It is therefore possible to write down an expression for the expected value of the exchange rate in period $t + 1$ given information available at period t. The relevant expression is:

(8) $E_t(s_{t+1}) = \Phi(\overline{D} - D_t - \mu)\overline{s} + \left\{ \int_{\overline{D}-D_t-\mu}^{\infty} \emptyset(\omega)\tilde{s}(\omega)d\omega \right\}$

where $\varnothing(.)$ is the probability density function of ω, $\Phi(.)$ is the corresponding cumulative probability function and $\tilde{s}(.)$ is the shadow rate expressed as a function of the shock variable.

The position of $\overline{D}$ can be deduced using Figure 4.1. Here the shadow rate is plotted against the level of domestic credit. The critical level of domestic credit in the deterministic case is $\overline{D}'$ where the shadow rate schedule crosses the fixed rate. Is this also the critical level in the stochastic case? It is simple to show that in fact the critical level must be to the left of this point. If $\overline{D}'$ were the critical level consider the situation where D is precisely equal to $\overline{D}'$ and compare the level of the interest rate in the floating and fixed rate regimes for that level of D. The level of the interest rate is determined by the expected change in the exchange rate. In the floating rate regime the expected change in the exchange rate is the average of possible movements up or down the shadow rate schedule. In the fixed rate regime, on the other hand, the expected change in the exchange rate is formed by averaging over the shadow rate schedule to the right of $\overline{D}'$ and over the fixed rate to the left of $\overline{D}'$. It is clear that in the fixed rate regime there is no potential for the exchange rate to appreciate (as there is in the floating rate regime). It must follow therefore that the expected change in the exchange rate in the fixed rate regime is greater than in the floating rate regime. Hence the interest rate in the fixed rate regime must be higher. This in turn must imply that the level of reserves in the fixed rate regime is lower than in the floating rate regime. This is, however, a contradiction. Reserves in the floating rate regime are by definition at their lowest possible level. It must therefore be the case that $\overline{D}$ is to the left of $\overline{D}'$, as shown in Figure 4.1.

At first sight this many seem to be something of a paradox. At $\overline{D}$ it seems to be the case that the exchange rate appreciates after the collapse of the fixed rate. Surely profit maximising speculators will not attack a currency that is about to appreciate? There are two points to be made here. Firstly the collapse of the fixed rate at $\overline{D}$ is not in fact caused by a speculative attack. It is caused by the monetary authority simply running out of reserves. Beyond $\overline{D}$ the monetary authority does not have the means to contract the money supply sufficiently to protect the exchange rate. Secondly at no point is there any forecastable profit to be made. The fact that some realisations of D may produce an appreciation is outweighed by the fact that other realisations will produce a depreciation. The expectation is therefore always for a depreciation.

Figure 4.1: The shadow rate and the critical level of domestic credit.

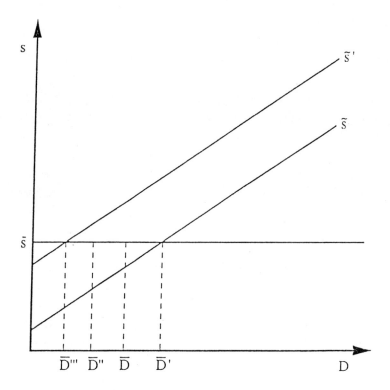

There are two ways of modifying the set-up so that the appreciation at the switch point disappears. The first is to make the switch of regime reversible (as in Krugman and Rotemberg (1992)). This would have the effect of eliminating the potential for appreciation in the floating rate regime. The second is to make the stochastic shocks driving domestic credit one-sided in the sense that domestic credit only ever grows. This is the approach taken in Flood and Garber (1984). In the latter case the switch point becomes $\overline{D}'$. It remains the case, however, that the collapse is triggered by a natural depletion of reserves to $\overline{R}$ rather than by a stock shift in reserves caused by a speculative attack.

4 A digression into continuous time

Consider for a moment a continuous time version of the above model. First of all assume that there are no stochastic shocks and that domestic credit evolves according to:

$$(9) \quad \dot{D}=\mu$$

In this case the shadow rate is again given by equation (6) and, as in Krugman (1979) and Flood and Garber (1984), the breakdown of the fixed rate is given by the point where $\tilde{s} = \overline{s}$. The complications caused by discrete steps in domestic credit do not arise in the continuous time case. At this point there is a single speculative attack which reduces reserves to the minimum level. The deterministic discrete and continuous time cases are therefore essentially identical.

Now consider a continuous time stochastic case where domestic credit evolves according to:

$$(10) \quad dD = \mu\,dt + \sigma\,dz$$

where z is a standard Brownian motion process with unit variance per unit time. Again the shadow rate is given by equation (6). There is, however, now a major difference between the discrete and continuous time cases. In the discrete time case the interest differential played a major role in determining the critical value of D at which a breakdown occurs. This is because in discrete time it is possible from any level of D for a single shock to produce a discrete jump in the exchange rate. The interest rate must therefore adjust so as to compensate investors. In the simple continuous time case considered here it is necessary and usual to regard the interest rate as the instantaneous rate. In contrast to the discrete time case, this rate will only adjust an instant before any forecastable jump in the exchange rate takes place. At that point the rate rises to infinity. But if the interest rate rises to infinity the level of reserves must go to minus infinity. Given the assumption of a lower bound on reserves it is therefore impossible for any breakdown to involve a discrete jump in the exchange rate. Thus the stochastic continuous time case gives rise to exactly the same solution as the deterministic continuous time case, namely that the collapse takes place the first time $\tilde{s} = \bar{s}$. As with the deterministic case, the collapse involves a speculative attack which generates a step change in the level of reserves. This is in complete contrast to the stochastic discrete time case where no such attack takes place.

There are two ways of reproducing the properties of the discrete time case in a continuous time framework. The first is to consider interest rates with a longer maturity than the instantaneous rate. This is the approach adopted in Ozkan and Sutherland (1994a and 1994b). When longer maturity interest rates are considered a forecastable discrete jump in the exchange rate does not require an infinite interest differential. There is therefore no problem in considering breakdown points away from $\tilde{s} = \bar{s}$. The second approach is to assume that stochastic shocks are generated by a compound Poisson process rather than a Brownian motion process. A compound Poisson process is a continuous time process that moves in discrete jumps. Both the timing and the size of the jumps are stochastic. The fact that a discrete jump in the level of domestic credit in the next instant has a probability strictly between zero and unity implies that the instantaneous interest differential is positive but not infinite. It therefore becomes possible (and in fact necessary) to consider solutions to the model where the exchange rate makes a discrete jump. When these alternative approaches are considered it appears that the fact that the continuous time stochastic case outlined above produces a collapse at $\tilde{s} = \bar{s}$ is an artefact of the assumption of Brownian motion shocks and the concentration on the instantaneous interest rate.

5 Change in domestic credit policy at the collapse point

In all the cases considered above it is assumed that domestic credit policy is unaffected by the switch from fixed to floating rates. Thus there is neither a (policy induced) change in the level of domestic credit at the time of the switch nor is there a change in the process driving the on-going evolution of domestic credit. This section considers the implications of a partial relaxation of this assumption. The particular example that will be considered here is one where the switch from a fixed to a floating exchange rate causes an increase in the rate of growth of domestic credit. This case is analysed by Obstfeld (1986) who suggests that such an increase may be induced by an increase in foreign debt service costs for the fiscal authority after a switch of exchange rate regime. This increases the amount of monetary financing in the post collapse regime.

The effect of an increase in domestic credit growth in the post attack regime affects the solution of the model through the shadow rate. Equation (6) shows that an increase in μ causes an upward shift in the shadow rate schedule. Consider Figure 4.1 where the schedule $\tilde{s}$ is the shadow rate schedule that applies to the case where there is no increase in μ after a collapse and the schedule $\tilde{s}'$ is the schedule that applies when there is such an increase. The question that now needs to be tackled is, at what level of D will the fixed rate system collapse? It is simple to see that the collapse point must be to the left of $\overline{D}$ (where the latter is the collapse point arising in the case where there is no loosening of domestic credit policy after a collapse). This must be so because the prospect of a loosening of policy after a collapse increases the expected depreciation of the exchange rate at all levels of domestic credit in the fixed rate regime. This raises the interest rate and reduces reserves. Reserves must therefore run out at a lower level of D. The breakdown point is indicated by $\overline{D}''$ which is to the left of $\overline{D}$.

There is, however, a more significant difference between this case and the previous cases considered. Notice in Figure 4.1 that the shadow rate schedule $\tilde{s}'$ cuts $\tilde{s}$ at point $\overline{D}'''$ which is to the left of the breakdown point $\overline{D}''$. There is therefore a range of realisations of D for which the fixed rate remains in force but where the shadow rate is higher (i.e. more depreciated) than $\tilde{s}$. Obstfeld (1986) showed that these are precisely the circumstances in which a "self-fulfilling" speculative attack may occur.[2] The logic of a self-fulfilling attack is as follows. Speculators know that for realisations of D in the range $\overline{D}'''$ to $\overline{D}''$ the shadow rate is higher than $\tilde{s}$. They also know that if the authorities run out of reserves they will switch to the post attack domestic credit rule and the exchange rate will jump onto the shadow rate schedule. Speculators therefore know that they can make a profit by mounting a selling attack on the currency which instantaneously results in the elimination of remaining reserves and causes a jump in the exchange rate. Those speculators who succeed in buying up the authorities' stock of reserves will make a profit on the transaction.

The problem with this theory of speculative attacks is that, if individual investors are small relative to the government, it is not clear how they can coordinate to produce an attack sufficient to exhaust the stock of reserves. In Obstfeld (1986) this problem is side-stepped by assuming that whenever the level of domestic credit falls within the critical range there is an exogenous lottery which determines whether an attack will take place or not. If an attack takes place then it is assumed to be successful. The lottery is such that an attack takes place with probability π. The expectation of the exchange rate is therefore now given by:

(11)
$$
\begin{aligned}
E_t(s_{t+1}) = \Phi\left(\overline{D}''' - D_t - \mu\right)\overline{s} + (1-\pi)\left\{\int_{\overline{D}'''-D_t-\mu}^{\overline{D}''-D_t-\mu}\phi(\omega)d\omega\right\}\overline{s} + \\
\pi\left\{\int_{\overline{D}'''-D_t-\mu}^{\overline{D}''-D_t-\mu}\phi(\omega)\tilde{s}(\omega)d\omega\right\} + \left\{\int_{\overline{D}''-D_t-\mu}^{\infty}\phi(\omega)\tilde{s}(\omega)d\omega\right\}
\end{aligned}
$$

The third term on the right hand side of this expression reflects the possibility that in the next period D may fall within the critical range and that a self-fulfilling attack may occur. This has the side-effect of raising interest rates at all levels of D and further bring forward the point of a natural collapse. Obstfeld argues that the model has multiple equilibria in the sense that there is a different equilibrium for each value of π.

6 An optimising policy-maker

It is now possible to consider the underlying assumptions in the above models concerning the behaviour of the monetary authority and thus to consider ways of introducing an optimising policy-maker. There are two significant and debatable aspects of the behaviour of the monetary authority in the above models. Firstly, there is an assumption that there is some exogenously given minimum level of reserves. In a world with a large international capital market it is not unreasonable to suppose that a developed country is able to borrow reserves and thereby sustain a negative reserve level. It is therefore not clear why any particular level of reserves should be regarded as an absolute minimum. The second significant assumption in the models described so far is that the level of reserves in the post collapse regime is fixed at the minimum. Even if it is accepted that there is an absolute minimum level of reserves, it is clearly possible for the monetary authority to buy back reserves in the post attack regime and set R at whatever level it chooses above the minimum.

It is possible to argue that, in some countries, the monetary authority has very little room to manoeuvre and is constrained in its ability to set policy.[3] The assumptions underlying the above models may well be relevant to such cases. However, it is apparent that for many countries the monetary authority has both the ability to choose the critical level of reserves at which to abandon a fixed exchange rate and thereafter the ability to choose the level of reserves in the post collapse regime. This discussion immediately suggests that the appropriate way to model these choices is by considering the optimising behaviour of the monetary authority. This section demonstrates how this can be done within the context of the models already described.

Allowing for the optimising behaviour of the monetary authority raises many complex issues. Firstly, there is the question of specifying an appropriate objective function. What are the variables that the policy-maker cares about and why? Secondly, there is the question of why the policy-maker chooses to operate a fixed exchange rate rather than any other open– or closed-loop policy rule. Thirdly, if optimising behaviour can be used to explain the choice of such a rule can it also explain why the rule is abandoned in some circumstances? Finally, how will an optimising policy-maker set policy in the floating rate regime and will re-entry into the fixed rate regime be possible?

It is not practical to deal with all these questions in one model so the approach taken here is to suppress a number of aspects of the problem and concentrate on some of the key issues. The discussion will proceed in two stages. In the first stage an objective function for an optimising policy-maker will be added to the model discussed in the previous sections of the paper to illustrate the basic principles. This objective function and some of the associated assumptions will, however, be rather implausible for some obvious reasons. The formal structure of this model will nevertheless have very close parallels with the model of Ozkan and Sutherland (1994a and 1994b). Therefore, in the second stage, this alternative model will be described and its links to the model of this section will be discussed.

Consider the monetary model framework which is given in equations (1) to (4). This model is not based on explicit microeconomic foundations so it is not immediately clear how to construct a welfare function for an optimising policy-maker. Since the model is one where output and employment are permanently at their equilibrium levels it is clear that there are no useful results to be obtained by assuming that the policy-maker is concerned about real economic activity. In fact the only variables that fluctuate at all are nominal variables such as the exchange rate, prices, the money supply and the nominal interest rate, so, if the above framework is to be used, it is necessary to define policy objectives in terms of one of these variables. As an illustrative exercise it will be assumed that the policy-maker dislikes deviations of reserves from some target level. Call this target level $\overline{R}$ and assume that the policy-maker's welfare declines linearly in $(R_t - \overline{R})^2$.

It is immediately apparent that such a welfare function could not explain why this policy-maker would ever want to join a fixed rate system. The need to defend the fixed rate causes fluctuations in the level of reserves which reduce welfare. On the other hand, in the floating rate regime the policy-maker is free to set R at $\overline{R}$ where maximum welfare is achieved. There is therefore no incentive to operate a fixed rate. This problem can be overcome if it is assumed that there are some other benefits which a country receives from membership of a fixed rate system but which are not explicitly modelled. Thus assume the policy-maker has the following welfare function:

$$(12) \quad W_t = \sum_{\tau=t}^{\infty} \beta^{(\tau-t)} E_t \left[Z - (\overline{R} - R_\tau)^2 \right]$$

Here β is the policy-maker's discount factor and Z is assumed to reflect the unmodelled benefits that the policy-maker receives from membership of a fixed rate system. As an example assume that the fixed rate system (such as the ERM) is part of a wider agreement on trade barriers and political cooperation. Agreement to abide by the rules of the fixed rate system may give the policy-maker greater bargaining power over other aspects of economic cooperation. It is assumed that Z is equal to a fixed positive value while the country is a member of the fixed rate system. On switching to a floating rate system Z is set to zero. The analysis is further simplified if it is assumed that once the country has switched to the floating rate system it cannot regain positive Z by re-entering the fixed rate system. It is obvious that this final assumption implies that it is never optimal for a country to re-enter the fixed rate system. It is also obvious that once in the floating rate system it is optimal to set R at $\overline{R}$ and to fix it at that level permanently.

Some of the features of the solution to this model are already becoming apparent and these can be illustrated more clearly with reference to Figure 4.2. It has just been established that in the floating rate regime the policy-maker will fix reserves at $\overline{R}$. Given the assumption concerning the process followed by domestic credit the exchange rate in the floating rate system will again be determined by equation (6). This is marked $\tilde{s}$ in figure 4.2. This is in effect equivalent to the shadow rate schedule that emerges in the traditional models. The main difference is that the level of reserves that is set is emerging from the policy-maker's optimising problem rather than from some exogenous assumption about the minimum level of reserves. Of course, it may be objected that the assumption about a target level of reserves in the policy-maker's objective function is no more soundly based than the assumption of an exogenous minimum level of reserves. It is true that, in this illustrative example, there is no satisfactory explanation for a target level of reserves. However, the important point is that the critical level of domestic credit at which this policy-maker optimally chooses to leave the fixed rate system will typically not correspond to a reserve level of $\overline{R}$. The switch of regime will therefore be accompanied by a step change in the reserve level which is the result of some optimising process. This is a feature which is very different from traditional models.

Now consider how this policy-maker will choose between exchange rate regimes. It is clear from the form of the objective function that the policy-maker's willingness to maintain a fixed exchange rate depends on how far reserves are away from the target level. Using the equations of the model it is simple to show that the level of reserves is determined as follows:

$$(13) \quad R_t = \frac{1}{1-\gamma}(\tilde{s} - \lambda i_t - \gamma D_t)$$

Thus R depends on the nominal interest rate and the level of domestic credit. Assume for the moment that $\lambda = 0$. This implies, from equation

Figure 4.2: Optimal regime switching.

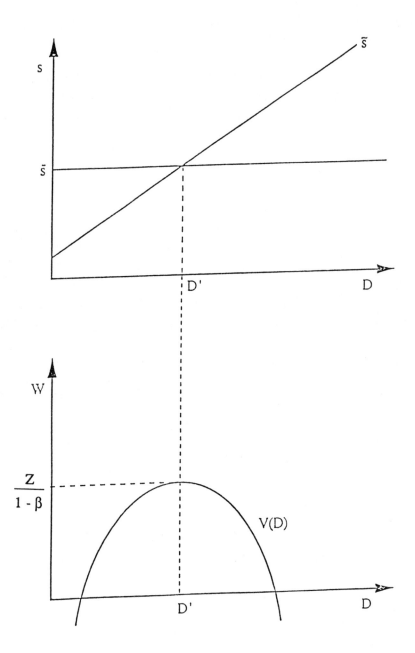

(13) that reserves follow a stochastic process which has the same characteristics as that of domestic credit (albeit with the opposite sign). In particular R has the same degree of persistence as D. A stochastic shock to D therefore not only moves the current value of R away from the target level it also moves all future expected values of R in the same direction. In fact for each value of D_t there is a corresponding expected path for R and therefore a corresponding value for the objective function. It is possible to write the value of the objective function as a function of D_t, i.e. $W_t = V(D_t)$. If the drift in the stochastic process driving D is set to zero (i.e. $\mu = 0$) so $E_t(D_\tau) = D_t$ for all $\tau > t$, the following expression for $V(D_t)$ can be derived:

$$(14) \quad V(D_t) = \frac{1}{1-\beta} \left\{ Z - \left[\overline{R} - \frac{1}{1-\gamma}(\overline{s} - \lambda i_t - \gamma D_t) \right]^2 \right\}$$

An example of the function $V(D_t)$ is sketched in the lower panel of Figure 4.2. It can be seen that it reaches a peak at D' and falls as D diverges to positive or negative values. The point D' is the level of D at which current R is equal to $\overline{R}$. (If the drift term is positive then the peak in the value function is to the left of D'.).

Having derived this function the natural next step is to compare it to the level of welfare that is obtained in the floating rate regime. The latter is very simply derived since, in the floating rate regime, Z is zero and R is set equal to $\overline{R}$. The level of W is therefore zero for all levels of D. The obvious conclusion from this reasoning is that the policy-maker will choose to remain in the fixed rate system while $V(D_t) > 0$ and switch to the floating rate regime (and remain there forever) the first time $V(D_t) < 0$.

The solution to the model is in fact rather more complicated than this for reasons which will be discussed below. Before turning to these complications notice two factors which are revealed by the case sketched in Figure 4.2. Firstly, the vital role of the variable Z is clearly revealed. If the benefits arising from a fixed rate system represented by this variable do not exist then the function $V(D_t)$ would lie entirely below the horizontal axis. There would therefore be no range of D for which membership of the fixed rate system would be desirable. Secondly, notice that the case illustrated in Figure 4.2 suggests that there will in fact be two critical values of D at which the breakdown of the fixed rate regime will occur. This is an obvious consequence of the choice of a quadratic welfare function. The policy-maker is assumed to dislike high values of reserves as well as low values.

Turn now to the complications mentioned above. There are two main issues to be discussed in this connection. Firstly there are the effects of (what may be described as) the "option value" attached to membership of a fixed rate system. Secondly there are the implications of private sector expectations of a regime switch on the interest rate and the level of reserves when $\lambda \neq 0$. These points will be discussed in turn.

To understand the role of the "option value" of the fixed rate it is necessary to consider an implicit (and incorrect) assumption that is embodied in equation (14). Equation (14) is based on the entire expected future path of R. The expected path for D is simple to derive and it thus seems simple to derive the expected path for R using equation (13). This is the approach adopted in deriving equation (14). It is however incorrect to use equation (13) to derive the expected path for R. The expected path for R must take into account the possibility of switching from the fixed rate regime (where equation (13) holds) to the floating rate regime, where $R = \overline{R}$. In effect equation (14) is ignoring the possibility that, for some realised paths of D, there will be a regime switch and a change in the process followed by R. It should be clear that the option to switch regimes when D reaches extreme values allows the policy-maker to avoid the effects of very bad realisations of the stochastic process. The value of being in the fixed rate regime is therefore higher than that indicated by equation (14). The difference between the true value of W in the fixed rate regime and the value indicated by equation (14) is the option value attached to the fixed rate regime.

It is immediately clear that the effect of this option value is to increase the total value of the fixed rate regime. The option value will therefore encourage the policy-maker to stay in the fixed rate regime for longer. It should also be apparent that the option value depends on the trigger points that the policy-maker chooses for switching regimes. At first as the trigger points are moved apart the option value increases. But beyond some point a further widening of the trigger points produces a decline in the option value. This latter effect arises because trigger points which are very extreme only eliminate very extreme realisations of R. The optimal trigger points will obviously be those which maximise the option value.

Turn now to the second complication that was mentioned above, namely the effect of regime switching on private sector expectations and the interest rate. In moving from equation (13) to equation (14) it was explicitly assumed that $\lambda = 0$. This meant that interest rate movements could be ignored. It has already been established that an optimising policy-maker will establish trigger points at which a step change in the exchange rate will be implemented. If private sector agents know that such trigger points exist then, as is well known from the traditional currency crisis models discussed in previous sections, the domestic interest rate will be affected. In particular, as domestic credit moves towards a trigger point at which a depreciation is expected the nominal interest rate rises (and the opposite occurs at a trigger point where an appreciation is expected). It can be seen from equation (13) that when $\lambda \neq 0$ a rise in the domestic interest rate reduces reserves. A rise in domestic credit therefore has both a direct and an indirect effect on the level of reserves. The net result must therefore be to encourage the policy maker to switch regimes sooner than is the case when $\lambda = 0$. A symmetric effect works at low levels of domestic credit.

The interest rate effects in the previous paragraph are only the most obvious that arise from relaxing the assumption of $\lambda = 0$. There is also a more subtle effect that arises. The fact that a movement in domestic credit towards a trigger point causes a change in the interest rate has already been described. It must also be true that, for a given level of domestic credit, a change in the position of a trigger point will produce a change in the interest rate and therefore a change in reserves and welfare. Thus the policy-maker appears to have an indirect means of affecting W through manipulation of private sector beliefs about the position of the trigger points.

The important feature to note about this indirect effect is that its strength is not constant. When D is close to a trigger point, changes in the position of that trigger point (if they are credible) will have powerful effects on the rate of interest and the level of reserves. But when D is far from a trigger point, changes in the trigger point will have relatively little effect. The policy-maker's incentive to manipulate private sector expectations therefore varies as the level of domestic credit varies. This in turn means that the policy-maker would like to choose a different pair of trigger points for every value of D.

If it is assumed that the optimising problem faced by the policy-maker is known to private sector agents then the incentive to manipulate expectations will also be apparent to those agents. In particular they will realise that the policy-maker would like to choose a different set of trigger points for every level of D. For this reason it is clear that, at any given level of D, the policy-maker's most preferred pair of trigger points will in fact not be credible. Private sector agents will be able to predict that those trigger points will not be optimal once D has changed.

It is clear from the foregoing discussion that the appropriate solution to this model does not consist of simply locating the trigger points that the policy-maker would like to announce at any given level of D. Rather, the appropriate solution must involve locating those trigger points which the policy-maker has an incentive to implement given the beliefs of private sector agents.

It should be clear by now that the process of obtaining a full solution to the model outlined in this section is not straightforward. Adding explicit policy optimisation to traditional balance of payments crisis models clearly raises a number of intricate problems which are too complex to be resolved explicitly in this paper. An explicit solution to a model which is formally similar to the one discussed here is however fully discussed in Ozkan and Sutherland (1994a and 1994b). The parallels between the model under consideration here and the Ozkan and Sutherland model are the subject of the next section.

7 An alternative model

The model of the previous section was presented as an illustrative example of how explicit policy optimisation could be introduced into a traditional balance of payments crisis model. It is clearly rather difficult to justify the objective function given in equation (12) in economic terms so the wider economic interpretation of the results described in the previous section is not of much interest. It will be shown below, however, that the model needs only very few amendments to produce a structure which is of more interest. The resulting model will have the same formal mathematical structure as the above model and will in fact be a discrete time equivalent of the model used in Ozkan and Sutherland (1994a and 1994b).

Consider first the structure of the objective function. Equation (12) assumes that the policy-maker cares about the deviation of reserves from some target level. It is much more plausible to assume that the policy-maker is concerned with variables that are linked to the welfare of the public in some way. Thus, as is common in the literature on policy optimisation, it could be assumed that the policy-maker cares about the deviation of output and inflation from target levels. Thus an objective function of the following form could be postulated:

$$(15) \quad W_t = \sum_{\tau=t}^{\infty} \beta^{(\tau-t)} E_t \left[Z - (\bar{y} - y_\tau)^2 - \pi_\tau^2 \right]$$

where $\bar{y}$ is the output target and π is the rate of inflation (the target level of inflation is zero). It is obvious from this structure that the motive for switching exchange rate regime will be excessive deviations of output and/or inflation from their target levels.

There would of course be no point in combining an objective function of the form of (15) with the monetary model structure used so far in this paper. The level of output in the monetary model is assumed to be completely fixed at its equilibrium level. The output term in equation (15) would therefore be irrelevant. In addition, the rate of inflation in the monetary model is completely determined by the exchange rate. Thus deviations of inflation from zero can best be achieved by completely fixing the exchange rate. The objective function given in (15), combined with the monetary model, would therefore predict a permanently fixed exchange rate.

An obvious way of generating fluctuations in output is to introduce some form of nominal stickiness in wages or prices. Thus, for instance, a Phillips curve relationship which links price adjustment to excess demand would allow output to deviate temporarily from its natural rate. It would also provide for more interesting behaviour of inflation. It turns out, however, to be very difficult to deal with the extra dynamics that a Phillips curve relationship introduces into the model. As a first step therefore it is better to consider a more extreme form of nominal rigidity, namely completely fixed nominal prices and wages. Thus assume p is fixed and, for simplicity, set $p = 0$.

With the introduction of nominal inertia it is also necessary to introduce an expression for aggregate demand. This could be given as follows:

$$(16) \quad y_t = -\gamma i_t + \eta s_t$$

Thus demand depends negatively on the interest rate and positively on the exchange rate. The assumption of fixed prices means that there is no need to distinguish between nominal and real variables. Assume output is demand determined.

There is one last amendment that is required to allow this model to generate a regime switching solution. Consider the fixed rate solution to this model with domestic credit following the stochastic process given in (6). A policy-maker in this model who is attempting to maximise (15) would clearly prefer to be in the fixed rate system since any other regime involves fluctuations in output. The policy-maker can maintain the fixed rate indefinitely since there are no constraints on reserves and there are no costs involved in using reserves perfectly to offset fluctuations in domestic credit. Unlike the previous model, the policy-maker in this model does not care about fluctuations in reserves. The fact that a regime switch is not generated is due to the assumption that shocks are hitting the economy through the money supply. If on the other hand the source of shocks is in the real economy then the policy-maker faces a trade-off between the benefits of a fixed rate system, represented by Z, and the costs, which take the form of fluctuations in output that cannot be stabilised in a fixed rate regime. (Notice that the fixed price assumption makes the inflation term in the objective function redundant.)

In Ozkan and Sutherland (1994a and 1994b) it is assumed that shocks enter the economy through the foreign interest rate. This is to represent the effects of German monetary policy on other ERM members during the lead up to the collapse of the ERM in 1992 and 1993. It is equally possible to assume that shocks enter the economy through real demand.

The model that emerges from these various amendments is very different in terms of its economic interpretation from the model outlined in the previous section. Formally however it has a very similar structure. The discussion of the main features of the solution contained in the previous section therefore applies to both models. First consider the parallels in the structures of the models. In the model of this section the policy-maker cares about deviations of output from a target level. In the fixed rate system output is shocked away from its target level by an exogenous stochastic process. If the stochastic shocks are in i^* then, through uncovered interest parity, they result in shocks in i and therefore in y. In the model of the previous section the policy-maker cared about R which is shocked way from its target level by movements in D. Equation (13) in the previous model plays the same role as equation (16) in the current model.

In the model of the previous section the policy-maker chooses to set R at its target level in the floating rate regime. This generates a shadow rate schedule which implies a step-change in monetary policy and the exchange rate at the time of a regime switch. In the model of the current section the policy-maker would choose to set y at its target level in a floating rate regime. Again this generates a step change in monetary policy and the exchange rate at the time of a switch.

Finally notice that the domestic interest rate behaves in essentially the same way in both models. For instance, as the shock variable approaches a trigger point which will produce a depreciation, expectations of a regime switch cause domestic interest rates to rise. In the previous model this accelerates the loss of reserves (see equation (13)) and encourages the policy-maker to switch regimes sooner. In the current model the rise in the interest rate further depresses output and likewise encourages the policy-maker to switch regimes.

It can thus be seen that the formal structure of the models is very similar. The discussion concerning the option value of the fixed rate regime and the credibility problems relating to the optimal choice of trigger points therefore applies equally to both models.

An explicit solution to a continuous time version of the model presented here is derived and extensively analysed in Ozkan and Sutherland (1994a and 1994b). The properties of this solution will therefore not be discussed here. It is however interesting to finish this section by considering some of the implications of the model for the behaviour of reserves. Given the assumptions, firstly that the policy-maker does not care about the level of reserves and secondly that there is no external constraint on the level of reserves, it is clear that the model can be solved without any explicit reference to R. It is however possible to deduce the behaviour of R that is implied by the policy-maker's behaviour. While in the fixed rate regime the policy-maker uses reserves to stabilise the exchange rate. In effect this requires that R be continually expanded or contracted so as to accommodate changes in money demand that arise from movements in *i* and *y*. On switching to the floating rate regime it becomes optimal for the policy-maker to stabilise output at its target level. This is achieved by an appropriate step change in the level of reserves. Thereafter reserves are continually expanded or contracted in such a way that output is maintained at its target level.

The model of this section was introduced as a framework which offered a better motivation for considering optimising policy making.

However as a final point, it is worth noting that it is perfectly possible to disregard the policy-maker's objective function and use this model to consider the traditional type of balance of payments crisis solution (as outlined in sections II to V) where the policy-maker is forced to abandon the fixed rate when reserves reach some exogenous lower bound.

8 Conclusion

This paper started with a description of a version of the deterministic Krugman (1979) model of balance of payments crises. This was extended firstly to allow for stochastic shocks (as in Flood and Garber, 1984) and secondly to produce self-fulfilling speculative attacks (as in Obstfeld, 1986). The central feature of all these models is that the policy-maker defends the exchange rate while there are sufficient reserves and switches to a floating rate regime when reserves reach some exogenous lower bound. The Obstfeld model introduces an assumption that monetary policy is relaxed after the breakdown of the fixed rate regime. The policy-maker, however, continues to perform an essentially passive role.

In section VI it was shown how a simple objective function for the policy-maker could be introduced into the model which allows an explicit analysis of the policy-maker's optimising behaviour. It was briefly shown that the policy-maker's optimisation problem is complicated by two factors. Firstly there is an option value that is attached to membership of a fixed rate regime. Secondly the fact that interest rates are affected by private sector perceptions of the policy-maker's optimising behaviour gives rise to credibility effects.

The model discussed in section VI is sufficient to demonstrate the issues involved in introducing an optimising policy-maker into traditional currency crises models. The underlying economic interpretation of the resulting model is however rather unsatisfactory. For this reason in section VII it was shown how, with a few more modifications, the model can be given a more meaningful structure. The resulting model is in fact a discrete time version of the model in Ozkan and Sutherland (1994a and 1994b). One of the basic themes of this paper is, therefore, a demonstration of how, by a series of modifications, this model can be derived from more traditional currency crises models.

As stated in the introduction, the Ozkan and Sutherland model is related to another set of models. These are the so called "escape clause" models of Flood and Isard (1989), Obstfeld (1991), De Kock and Grilli

(1993) and Obstfeld (1994). The origin of these models lies in the literature on time inconsistency and pre-commitment in economic policy. The basic proposition that gave rise to the development of these models is that a policy which involves pre-commitment to a simple rule (such as a fixed exchange rate) can be improved if an escape clause is explicitly written into the rule which allows it to be abandoned in extreme circumstances. The definition of an extreme circumstance is when a shock variable crosses an explicitly announced trigger value. It is clear that it requires only a reinterpretation to use this style of analysis to consider the collapse of a fixed rate. This is the approach adopted by Obstfeld (1994).

The parallel between the escape clause approach and the Ozkan and Sutherland model is also very clear. Indeed it is perfectly possible to regard the Ozkan and Sutherland model as a development of the escape clause literature rather than a development of the balance of payments crisis literature as described in this paper. The main difference between the Ozkan and Sutherland model and the structure of a typical escape clause model is that the latter is usually a static framework. The typical escape clause model is one where each period the economy is hit by a single temporary shock and the policy-maker has to decide whether to fix or float in that period. In the following period the problem is repeated from the same starting point. The Ozkan and Sutherland model is, on the other hand, a fully dynamic structure where the policy-maker faces a serially correlated shock and is attempting to maximise an intertemporal welfare function. It is this structure which makes it necessary to consider the option value of a fixed rate system. It also allows the dynamic development of a currency crisis to be modelled.

It is worth considering briefly some of the extensions that can be made to the models described in sections VI and VII of this paper. One aspect of these models, which has not been sufficiently discussed, is the link with the self-fulfilling attack model of Obstfeld (1986). It was described in section V how that model depended on the policy-maker implementing a step change in monetary policy at the time of a switch in regime. This is precisely what the optimising policy-maker does in the models of sections VI and VII, so it is possible that these models allow for self-fulfilling attacks. Thus, for instance, in the model of section VI it is possible for speculators to mount a selling attack on the domestic currency and push reserves down to a level which induces the policy-maker to switch regimes and relax monetary policy. In the model of section VII the chain of events would be slightly different. In that model the contraction in reserves would force up the interest rate and reduce aggregate demand. The resulting contraction in output would induce the policy-maker to switch regimes and relax monetary policy.

The explicit modelling of such attacks was not considered in the context of the above models.[4] To do so would raise some interesting but very intricate issues. For instance, self-fulfilling attacks in themselves are a source of stochastic shocks which an optimising policy-maker would have to build into the setting of policy. The nature of the stochastic shocks coming from speculative attacks would, however, be different from other stochastic shocks in that a speculative attack can be reversed if speculators can be persuaded that an attack is misguided. It is not immediately apparent, therefore, that the optimal way to set policy in the presence of speculative attacks is in terms of trigger points. It may be better to set a time limit on how long to withstand a speculative attack and only give in once the duration of an attack has exceeded that limit. If the optimal behaviour of the policy-maker is of this form then, in turn, the optimal behaviour of speculators must take this into account.[5]

The discussion of the previous paragraph is sufficient to demonstrate that the modelling of self-fulfilling speculative attacks in the presence of an optimising policy-maker is a difficult but potentially very interesting problem. It may be that a fully satisfactory explanation for the collapse of the ERM will require a model which combines self-fulfilling attacks with an optimising policy-maker. However, a first step in moving towards such a model is to gain more understanding of the implications of incorporating an optimising policy-maker into traditional currency crises models. It has been the purpose of this paper to show how the model of Ozkan and Sutherland performs this task.

Notes

[1] I am grateful to participants at the conference "European Currency Crises and After" for many useful comments and suggestions. I am also greatly indebted to Gulcin Ozkan for many enlightening discussions on the subject of currency crises.

[2] In contrast to the situation being described above, Obstfeld assumed that the stochastic process followed by domestic credit was such that a natural collapse could not occur. He was thus able to show that a speculative attack could occur even when domestic credit policy was

consistent with a fixed rate. In the model described here both natural and self-fulfilling collapses are possible.

[3] The constraints in question here are those created by lack of access to developed financial markets rather than those created by the constitutional or institutional set-up of the central bank.

[4] Implicitly such attacks are being ruled out by assuming that individual speculators are too small and too uncoordinated to mount an attack.

[5] Some of the features of this problem are reminiscent of the budget crisis model of Alesina and Drazen (1991). There two groups of tax payers are fighting over the share of tax to be paid. This gives rise to a waiting game as each group waits to see if the other group gives in. Bensaid and Jeanne (1994) have proposed a model of speculative attacks which has some of the elements of this structure.

References

Anderson, T.M. (1994), "Shocks and the Viability of a Fixed Exchange Rate Commitment," *CEPR Discussion Paper,* N° 969.

Alesina, A., and A. Drazen (1991), "Why are Stabilisations Delayed?" *American Economic Review,* 81, pp. 1770-1188.

Bensaid, B., and O. Jeanne (1994), "The Instability of Fixed Exchange Rate Systems when Raising the Nominal Interest Rate is Costly," mimeo, University of Paris I.

De Kock, G., and V. Grilli (1993), "Fiscal Policies and the Choice of Exchange Rate Regime," *Economic Journal,* 103, pp. 347-358.

Flood, R.P., and P. Garber (1984), "Collapsing Exchange Rate Regimes: Some Linear Examples," *Journal of International Economics,* 17, pp. 1-13.

Flood, R.P., and P. Isard (1989), "Monetary Policy Strategies," *IMF Staff Papers,* 36, pp. 612-32.

Krugman, P.R. (1979), "A Theory of Balance of Payments Crises," *Journal of Money, Credit and Banking,* 11, pp. 311-325.

Krugman, P.R., and J. Rotemberg (1992), "Speculative Attacks on Target Zones," in P. Krugman and M. Miller (eds), *Exchange Rate Targets and Currency Bands,* Cambridge University Press.

Obstfeld, M. (1986), "Rational and Self-Fulfilling Balance of Payments Crises," *American Economic Review,* 76, pp. 72-81.

Obstfeld, M. (1991), "Destabilising Effects of Exchange Rate Escape Clauses," *NBER Working Paper*, N° 3603.

Obstfeld, M. (1994), "The Logic of Currency Crises," *Cahiers Economiques et Monétaires*, Banque de France, 43, pp. 189-213.

Ozkan, G., and A. Sutherland (1994a), "A Currency Crisis Model with an Optimising Policy-Maker," mimeo, University of York.

Ozkan, G., and A. Sutherland (1994b), "Policy Measures to Avoid a Currency Crisis," mimeo, University of York, forthcoming in the *Economic Journal*.

82-88   F31

p57: **Discussion**   E52

JEAN-SEBASTIEN PENTECOTE & MARC-ALEXANDRE SENEGAS

A. Sutherland provides us with a very insightful approach about speculative attacks on fixed exchange rates regimes, at least from two points of view.

On one hand, he makes a very relevant synthesis of the "traditional" literature on the subject, as it was initiated by, inter alia, Krugman (1979) and Flood and Garber (1984). He wants to put an emphasis on the role played by the specification of the models used in this literature: most of the speculative attacks features depend on the modelling framework which is retained. Hence it is not indifferent whether a deterministic or a stochastic framework is specified or whether a discrete time or a continuous time modelling is chosen. Furthermore, whether the process followed by the credit component of the money base is contingent or not on the exchange rate regime, will determine if self-fulfilling attacks can arise in these traditional models (cf. Obstfeld (1986)).

On the second hand, the author lays, in a rigorous manner, the foundations of a parallel between the former literature and the one which analyses exchange rate crises in an optimising framework (i.e. the monetary authorities max(min)imize an objective-function). This enterprise is motivated in part by an empirical evidence: Central Bank reserves have not played a major role in the triggering of recent EMS crises (1992-1993), what one could have predicted according to the results drawn from the "traditional" literature. It seems, rather, that these crises, in some cases, have been associated with a conflict between, on one side, some monetary authorities which were actively committed to a fixed exchange rate regime and, on the other side, a private sector which rationally analysed the implications of a given path of some "fundamentals" (e.g. credit, interest rates, output, ...). This leads then to establish, theoretically, some comparisons with the literature on escape clause rules (this is done in greater detail in the two articles Sutherland wrote with Ozkan (1994a,b)).[1] In this configuration (e.g. De Kock and Grilli (1989)), the exchange rate crisis can be considered not so much as arising from an incompatibility between the behaviour of the "fundamentals" and the "rules of the game" of a fixed exchange rate regime, as, rather, being associated with an optimal reaction adopted by the monetary authorities confronted to shocks.

By "bridging the gap between old and new approaches", Sutherland seems to favour the distinction (or more precisely the complementarity) between, on the one hand, speculative attacks prompted by the behaviour of the "fundamentals" eventually incompatible with a passive commitment by the monetary authorities to a fixed exchange rate regime and, on the other hand, crises occurring in the context of optimising and active monetary authorities which face a private sector with rational expectations. This boundary line, which Sutherland sheds light on, is quite new, compared, in particular, to the commonly and traditionally acknowledged one which is drawn between crises which are logically triggered given the path of the "fundamentals" and those which may occur (arbitrarily?) even if the regime is a priori sustainable. This latter distinction has been mentioned, in particular, in the analysis of recent EMS crises (cf. Eichengreen and Wyplosz (1993) for an excellent presentation). For Sutherland the problem of self-fulfilling speculative attacks could be addressed in an optimising framework (see Obstfeld (1991, 1994)): these crises must be considered as rational and triggered by the process followed by the "the fundamentals", which is, in this case, contingent on the exchange rate regime considered (this contingency is precisely what makes the difference with the other type of "traditional" exchange rate crises).

Furthermore the bridge that Sutherland establishes, brings out the central role that the rationality of private sector expectations plays in the models used in both approaches : this "common status" justifies, in a way, the connection emphasised by Sutherland.

In the "old" literature the incompatibility of the path followed by the "fundamentals" with "the rules of the game" of a fixed exchange rate regime would (in most cases) inevitably lead to a collapse of this unsustainable regime. However the private sector expects rationally this inconsistency and the " natural death " of the regime which follows it. This behaviour prompts it in turn to hasten the collapse in order not to be "fooled" by the switch to the floating exchange rate regime. Thus, due to this key role played by rational expectations, we can see under the "balance-of-payments crisis" generic term a two-fold process.

Private sector rational expectations occupy a strategic place in the literature based upon an optimising framework as well. Since the works of Kydland and Prescott (1979) and their application by Barro and Gordon (1983) to monetary policy games, we know that taking into account these rational expectations in the derivation of the "optimal" policy by monetary authorities has strong implications on the nature of the solutions in the models considered by this literature. The related temporal inconsistency and credibility issues are mentioned by Sutherland (but more profoundly addressed by him and Ozkan in their two articles (1994a,b)). In the model presented, the authorities, which are subject to the constraint of a given path followed by the credit component, try to derive a point on this path which will trigger, if attained, the regime switch - in Ozkan and Sutherland's model this optimal value concerns the level of the shock on the domestic interest rate. However the equilibrium point depends eventually on how private sector expectations have been treated by the monetary authorities when the latter determine their optimal policy. In this determination it is important, in particular, to consider whether, in the case where the monetary authorities pre-commit to a rule, private agents are able to take into account that this pre-commitment is de facto contingent on a position on the dynamic-but-with-persistence path followed by the credit component (for a parallel see Cukierman's analysis (1992) in a Barro-Gordon model with persistence in the inflation rate).

The central feature of the new approach is the objective-function that the policy-maker wants to maximise. Sutherland's original way of explaining the occurrence of exchange-rate regimes switches raises two series of questions : the first one concerns characteristics that are common to both alternative models suggested by the author, while the second one will point out particular aspects or assumptions distinguishing each of these models.

The starting point of Sutherland's analysis is to suppose that the policy-maker has to trade-off the costs against the benefits involved by its membership of a fixed exchange rate system. The author gives, however, *an asymmetric treatment* of this trade-off. Indeed Sutherland extensively discusses the true nature of welfare losses resulting from the maintenance of a preannounced parity. Even though Sutherland is conscious of *the crucial role played by the benefits* that the policy-maker receives from its participation to a fixed exchange-rate regime and without which this study loses all of its substance, the fundamental determinants of these gains should be examined in greater detail. The author mentions the benefits arising from international trade when the bilateral exchange-rate remains fixed, although the measurement and significance of these gains are still questionable. Future works should undoubtedly be done in this respect in order to give a more comprehensive view of the policy-maker's choice of a particular exchange-rate regime.

A noticeable feature of Sutherland's analysis is *the irreversibility of the switch* from the fixed parity to the floating rate regime. This implicit assumption in the paper has the convenient property to make the analytical resolution of the model tractable, but it considerably lowers the explanatory power of the analysis. A crude historical retrospective shows that since the Gold Standard most countries successively experienced periods during which exchange-rates remained (practically) fixed and periods of a higher degree of exchange-rate flexibility. Allowing the policy-maker to make his decision reversible, as Krugman and Rotemberg (1992), Buiter and Grilli (1992) and Giovannini (1992) have already done, would surely shed light on questions unresolved by this new approach of currency crisis. To deal with this problem requires a closer examination of the precise nature of the costs and the benefits that the policy-maker has to take into consideration in its welfare-function.

The qualitative nature of this objective-function brings up another question to which Sutherland gives no convincing answer. *The quadratic form* considered in the text leads to the determination of two critical values for the level of domestic credit, that is values at which the policy-maker prefers to give up the fixed exchange-rate system. Nevertheless, nothing prevents from obtaining negative trigger values. What economic interpretation shall we give to such results? Moreover the author does not seem to convincingly explain why the policy-maker cannot tolerate high as well as low stocks of reserves (or levels of activity depending on the model which is used). The description of the policy-maker's optimising behaviour certainly needs further refinements to give an endogenous determination of these target levels.

To conclude with these general remarks, we would like to underline and *to question the partial equilibrium nature of Sutherland's models.* In reality it is often the case that domestic *and* foreign policy-makers decide of one accord to fix the relative price of their moneys at a given agreed level: the viability of the fixed rate regime depends not only on the attitude of the domestic policy-maker, but also on that of its foreign counterpart (cf. Dumas and Svensson (1994) in the context of a bilateral exchange-rate target zone). Each policy-maker may have to take its optimal decision knowing the reaction of its counterpart. Furthermore, members of the Exchange-Rate Mechanism have to focus (perhaps in a hierarchical manner) on *several bilateral parities,* a crucial feature that Sutherland neglects in his models.

We would like now to point out some weaknesses that are specific to each of the two approaches developed by Sutherland.

Wishing to stress the analogies between traditional currency crisis models and his study, the author first suggests that the policy-maker only cares about the deviation of its stock of reserves from a target level. Retaining an *exogenous determination* of this target level is quite disturbing. It is hard to understand the true motives that guide the policy-maker to hold indefinitely a non-zero amount of exchange-rate reserves in the post-collapse (flexible) exchange-rate system.

The role of reserves in a floating rate system (described by Sutherland in section VII of his article) is far from convincing: why should the policy-maker modify its stock of reserves to stabilise the real product to its (exogenous and undefined) target level while, by nature, this objective can be instantaneously and automatically achieved by an appropriate adjustment of the flexible exchange-rate?

In a final section Sutherland wishes to give an alternative insight into how the dramatic 1992-1993 events experienced by EMS members went on. To this end, the author takes nominal rigidities explicitly into account. This interesting work may stimulate future research in two possible directions. *First,* the author assumes that domestic prices are completely fixed. This is a convenient but unrealistic assumption because it gives no role to the domestic inflation rate (and thus to competitiveness problems) in the policy-maker's objective function (as it had been previously specified). Taking into account a *dynamic adjustment process* of domestic prices in this new approach to currency crisis models still remains to be considered. *Second,* Sutherland implicitly supposes that shocks, whatever their origin, *instantaneously* transmit to the level of real activity. This does not explain delays observed between the occurrence of shocks and their impact on aggregate demand in most EEC countries.

Sutherland's contribution clearly establishes analogies between two different ways of modelling the currency crises. It also stresses the need to offer a more rigorous treatment of the policy-maker's behaviour if one wishes to give convincing explanations of recent events. *Empirical investigation* remains to be done in order to evaluate the respective explanatory powers of old and recent theoretical views.

Note

[1] To tackle this issue Sutherland examines reserves holding by Central Banks in an optimising perspective. Taking into account the agents behaviour in the model through an optimisation program is considered by Obstfeld (1986) in a representative agent framework with intertemporal utility maximisation. Willman (1989) extends this analysis to address problems concerning the minimal reserves level hypothesis retained in traditional speculative attacks models.

References

Barro, R., and D. Gordon (1983), "A Positive Theory of Monetary Policy in a Natural Rate Model," *Journal of Political Economy,* 91, August, pp. 589-610.

Buiter, W., and V. Grilli (1992), "Anomalous Speculative Attacks on Fixed Exchange Rate Regimes: Possible Resolutions of the 'Gold Standard Paradox'," chapter 9 in Krugman, P., and M. Miller (eds), *Exchange Rate Targets and Currency Bands,* Cambridge University Press.

Cukierman, A. (1992), *Central Bank Strategy, Credibility and Independence: Theory and Evidence,* Cambridge: MIT Press.

De Kock, G., and V. Grilli (1989), "Endogenous Exchange Rate Regime Switches," *NBER Working Paper,* N° 3066.

Dumas, B., and L. Svensson (1994), "How Long Do Unilateral Target-Zones Last?" *Journal of International Economics,* 36, N° 3/4, May, pp. 467-481.

Eichengreen, B., and Ch. Wyplosz (1993), "The Unstable EMS," *CEPR Discussion Paper,* N° 817.

Flood, R., and P. Garber (1984), "Collapsing Exchange Rate Regimes: Some Linear Examples," *Journal of International Economics,* 17, pp. 1-13.

Giovaninni, A. (1992), "Bretton Woods and its Precursors: Rules versus Discretion in the History of International Monetary Regimes," *CEPR Discussion Paper,* June, N° 661.

Kydland, F., and E. Prescott (1979), "Rules rather than Discretion: The Inconsistency of Optimal Plans," *Journal of Political Economy,* 85, June, pp. 473-491.

Obstfeld, M. (1986), "Speculative Attack and the External Constraint in a Maximising Model of the Balance of Payments," *Canadian Journal of Economics,* 19, N° 1, February, pp. 1-22.

Obstfeld, M. (1986), "Rational and Self-fulfilling Balance of Payments Crises," *The American Economic Review,* 76, pp. 72-81.

Obstfeld, M. (1991), "Destablising Effects of Exchange Rate Escape Clauses," *NBER Working Paper,* N° 3603.

Obstfeld, M. (1994), "The Logic of Currency Crises", *Cahiers Economiques et Monétaires,* Banque de France, 43, pp. 189-213.

Willman, A. (1989), "Studies in the Theory of Balance of Payments-Crises," Suomen Pankki.

Choosing a Target Zone: Rules versus Discretion[1]

$89 - 103$

$F31$
$E52$
$F33$

1 Introduction

A government can try to stabilise the external value of its currency by announcing that it intends to keep it in a currency band ("target zone"). But it will succeed on if there are sufficient reserves of foreign currency available and if the intervention limits are regarded as incentive compatible. Market participants must see that the government has both the resources and the will to intervene.

In this paper we focus on the second of these two factors. Assuming that the government seeks to minimise the expected costs of stabilisation, we apply the techniques of inventory theory to the canonical target zone model of Krugman (1991) to determine the cost-minimising discretionary currency band. The band we determine in this way is incentive compatible because it satisfies the Principle of Optimality, which requires that "an optimal policy has the property that whatever the initial state and initial decision are, the remaining decisions must constitute an optimal policy with regard to the state resulting from the first decision." (Bellman, 1957, p. 83).

It turns out, however, that there are gains to precommitting to a band which is narrower than this. After suggesting the reason for this, we present a numerical example where precommitment cuts the bandwidth by a third. This suggests that a key function of an Exchange Rate Mechanism (ERM) in theory is to do just this, replacing discretion by a rule (for a narrower band). In practice, the ERM of the European Monetary System seemed to function in this way, at least until 1993. When the official bands were widened dramatically in response to speculative attacks. Exchange rates may have stayed close to their old parities since then, but the analysis of the paper casts doubt on the sustainability of narrow bands without formal precommitment.

The exposition that follows is intuitive rather than rigourous, relying largely on graphical techniques and using only an approximation to the value function. A more exact derivation of the results reported here can be found in Miller and Zhang (1994). Note that the same logic has also been applied to managing exchange rates not by target zones, but by continuous intervention, see Papi (1993) and Svensson (1992).

2 Discretion: finding the optimal, discretionary target zone

Before considering optimisation, we first recall the key features of the canonical target zone model of Krugman (1991). Let s denote the log of the exchange rate (defined as the price of foreign currency) which is assumed to satisfy the equation of motion

(1) $E(ds)/dt = \beta(s-k)$

where E is the expectations operator and k refers to economic fundamentals. In this simple monetary model k represents the log of the money supply, adjusted for a velocity "shock" which follows a random walk. The exchange rate is a good proxy for the price level on the assumption of Purchasing Power Parity.

Equation (1) represents equilibrium in the domestic money market. The expected rate of increase in the foreign exchange rate on the left hand side measures the opportunity cost of holding local currency; the term k-s on the right hand side represents real balances adjusted for the velocity shock and the parameter β is the inverse of the semi-elasticity of demand for money. Note that equation (1) is consistent with the exchange rate being the present discounted value of expected future fundamentals, i.e.

(2) $s = E\int_t^\infty \beta k(x)e^{-\beta(x-t)}dx.$

Let the fundamental k evolve as the result of two influences – the random walk followed by velocity and official intervention (which involves buying and selling foreign currency in exchange for domestic currency); so

(3) $dk = \sigma dW + dR - dL,$

where W is a standard Brownian motion, σ measures the volatility of fundamentals,   and R/L are two right continuous processes which represent the effects of intervention to buy/sell foreign currency respectively.

Assume that the authorities want to intervene so as to stabilise the exchange rate around a fixed target value, subject to intervention costs of c per unit which we treat as a constant in what follows. (In other work we are examining the case where c is variable, depending on the profitability of intervention.) If it is the squared deviation from s = 0 that they aim to minimise, then we can measure the minimised expected discounted costs by the value function

$$(4) \quad V(k) = \min_{R,L} E\left[\int_0^\infty s^2 e^{-\rho t} dt + \int_0^\infty ce^{-\rho t}(dR + dL)\right],$$

subject to (2) and (3), where ρ is the discount rate.

The reason for assuming a constant marginal intervention cost is because the optimal policy in such a case is the infinitesimal intervention analysed by Krugman (1991); see for example Dixit (1991, 1992). The symmetry of costs implies that the value function is symmetric, so we need only consider the upper barrier denoted $\bar{k}$. There may be a temptation to "cheat" by announcing narrow barriers so as to induce stabilising expectations without ensuring that they will be judged   worth defending when they are reached. But such barriers would not be credible. To ensure credibility, one needs to choose $\bar{k}$ so as to minimise V while ensuring that intervention will satisfy the Principle of Optimality (which requires that the announced policy still be optimal even when the intervention points are reached).

One strategy for doing this was outlined by Cohen and Michel (1988), namely to apply standard optimising conditions to the value function on the assumption that expectations are a   predetermined function of the economic fundamentals. They actually considered the case of linear quadratic optimal control where the conjecture that expectations are a linear function of fundamentals is in fact true under the linear feedback policy which is chosen. To find the desired optimal solution, one needs to find a "fixed point" – where the conjecture made about expectations is consistent with the optimal policy itself.

In context of barrier policies considered here, the conjecture that the exchange rate is a linear function of fundamentals is no longer strictly appropriate. Instead the functional form should be hyperbolic or S-shaped, specifically

$$(5) \quad \begin{aligned} s &= \frac{A}{2}\left(e^{\lambda k} - e^{-\lambda k}\right) + k \\ &= A\sinh(\lambda k) + k. \end{aligned}$$

with parameters λ and A defined as $\lambda = \sqrt{2\beta / \sigma^2}$ and

$$(6) \quad A = -\frac{1}{\lambda\cosh(\lambda\bar{k})},$$

see Krugman (1991).

In this paper, however, we will continue to make the assumption of linearity. This greatly simplifies the analysis without substantially changing the results. Assume therefore that the exchange rate is expected to be a linear function of k; specifically assume the expected rate can be represented as

$$(7) \quad s = (\lambda A + 1)k$$

which is the linear approximation at the origin of the hyperbolic solution in (5) above. Then the value function giving expected costs as a function of fundamentals can be written as

$$(8) \quad V(k; A, B) = \frac{(1 + A\lambda)^2}{\rho}\left(\frac{\sigma^2}{\rho} + k^2\right) + B\cosh(\mu k).$$

where A represents expectations and B reflects the boundary conditions determined by the barrier chosen for intervention. To fix ideas, consider first a free float where no intervention takes place.

2.1 A free float

With no intervention the appropriate values for *A* and *B* are zero, so expected costs will be given by

$$(9) \quad V(k;0,0) = \frac{1}{\rho}\left(\frac{\sigma^2}{\rho} + k^2\right).$$

This quadratic form is illustrated in the upper panel of Figure 5.1 by the symmetric function labelled V_N: and the expected marginal cost under a free float, $V'(k;0,0)$, is shown by the line labelled ON in the lower panel. Now we turn to intervention.

2.2 *Optimal discretionary intervention*

We consider the policy of choosing a barrier for the fundamental and using infinitesimal intervention to prevent this being crossed. The value function is conditioned on a given set of expectations, signified by the parameter A. The first order conditions (FOCs) determining the optimal upper barrier, $\bar{k}$, are as follows

$$(10) \quad V'\left(\bar{k}; A, B\right) = 2(1 + A\lambda)^2 \frac{\bar{k}}{\rho} + \mu B \sinh\left(\mu\bar{k}\right) = c,$$

$$(11) \quad V''\left(\bar{k}; A, B\right) = \frac{2(1 + A\lambda)^2}{\rho} + \mu^2 B \cosh\left(\mu\bar{k}\right) = 0.$$

see Dixit (1991, 1992). These conditions, taken together with (6) above, suffice to determine $\bar{k}$, A and B. (Equation (6) ensures that we have a "fixed point", where expectations are consistent with the optimal policy).

The first of these conditions simply requires that on the margin the benefit of stabilising - checking a cost of V' - matches the cost of intervention, c. The other condition, so-called second order smooth-pasting, is easier to explain with the aid of Figure 5.1.

In the upper panel the cost function for optimal intervention is given by the schedule V_E between the barriers $\bar{k}$ and $-\bar{k}$. At the point labelled D, i.e., at the upper barrier $\bar{k}$, the slope of V_E reaches c - a local maximum as there is a point of inflexion at D. This is illustrated clearly in the lower panel by the schedule OE which measures the expected marginal cost given optimal intervention. Note that OE is flatter than ON at the origin; this reflects in part the effect of changed expectations - the so-called "honeymoon" effect - and in part the operation of the boundary conditions. From the origin the schedule OE follows a nonlinear path so as to satisfy the two boundary conditions just described at point D, where

Figure 5.1: The value function and optimal target zone.

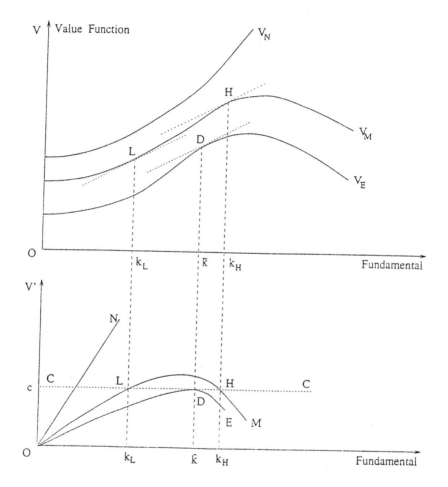

it reaches a maximum as it "smooth pastes" against the line CC showing the cost of intervening.

To see why this smooth pasting condition is necessary for optimality consider the alternative value function shown as V_M in the upper panel, with expected marginal cost given by the schedule OM. (The value of A is the same as for V_E, but B is closer to zero in absolute value.) There are two points, H and L, where the slope of V_M satisfies the value-matching condition (10); but neither is a point of inflexion - so condition (11) is not met. This is apparent from the lower panel where the line OM *crosses* CC at L and H at levels of the fundamental labelled k_L and k_H. In the absence of smooth-pasting one can use the following reasoning to rule out k_L and k_H as optimal barriers. Take a point just to left of k_L, where V' will be close to c. Consider the effect of movements of k to the left and right, assuming that rightward shifts will be truncated at k_L. Since V' will fall when k moves left, but will be checked when k goes right, the expected value of V' will be pulled below its current value. But this implies that intervention should be postponed, as expected V' at k_L would no longer satisfy the value matching condition. (Similar reasoning applied to points just to the left of k_H implies that expected V' will tend to exceed c, so intervention should take place earlier.)

Since intervention at $\bar{k}$ satisfies both value-matching and smooth-pasting conditions it is incentive compatible. But is it consistent with market expectations regarding the exchange rate? The answer is yes, so long as the parameter A measures the honeymoon effect for a band on fundamentals defined by $\bar{k}$ (i.e., so long as $A\lambda = -1/\cosh(\lambda \bar{k})$; and this has been imposed in finding $\bar{k}$. This can be illustrated by a numerical example.

Let $\beta = 1$ and $\sigma^2 = 0.1$ as in Svensson (1991, p. 33) and $\rho = 0.1$ as in Svensson (1992, p. 16). These imply values for λ and μ of $\sqrt{20}$ and $\sqrt{2}$, respectively. From equations (5) and (6), we find that a currency band of $\pm 4\%$, i.e., $\bar{s} = 0.04$ and an intervention point of $\bar{k} = 0.20$ are chosen as optimal when the cost parameter c is set at 0.01, approximately. (See Appendix 5.A for the "inverse optimal" calculation.) These results are displayed in Figure 5.2, where the schedule OE shows the derivative of the value function and the first order conditions are both met at the point of smooth pasting labelled D. The value of the exchange rate is given by the hyperbolic curve OS, whose slope at the origin, $1 - \lambda A$, is approximately 0.3. The exchange rate lies inside the band except at the point P where it too smooth pastes, against the edge of the currency band. The smooth-pasting of the exchange rate will be observed for any credible band, as it is an implication of efficient arbitrage, see Dixit (1992) or Krugman (1991). But the second order smooth pasting of the value function only occurs if the band is chosen according to the Principle of Optimality.

The nature of the approximation involved here can be seen by comparing the hyperbolic curve OS which shows the actual rate, with the dashed line OX, the linear approximation with slope $1 - \lambda A$ which was used in the value function as a proxy for market expectations. The approximation is perfect in the middle of the band, but it is at its worst at the edges where it exaggerates the deviation of the rate by half (0.6 instead of 0.4). To get an exact result one needs to use a hyperbolic function to characterise expectations. The formulae for calculating the optimal target become a good deal more complicated, but the principles remain the same, see Miller and Zhang (1994).

3 The gains from precommitment

It is well known that, where expectations are important, the results of applying the Principle of Optimality can be improved upon by precommitment. Currency bands are no exception: stabilisation can be achieved at lower cost if the Government can tie itself to defending a band narrower than the optimal discretionary band we have just solved for!

The reason for this is easy to see. Recall that the optimal discretionary band was selected under the (very strong) restriction that expectations were taken as given: the value-matching and smooth-pasting conditions were applied to the value function conditional on A. The fact that A is linked to the choice of $\bar{k}$ by equation (6) was not taken into account when choosing where to intervene; so any stabilisation benefits arising from the "honeymoon" effect come as a by-product of intervention and not by design. Rule-governed intervention, on the other hand, does not have to satisfy the Principle of Optimality - it just has to obey the rule: and the rule itself can be chosen with the effect on expectations included as a design feature. This is the source of potential gains.

How to choose the rule - that is the question. One might, for example, choose a rule that minimised the value function using the flat asymptotic distribution to weight the different possible outcomes for fundamentals. One could; but what we do here is much simpler - namely to minimise the value function at the mean of fundamentals, i.e., at k = 0. This is sufficient to make the point that precommitment pays.

Evaluating the approximate value function of (8) above at the origin yields

$$(12) \quad V(0;\bar{k}) = \frac{(1+A\lambda)^2 \sigma^2}{\rho^2} + B.$$

The notation on the left hand side indicates that the underlying determinant of the expected costs is the width of the band working through expectations (A) and the boundary condition (B). To make this explicit one can substitute for A from equation (6) and for B using (10) - the boundary condition that does not involve second-order smooth pasting - so as to obtain V(0) as an explicit function of $\bar{k}$,

$$(13) \quad V(0;\bar{k}) = \left(1 - \frac{1}{\cosh(\lambda\bar{k})}\right)^2 \left(\frac{\sigma^2}{\rho^2} - 2\frac{\bar{k}}{\rho}\frac{1}{\mu\sinh(\mu\bar{k})}\right) + \frac{c}{\mu\sinh(\mu\bar{k})}.$$

Minimising with respect to $\bar{k}$ given c yields $\bar{k}_R$, the desired intervention rule; i.e., setting

$$(14) \quad \frac{\partial V(0;\bar{k})}{\partial\bar{k}} = 0$$

determines the intervention rule for precommitment.

Formal details are omitted here, but we continue with the numerical example, as illustrated in Figure 5.2. Though this is not drawn precisely to scale, it does indicate that the barrier selected by the criterion of minimising $V(0;\bar{k})$ is about 15% smaller than under discretion - 0.17 rather than 0.20.

The effect on the currency band itself is rather more dramatic, as can be seen from the S-shaped curves for the exchange rate given in the figure. With discretion the rate lies on OS and reaches the edge of the ±4% band at P (i.e., $\bar{s} = 0.04$). Under the rule the rate is a good deal more stable as the band is only two thirds as wide! Now the exchange rate follows OS_R which reaches the edge of the band at Q where $\bar{s}_R$ is 0.027.

Figure 5.2: Why a narrow band needs precommitment.

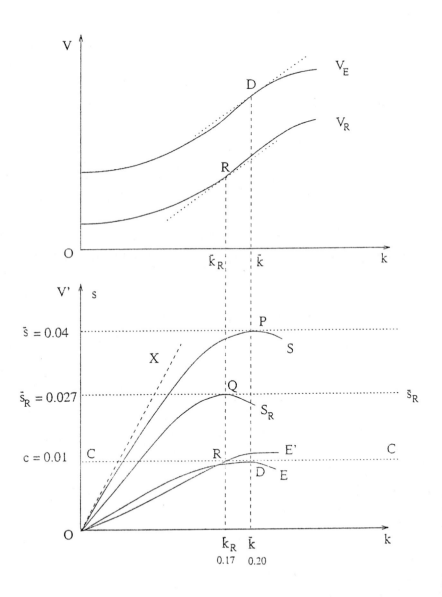

What about expected costs? They are less dramatically affected since the narrower band takes more defending. The extra honeymoon is no free lunch, one might say! Thus expected costs fall by only about 8% at the origin, the point where they were being minimised (see Appendix 5.B). What is perhaps surprising is that expected costs fall by about the same percentage *even at the edge of the (narrower) band.* So the rule strictly dominates discretion. This is indicated in the upper panel of Figure 5.2 where the V_R, the value function under the rule, lies below its discretionary counterpart V_E for all k between zero and $\bar{k}_R$.

That such a narrow band needs some mechanism of precommitment is also evident from the figure, see the lower panel. Unlike the curve OE which value-matches and smooth-pastes at D (the discretionary equilibrium), the curve OE' showing marginal costs under the rule crosses the line CC at R. This means that there would be an incentive to postpone intervention in the absence of a rule, as we have argued above.

The numerical results obtained here are in line with conclusions we have reported elsewhere that precommitment could support optimal bands only half as wide as under discretion, Miller and Zhang (1994). (The differences are due to the fact that the approximation tends to understate the value of stabilising expectations.)

4 Conclusion

Inventory theory suggests that one should be able to derive Krugman's target zone as the outcome of minimising expected stabilisation costs, see Avesani (1990). But prevalence of forward-looking behaviour in this case means that the Principle of Optimality must also be respected. This has been done by applying a conjectural method due to Cohen and Michel to a somewhat simplified value function. It was easy to show, however, that narrower bands would improve welfare, if only some mechanism of precommitment were available.

One does not have to look very far back in time to find an example of the sort of institution required for this purpose. Until 1993 the Exchange Rate Mechanism of the European Monetary System, with its strict obligation for marginal intervention by countries whose currencies reached the edge of preannouced narrow bands of $\pm2\frac{1}{4}\%$, seemed to fit the bill very closely. So one could interpret the European ERM as a device for imposing rules in place of discretion.

But immediately after the speculative attacks in 1992 and 1993, these narrow bands were abandoned and replaced with bands about six times as wide (i.e., ±15%). Thus, according to Neils Thygesen (1994), "almost by default the EMS ended up with the present regime, the crucial element of which is the central rates, their margins having become so wide that they may never be tested" - a situation which he says could be labelled "exchange rate targets without a zone". (That such wide bands may have very little value in terms of precommitment is borne out by the illustrative example we worked through: there the discretionary equilibrium was only one and a half times the narrow band, implying that individual governments would choose to intervene well before such very wide bands were reached.) Nevertheless, one observes that "over the first year since the introduction of the wide margins, most of the eight currencies linked to the Deutsche mark in the EMS have returned to their previous narrow margins" (Thygesen (1994, p. 125)).

But is the current situation a sustainable equilibrium? Surely not; for if there are no obvious rules to enforce intervention in support of narrow bands, then the market should expect rates to fluctuate more - and this will make it more difficult to maintain the old narrow margins. That is the logic of this paper. Similar doubts are expressed by Thygesen as follows: "There is no formal requirement to reintroduce the narrow margins as a step toward EMU, but there is a concern, particularly if the transition is lengthy (and it may take another four years), that some participants will find irresistible pressure to avail themselves of the freedom of action that the wide margins have left... [My] attitude toward the present regime - 'exchange rate targets without a zone'- is therefore mixed: satisfaction with short term stability, but doubts about long-term robustness."

Note

[1] Acknowledgements: This paper has benefited from discussion at the Conference "European Currency Crises and After," and from comments by Laura Papi and Steven Turnovsky. It was substantially revised when Marcus Miller was a Visiting Fellow at the Institute for International Economics, and he is most grateful for their hospitality.

Appendix 5.A
The "inverse optimal" problem

If the optimal discretionary band is 4% wide, what are intervention costs, c? Let $\sigma^2=0.1$, $\beta=1$, $\rho=0.1$ and $\bar{k}=0.1991$ (which is consistent with $\bar{s}=0.04$). It follows that

$$\lambda = \sqrt{2\beta/\sigma^2} = \sqrt{20} \text{ and } \lambda\bar{k} = 0.8906,$$
$$\mu = \sqrt{2\rho/\sigma^2} = \sqrt{2} \text{ and } \mu\bar{k} = 0.2816;$$

and

$$A\lambda = -1/\cosh(\lambda\bar{k}) = -0.7025,$$

so

$$1 + A\lambda = 0.2975.$$

To find B we note from (11) that

$$V'' = 2(1+A\lambda)^2/\rho + B\mu^2\cosh(\mu\bar{k}) = 0,$$

i.e., 1.7699 - 2.0798 B = 0 so B = -0.8510.

To find c we note from (10) that

$$V' = 2(1+A\lambda)^2\bar{k}/\rho + B\mu\sinh(\mu\bar{k}) = c,$$

i.e., 0.3524 - 0.3434 = 0.009 = c.

Appendix 5.B
On evaluating a narrow ERM band

To find the intervention rule $\bar{k}_R$, one has to minimise $V(0;\bar{k})$ given c, using numerical methods. To evaluate this rule (or any other), one calculates A and B given $\bar{k}_R$, which is a lot simpler. Thus for λ, μ, ρ and c as in Appendix 5.A but $\bar{k}_R = 0.17$ we find from (6) that

$$A\lambda = -1/\cosh(\lambda\bar{k}_R) = -0.7673, \text{ so } 1 + A\lambda = 0.2327;$$

and from (10) that

$$B = \left(c - 2(1 + A\lambda)^2 \bar{k}_R / \rho\right) / \left(\mu \sinh(\mu\bar{k}_R)\right)$$
$$= (0.009 - 0.1840) / 0.3433 = -0.5099.$$

Hence, for example,

$$V(0; \bar{k}_R) = (1 + A\lambda)^2 \sigma^2 / \rho^2 + B$$
$$= 0.5413 - 0.5099 = 0.0314.$$

This represents a fall of about 8% relative to what is found with discretion, where the values of A, B and $\bar{k}$ in Appendix 5.A would imply

$$V(0; \bar{k}) = (1 + A_D\lambda)^2 \sigma^2 / \rho^2 + B_D$$
$$= 0.8845 - 0.8506 = 0.0339.$$

References

Avesani, R.G. (1990), "Endogenously Determined Target Zone and Central Bank Optimal Policy with Limited Reserves," Mimeo, Presented at CEPR/NBER Conference on Exchange Rates and Currency Bands, University of Warwick.

Bellman, R. (1957), *Dynamic Programming,* Princeton University Press.

Cohen, D., and P. Michel (1988), "How should Control Theory be Used to Calculate a Time Consistent Government Policy?" *Review of Economic Studies,* (55), pp. 263-274.

Dixit, A.K. (1991), "A Simplified Exposition of the Theory of Optimal Control of Brownian Motion," *Journal of Economic Dynamics and Control,* 15(4), pp. 657-73.

Dixit, A.K. (1992), *The Art of Smooth Pasting,* Reading, England: Harwood Academic Publishers.

Krugman, P. (1991), "Target Zones and Exchange Rate Dynamics," *Quarterly Journal of Economics,* 163(3), pp. 669-682.

Miller, M., and L. Zhang (1994), "Optimal target zones: how an exchange rate mechanism can improve upon 'discretion'," *CEPR Discussion Paper*, N° 1031.

Papi, L. (1993), *Essays on Optimal Government Policy*, Ph.D. Thesis, University of Warwick.

Svensson, L.E.O. (1991), "Target Zones and Interest Rate Variability," *Journal of International Economics*, 31, pp. 27-54.

Svensson, L.E.O. (1992), "Why Exchange Rate Bands? Monetary Independence in spite of Fixed Exchange Rates," *CEPR Discussion Paper*, N° 742.

Thygesen, N. (1994), "Managing the Monetary System: Comment," in Kenen, P.B. (ed.), *Managing the World Economy*, Washington, D.C.: Institute for International Economics.

p 89.)

103 - 05   F 31
                  E 52
⇔ **Discussion**   F 33

JEAN-PIERRE LAFFARGUE

Marcus Miller and Lee Zhang have written an important paper. Most of the literature on target zones presents two limits.

1) The existence of the target zone and the width of the band of variation of the exchange rate are assumed a priori. Why a target zone would be better than a pegged exchange rate, or an exchange rate which might vary in a loosely defined neigbourhood of a central parity, is not really discussed. How to chose the bandwidth is not discussed either.

This literature a priori assumes that interventions are marginal and infinitesimal (Krugman) or intra marginal and discrete (Flood and Garber). But what are the respective advantages of these principles of intervention? And comparatively what would be the advantages and costs of infinitesimal interventions at each instant of time?

Marcus and Lei bring convincing answers to my criticisms and questions. They assume that the Central Bank bears two costs.

1) A quadratic cost when the exchange rate differs from its central parity.

2) A cost proportional to the amount of intervention.

Under these assumptions they prove the superiority of a target zone of the Krugman sort.

My first question is: what interpretation might be given to the costs of intervention. They look very abstract to me. A numerical computation by Marcus and Lei suggests that these costs are very small. In the real world Central Bank interventions seem to be important, intra marginal, and not very frequent. This looks like the results of Flood and Garber. But I wonder if this behaviour of Central Banks might be related to something which could be interpreted as intervention costs.

I have another question. Could we find an intervention costs function which supports interventions which would be continuous, and proportional to the deviation of the exchange rate from its central parity? In this case I guess that the exchange rate would follow a linear Ornstein-Uhlenbeck process, instead of a nonlinear controlled Brownian motion. Actually I made some econometrics on the exchange rate in the EMS, using the multi process Kalman filtering method introduced in economics by Axel Weber (*Annales d'Economie et de Statistique*, n° 35, July-August (1994)). One of my results was for instance, that the French franc/mark parity used to be stabilised around unofficial central parities and followed around these parities an Ornstein-Uhlenbeck process with a very small amplitude. From time to time the unofficial central parity was revised. Of course in my research I minimized the role of official central parities and bands. Now I was puzzled by the justification which could be given to such an exchange rate policy by the Bank of France. Marcus and Lei suggest some elements of answer.

The paper by Marcus and Lei includes something very subtle which is developed in paragraphs 2.2 and 3. The Government announces a band for the fundamental. The private sector knows that intervention costs are proportional, thus that interventions will be infinitesimal and marginal. In paragraph 2.2. the band is chosen in order to be dynamically consistent. That means that it will never be in the interest of the Government to cheat the private sector: the announcement of the band creates expectations by the private sector, and for these expectations it is optimal for the Government to respect its announcement. In paragraph 3 the Government selects the band, announces it, and is forced to hold its engagement by an international agreement such as the ERM for instance. This arrangement creates expectations by the private sector, for these expectations it is optimal for the Government not to respect its announcement, but it cannot do that because of the ERM. Marcus and Lei show that the bandwidth is smaller under the second system than under the first. The costs of the policy are also lower. The gains in bandwidth and welfare appear to be large in the numerical examples.

On the Nature of Commitment in Flexible Target Zones and the
Measurement of Credibility: the 1993 ERM Crisis[1]

106 - 30

EU

F31

F33

1 Introduction

Some ten years ago John Williamson (1983, 1985) proposed a system of
target zones for the world's major currencies that differs in fundamental
respects from that established in the Exchange Rate Mechanism (ERM) of
the European Monetary System.[2] The effective collapse of the ERM
between September 1992 and August 1993 has raised obvious questions
regarding the objectives it was designed to serve and hence how the
system could be reformed. It has also raised questions as to the viability
of target zone systems in general but in this respect the recent experience
within the ERM must surely have had the positive impact of emphasising
the critical role of policy coordination (as consistently argued for by
Williamson) alongside the constraint imposed by the target zone on
exchange rates. It can also be argued that the lack of flexibility that
demonstrably led to the eventual collapse of the ERM arose, somewhat
paradoxically, because its original objectives of providing a zone of
financial stability had become inconsistent with and subjugated to the
movement towards European Monetary Union. The ERM became in
effect, not a mechanism for stabilising exchange rates but more a
surrogate and indirect device for enforcing convergence in those
economies that would seek to join a European Monetary Union. Little or
no evidence seems to exist that explicit coordination of policies took
place external to the ERM.

Williamson's original target zone proposal differs from that established in the ERM in two essential respects;

(i) The central parity in Williamson's proposal would coincide with the "fundamental equilibrium exchange rate" (FEER) which would be expected to move over time rather than some target parity that in the event remained *fixed* until a crisis forced a realignment. The FEER was defined in *real* terms and it was envisaged that relatively frequent and small realignments would be necessary to accommodate movements in the fundamentals.

(ii) The bands of the zone, "the soft buffers", would be wide enough apart to achieve a desired degree of stabilisation with a relatively *weak* commitment towards a *"partial direction of monetary policy to discourage the exchange rate from straying outside its target zone".*

In contrast, the ERM was based on relatively narrow band-widths for *nominal* exchange rates together with the strict obligation to intervene to prevent movement outside the band. The interventions were supposed to be mandatory and bilateral at the margin and discretionary intramarginally. The relative fixity of the nominal target or central parity, the narrow bands and the requirement to intervene ensured that the ERM became an inflexible and rigid tool for stabilising exchange rates in the face of real shocks let alone for achieving convergence. Williamson's proposal, on the other hand, would seem to have explicitly recognised the need for flexibility to accommodate the evolution of the credibility in the system and effects of adjusting to temporary asymmetric shocks. (see Williamson (1985) and Williamson and Miller (1987)).

This contrast between Williamson's notion of a Target Zone and that implemented in the ERM was highlighted in *The Economist* after the ERM came under pressure following the September 1992 crisis when the lira and the pound dropped out of the system. For instance, an article in the May 8th 1993 issue suggested, some three months before the 1993 crisis, that although the experience during 1992 was due to exceptional circumstances (the German unification process), it showed that deep changes in the way the ERM operated were required. In particular the need for more flexibility was stressed together with the need for wider bands, soft buffers at the edges in order to allow for temporary excursions from the band and the adoption of a policy of frequent realignments in order to compensate for inflation differentials; this last aspect being tantamount to establishing a band for the real exchange rate.

A reply to this article came some weeks later (on June 5th) with a letter by Barry Eichengreen and Charles Wyplosz criticising the feasibility of the *"Williamson-Economist"* proposal and suggesting the need to regulate forex markets by adopting a version of the Tobin's taxes or "sand in the wheels" proposal (Tobin (1978)) that financial institutions taking open positions in the forex should be required to keep non interest bearing deposits with Central Banks. Eichengreen and Wyplosz stressed that this suggestion would not prevent a crisis from taking place but would simply buy the time necessary for the Central Bank to engineer an orderly realignment. They also argue that the proposal for a more flexible system would undermine credibility suggesting that "nobody will believe that governments are likely to intervene when exchange rates move toward the edge of their bands".

In a companion paper, Avesani, Gallo and Salmon (1994) (AGS), we have developed a model of a *flexible* target zone which captures much of the spirit of Williamson's original notion. Moreover rather than acting somewhat passively in the face of an attack, as Eichengreen-Wyplosz suggest, the monetary authority acts strategically, potentially well in advance of the attack and although it may, in time, realign it will do so as part of an *optimal* strategy given that it has monitored its credibility and recognises that the existing band widths are no longer sustainable. Credibility will not necessarily be lost in practice by being flexible, in this sense, but it *will* be lost by attempting to defend an unsustainable band. We show in that paper that substantial exchange rate stabilisation may in fact be achieved by adopting a target zone management strategy that explicitly reflects credibility contrary to the point of view put forward by Barry Eichengreen and Charles Wyplosz. It is important to note that this is achieved by a clear commitment to consistently and continuously defend the announced band but the commitment also recognises the importance of credibility and the need to maintain a required degree of credibility. Since credibility is not completely lost if the exchange rate passes over the band limit and if the authorities can be seen to be active in maintaining the band then credibility may well be recovered and a realignment avoided. In this sense the AGS model provides a relatively weak commitment to defend the band limits themselves and this is similar to the form of commitment suggested by Williamson and quoted above and quite unlike the rigid and inflexible commitment imposed on the ERM. The central issues lie in the *endogenous* evolution of partial credibility in the target zone and how the policy maker responds as his commitment is tested and how he trades off the desire for flexibility against a potential loss in credibility. The model essentially develops a target zone strategy that rests on a commitment to a feedback rule rather than the open loop precommitment that has been implemented in the ERM and in the Bretton Woods System. The dependence on such open loop strategies both in practice and theory would seem to have rested on the misplaced belief that only such policies would be credible and stabilise exchange rates. Notice that this does not mean that capital controls of the form suggested by Eichengreen and Wyplosz should not also be implemented as part of the flexible feedback strategy. Indeed a mechanism to include processes that slow down the financial markets ability to respond to current events is included in the AGS model.

The dynamics of credibility necessarily involves learning and the resolution of uncertainty by the markets regarding the policymaker's commitment and ability to defend the announced band and hence the importance for the policymaker to monitor the target zone's credibility in the day-to-day operation of intervention policy within the band. This is the question we address in this paper within the specific context of French franc/DM exchange rate in the period leading up to the ERM crisis in 1993. In Section (2) we briefly present the flexible target zone model of Avesani, Gallo and Salmon (1994). Section (3) discusses three measures of credibility which are then compared over the 1993 crisis period. The first is a qualitative measure based on the historical evidence collected from the views expressed in various issues of *The Economist* which we treat as reflecting informed opinion in the market; the second is the computation of the "simplest measure" of target zone credibility, suggested by Svensson (1991), which is based on forward exchange rates or rates of return and the final measure is based on the concept of relative credibility put forward by AGS. Our empirical results show that the latter measure closely shadows the press accounts, whereas the Svensson measure tends to signal losses of credibility that are not accompanied by realignments and hence its power to predict realignments is likely to be low.

2 The AGS Flexible Target Zone Model

The starting point of the standard target zone model is:

$$(1) \quad s(t) = k(t) + \alpha E_t \left(\frac{ds}{dt} \right).$$

with the fundamentals $k(t)$ following a controlled Brownian motion process, with control being exerted when the fundamentals hit either limit of the implied band imposed on them. From (1), it is clear that the policy maker can affect the determination of the exchange rate in two ways: the first is directly through the fundamentals (ie. through unsterilised intervention), the second is by modifying the markets' expectations. The imposition of an upper and a lower limit on the fundamentals brings about the honeymoon effect and the typical S-shaped curve for the fundamentals/exchange rate mapping of the Krugman model (Krugman (1991)).

This basic model suggests a rigid target zone where full credibility of the band limits is assumed *ex ante*. Extensions to include imperfect credibility (see for instance, Krugman (1991), Pesenti (1990) and Bertola and Caballero (1992)) have generally assumed a probability ϕ that the policy maker will defend the zone at the edge of the band and a probability $1-\phi$ that he will not defend and that a realignment of the central parity would be needed. Thus there is always an expectation of a devaluation which depends on the *exogenously* given ϕ. It is crucial to recall that in this extension of the model interventions would occur only at the edge of the band and hence at that limit one would get unambiguous information about the commitment of monetary authorities to defend the announced band. If intervention occurs then the fully credible path remains valid, otherwise there is an immediate attack and a jump to a free-float regime.

Historically experience within the ERM has been different: interventions occur intramarginally and credibility is not evaluated by the markets only on the basis of what happens at the edges of the band but seems to follow more complex mechanisms. The events in the ERM in the Summer and Autumn of 1992 indicate the importance of credibility in determining the sustainability of a target zone and the need for the authorities to continuously monitor their credibility. These implications seem to point to the fact that instead of delaying the moment of the crisis as in the Eichengreen and Wyplosz proposal, there is room for implementing a more farsighted and flexible management strategy in a target zone that may consciously preempt the crisis, i.e. a band which evolves around a central parity that may possibly *but not necessarily* be recalculated, but most importantly having the clear capability of being enlarged or restricted according to the perceived credibility of policy actions. The policymaker would remain firm in his commitment to maintain that band which is deemed to be sustainable given his degree of credibility.

The AGS model starts from the recognition that full credibility cannot be assumed but it has to be earned as the result of the explicit proof of the commitment by the policy maker to actively pursue actions *at all times* which will keep the exchange rate within the band.[3] There are essentially three additional elements that are introduced beyond the standard target zone model:

(1) the strategic interaction between the policy maker and the markets and the dynamics of credibility;

(2) the recognition that external shocks may warrant the temporary adoption of more flexibility than that imposed by a rigid target zone;

(3) the need for learning by the financial markets about the policy maker's actions and hence credibility in an uncertain world.

The endogenization of credibility in the AGS model revolves around the distinction between absolute and relative credibility. *Absolute* credibility is related to the level of exchange rate stabilization that the policy maker wants to (or can) achieve through the announcement of a band-width around a central parity value. The initial announcement corresponds to a commitment to direct policy, both inside the band and at the margins, with the objective of keeping the exchange rate within the announced limits given the shocks hitting the system. The announcement also forms the yardstick against which the markets evaluate those policy actions. Zero absolute credibility corresponds to no target zone and hence represents a free-float regime; full absolute credibility is the tightest band manageable and we assume is enforced by some external commitment or institutional agreement.

In this framework, any exchange rate regime can be characterized by a band-width corresponding to a solution for the exchange rate. For a given level of the fundamentals k, the solution for the exchange rate can be characterized as a convex combination of the institutional commitment regime, hence perfectly credible, $g_{pc}(k)$ and the free-float $g_{ff}(k)$ solution:

(2) $\quad g_w(k) = w g_{pc}(k) + (1-w)g_{ff}(k)$.

The higher the degree of exchange rate stabilization desired, the higher will be the weight on the institutional agreement path, and vice versa. In the presence of a need for flexibility, though, the policy maker may want to deviate from the announcement and he could do so in two ways; given a certain level of fundamentals and a desire to accomodate some domestic shock, he could choose a less stabilizing path corresponding to an implicitly wider band-width (devious behaviour). The second class of actions is to behave as if the band-width in place were tighter (virtuous behaviour) and in this way he may invest in his stock of credibility perhaps for later use.

Relative credibility reflects the degree of confidence the markets hold in the initially announced band or effectively the corresponding value of w when comparing the observed behaviour of the exchange rate and the behaviour that would be in place were the policy maker to continually adhere to the announced band. In this respect, the announced band-width would be fully credible (in a relative sense) if the actions of the policy maker were at each point in time *consistent* with the implications of the announced band. Deviating from the announcement in the devious direction will be recognized by the markets (although not immediately) as eventually leading to a lack of sustainability of the announced band and will be reflected in a decrease in the relative credibility, but will not necessarily be immediately punished by a run on reserves while some degree of credibility is retained. In fact, experience within the ERM is characterised by many such instances, with large swings in the exchange rate towards the margins, corresponding to less credibility, yet not all of them forcing an immediate realignment of the central parity.

In the opposite case of virtuous behaviour, the level of commitment to exchange rate stabilization is higher than the one warranted by the announced band, and hence is rewarded by an increase in the relative credibility of the band itself as the markets adjust their expectations. Again, one can think of the experience of the Italian lira prior to the official tightening of the band at the beginning of 1991, when the exchange rate was kept in a tunnel within the official band of ±6% as a way to achieve credibility for the next phase.

In either case the policy maker's actions signal a deviation from the announcement, the consequences of which should be taken immediately into consideration. In the case of devious behaviour a (political) cost will be incurred and if repeated it may lead to the need for a new band-width announcement in line with the current reputation of the policy maker. In the case of virtuous behaviour a political bonus is gained which may eventually (if such behaviour is repeated) lead to the opportunity for the announcement of a tighter band-width. In AGS we endogenise this process of the evolution of relative credibility while the authorities, recognising their current level of credibility, determine their *optimal* sterilised intervention strategy by trading-off the desire for flexibility against potential losses in credibility.

The simplest expression for relative credibility is then just the ratio between the band-width implied by the current observed exchange rate and that originally announced. This follows immediately from (2) as;

$$(3) \quad rc_t = \frac{w}{w_a} = \frac{s_t - g_{ff}(k_t)}{g_a(k_t) - g_{ff}(k_t)} = 1 - \frac{s_t - g_a(k_t)}{g_{ff}(k_t) - g_a(k_t)}$$

Figure 6.1 characterises this nonlinear function in terms of the divergence between the observed exchange rate and that expected given the announced band. We can see in particular that $rc = 1$ when $s = g_a(k)$, and $rc = 0$ for $s = g_{ff}$; a symmetric function holds for the lower part of the band.

In the absence of learning the policy maker could expect to hold full relative credibility when he adheres to the (s, k) mapping consistent with the initially announced band-width, ie. along the path A $(s = g_a(k))$ in the left hand subpanel of the Figure. Beneath this "s-mapping" he may actually increase his credibility as he would be potentially adopting a tighter sterilised intervention or monetary policy than required given his initial announcement. Such credibility building is important if we wish to consider how policy can be directed towards achieving a narrower band. Above the path A, there will be a loss of relative credibility, in the region AB, which becomes more dramatic as the exchange rate passes over the upper threshold of the announced band, U_a, through B and into the region BC. The policy-maker achieves both zero relative and absolute credibility when the exchange rate coincides with the free float value.

The level of relative credibility then plays a central role in determining the exchange rate in the heterogeneous and atomistic structure assumed for the financial markets in the AGS model. This is largely as a result of the effect his credibility has on unifying the expectations of the market. Market power is initially biased towards the policy maker as a

Figure 6.1: Relative Credibility.

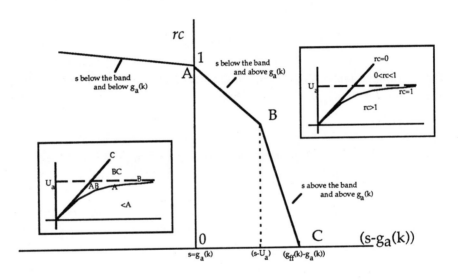

consequence of being a single large actor amongst the atomistic private agents in the market and from having greater monitoring capabilities given its institutional role. This market power however decreases with a decrease in relative credibility and is gradually shifted to the private sector to the point of being completely lost when all relative credibility is lost. This introduces a degree of asymmetric information between the policy maker and the financial markets, since the latter is uncertain about both the degree of market power held by the policy maker and his actions.

The strategic interaction between policy maker and the market then occurs as in a standard asymmetric information Stackelberg game where all players seek to maximize their objective function. The policy maker has to choose the implicit band-width he desires at each point in time which may deviate from the announced band-width depending upon the trade-off seen between the advantages from adopting a more flexible policy stance by deviating from the announcement and incurring the resulting political costs. This is carried out in the AGS model by constructing an objective function in which, apart from non-strategic elements related to exchange rate stabilization, both the deviation of the level of the exchange rate from central parity and volatility are penalised, strategic costs are included associated with the desirability :

- to gain more flexibility than that offered by the existing band;
- of not incurring the political costs that this higher flexibility entails;
- of not being forced through a realignment to a new announcement corresponding to a lower degree of absolute credibility.

Notice that this objective function intimately involves credibility in several places and is quite distinct from the standard approach to justifying the optimality of target zones through proportional costs of intervention. The private sector or financial markets on the other hand seek to minimize their prediction errors on the level of the exchange rate and this leads to their selection of an appropriate expectations formation mechanism.

The realised exchange rate is then determined by the interaction between the policy maker and the private sector in the foreign exchange market and is critically affected by the assumed general inability of the markets to directly observe the monetary authorities' actions, as pointed out above. Interventions are assumed to be fully sterilised and not immediately observable, as often seems to be the case in practice, so that the markets face a problem of signal extraction, from observations on the observed exchange rate, to determine the monetary authorities' *implicit degree of relative commitment* to the announced band. The initial fully credible (in a relative sense) announcement is subject to scrutiny by the market, in that the agents try to judge whether the observed exchange rate is consistent with the intention to defend the announced band. On his part, the policy maker takes into account the private sector's expectations and considers the trade-off between the desire for a greater monetary freedom and the political cost that devious behaviour brings about. In maximizing the objective function, therefore, he chooses an intervention policy corresponding to an exchange rate determined by a solution path lying between the free float and the institutional commitment solutions and identified by a value for the parameter w between zero and one.

In updating its aggregate expectations, the private sector acknowledges that it acts in a highly nonlinear and non-constant environment in which learning should never be switched off but should be able to track the instability of the exchange rate generating mechanism. In the presence of high credibility the markets adjust rapidly to surprises in the perceived band-width, whereas low credibility in fact implies less information on policy preferences as the market power of the policy maker has been eroded. To put it differently, the policy maker has to engage in proportionally greater effort to re-establish its reputation when its relative credibility is low, than when his relative credibility is close to high.

An initial endowment of credibility is granted to the policy maker, measured by the horizontal distance from the tangency point of the S-shaped curve to a free-float regime and corresponds to the amount of fundamental adjustment or speculative attack which would bring about an immediate collapse of the announced target zone. A stagewise game is then repeated with the policy maker cumulating the political costs that result from devious and virtuous behaviour. If an initial endowment of credibility is completely depleted, the announced band-width is no longer seen to be sustainable, and an enlargement of the band is needed (higher weight given to the free-float solution in (2)). The level chosen for the new announcement (new absolute credibility) is set at the band-width which was perceived by the markets as being that currently effective. This ensures that there are no jumps in expectations, nor in exchange rates, and hence the relative credibility function is reset to one and a new credibility endowment is available to the policy maker.

3 Alternative Measures of Credibility and the Crisis in the ERM in 1993

In this section we analyse the experience of the French franc within the ERM from the end of October 1991 to mid-August 1993 and compare the evolution of credibility as measured by press reports to the measure of credibility proposed by Svensson (1991) and that derived from the AGS model discussed above. The behaviour of the FF/DM deviations from central parity is shown in Figure 6.2. For future reference a band of 7.9% is superimposed to the period following August 1993.

3.1 *The French Franc Behaviour from Press Accounts*
One way of judging the credibility of an exchange rate band ex post is to reconstruct the market feelings as reported by the press, in our case the *Economist*, which is taken here to express the views of a well-informed agent.

Starting from the beginning of 1992 and stopping at the end of July 1993 (when the French franc was forced to an enlargement of the bands to ±15%), we can isolate four main phases in the French franc/Deutsche mark relationship. The first lasts until the end of June 1992 with a strengthening of the franc towards the central parity. It is interesting to note that this occurred in the presence of a stable short term interest rate differential between DM and FF denominated Eurodeposits around 50 basis points (bp) with the long term differential constantly increasing from 35-40 bp at the beginning of 1992 to 135-140 bp during the summer.

The second phase starts in July 1992 when the FF/DM weakened rapidly moving toward the upper limit of the ERM band. Short term interest rates became more volatile and the interest differential spread to more than 700 bp during the '92 crisis which forced the British pound and the Italian lira out of the ERM. The reason for this deterioration vis-à-vis the DM have been widely credited to the tight monetary conditions imposed by the German monetary authorities during the summer of '92. The official rates were locked until September 15 (right after the crisis) when the Bundesbank cut the discount rate by 50 bp to 8.25% and the Lombard 25 bp to 9.5%. During this period the FF/DM exchange rate fluctuated violently inside the band and the tensions were transfered to the short term rates and to an increased volatility in long term rates.

The third phase starts at the beginning of January 1993. In particular, the FF/DM exchange rate which was at the limit of maximum allowed

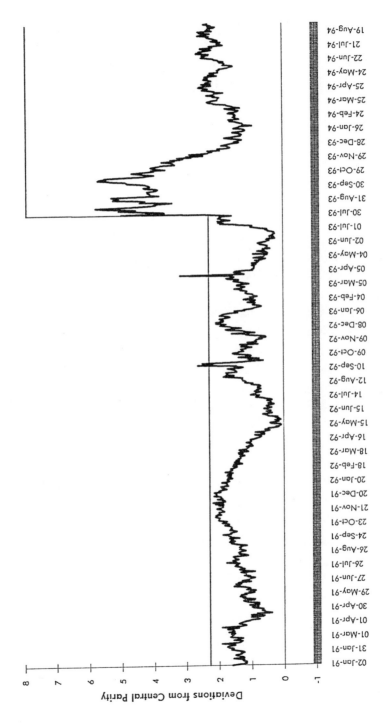

Figure 6.2: FF/DM Deviations from Central Parity.

depreciation recovered the losses (after Feb. 4 the German main intervention rates were cut by 25 bp, a move interpreted as a sign of the easing of monetary conditions), and moved rapidly toward and below the central parity, after a period of uncertainty surrounding the March elections. In the meanwhile the spreads on short and long term rates with respect to Germany also shrank to zero. Uncertainty still existed about the attitude of the new government towards monetary and fiscal issues and the reform of the Banque de France (BdF) in a direction of greater independence in line with the Maastricht Treaty. The formation of the new cabinet saw the appointment of two strong supporters of European integration and of the *Franc fort policy* as Finance and European Affairs ministers. Among the first measures adopted by the new government, the budget (May 10th - recognized as a tough one by the *Economist*) and the BdF reform plan sent a clear signal of commitment to the Maastricht Treaty and brought the short term interest rate differential in favour of the FF and the long term differential towards zero.

All these actions had the effect of dissipating the political fears that characterised the pre-election debate on the future course of French monetary policy. It seems however that while the uncertainties relating to the political will of the new French government disappeared, uncertainties hinging on the economic feasibility of the high interest rate policy seem to have remained. In fact, doubts concerning the tenability of the monetary policy in face of deteriorating expectations on GDP growth and unemployment had been a constant in the press before and after the elections.

The fourth phase starts in the second half of June when the French key intervention rate was lowered by 25 bp below the German discount rate to 7% (June 21st). While the FF was strengthening towards the edge of the band[4] the Bundesbank started to ease monetary conditions on July 1st, by cutting the discount rate by 50 bp to 6.75% and the Lombard rate by 25 bp to 8.25%. At the same time BdF was not able to match the Bundesbank and cut the intervention rate by only 25 bp. The hierarchy inside the ERM was reestablished and the market was left wondering whether the Banque de France had overstreched its position.

As usual market computations and reactions are fast and not always completely understandable being a mixture of short and long term forecasts, technical evaluations and an expression of animal spririts. *Ex post* we can say that the market looked at the following issues. First of all the market was disturbed by the emphasis with which the French government was pushing the issue of the low inflation rate. At the time the French inflation rate was half that in Germany, but the reverse had been true for the previous 20 years, and thus a different anti-inflationary reputation had been established in the two countries. Secondly, the fact that France was not able to match the Bundesbank interest rates cut and restablish the differential in her favour was interpreted as a sign of weakness. It was known that France needed to follow a fast track in cutting rates since there were worsening expectations for growth and unemployment plus a growing pressure from right wing politicians to follow a more independent monetary policy and abandon the franc fort policy.

Finally, in the second half of July the situation worsened very quickly: the franc moved to the upper limit of the band and the short term interest differential reached 6%. It is by now generally acknowledged that the uncooperative behaviour of the Bundesbank, which did not fulfill the expectations of further cuts before the summer recess, forced Belgium, France, Denmark, and Portugal to raise interest rates to defend their currencies. During the weekend of July 31st and August 1st, after a week of strong speculation against the French franc counteracted only by the BdF interventions in the forex, the ±15% band enlargement was announced.

3.2 Svensson's "Simplest Measure of Target Zone Credibility"

Svensson (1991) starts from the consideration of uncovered interest rate parity and of the exchange rate return over τ periods:

$$(4) \quad R_t^\tau = \left[\left(1 + i_{t,\tau}^*\right) \frac{S_{t+\tau}}{S_t} \right] - 1$$

where $i_{t,\tau}^*$ is the nominal foreign interest rate at time t for a τ maturity and S_t is the exchange rate at time t. He shows that if limits of fluctuations are imposed on the exchange rate of the kind $\underline{S} \leq S_t \leq \overline{S}$, an implicit band is imposed on the rate of return as well, $\underline{R} \leq R_t^\tau \leq \overline{R}$, defined as

$$(5) \quad \underline{R}_t^\tau = \left[\left(1 + i_{t,\tau}^*\right) \frac{\underline{S}}{S_t} \right] - 1, \qquad \overline{R}_t^\tau = \left[\left(1 + i_{t,\tau}^*\right) \frac{\overline{S}}{S_t} \right] - 1.$$

Since the tensions on the exchange rate market are passed onto the interest rate, one should see the exchange rate return move outside its implied band prior to a realignment. The reverse argument does not, however always prove to be the case. In fact in the case of the French franc for the period under examination the evidence regarding the rate of return for the Eurodeposit one-month maturity (shown in Figure 6.3) shows that apart from sporadic signals in late 1991, the period around the September 1992 crisis is characterized by a breech in the upper limit which lasted almost two months. While it was clear that the French franc was under attack, the crisis did *not* lead to a realignment. Similarly the five-month period marked by an exchange rate return above the upper limit in late 1992 and early 1993, as we have seen from the press accounts, was actually marked by fluctuating periods in which the French franc gained and lost credibility without generating a realignment of central parities. Finally, according to the Svensson's measure, the loss of credibility in the final period would originate somewhat around June 13, when the return hovers around the upper bound and breaks it around June 21 with a sudden downward shift in the bands following on July 1st (when German rates are cut).

3.3 *Measuring Credibility according to the AGS Model*

To apply the AGS model to measure the level of Relative Credibility over the relevant period we start by assuming the level of absolute credibility corresponding to the announced ±2.25% band which in turn implies a weight of $w_a = 0.78$ in the convex combination between the institutional commitment and the free floating regime. As there were no realignments for the French franc until the crisis of the end of July 1993, we keep this announcement as fixed in our analysis.

In order to extract the measure of relative credibility for the historical exchange rate, we face the problem of only having available the series of observed daily deviations from the central parity. Recall that relative credibility is a function of the difference between observed exchange rate and the exchange rate that would be observed if the policy maker completely adhered to the implications of the announcement. Under a flexible set of actions followed by the monetary authorities, the observed exchange rate would correspond to the outcome in the AGS model of the policy maker's optimization process and of the interaction between the policy maker and the markets. The "fundamentals" that gave rise to the observed exchange rate series are however not observed and now need to

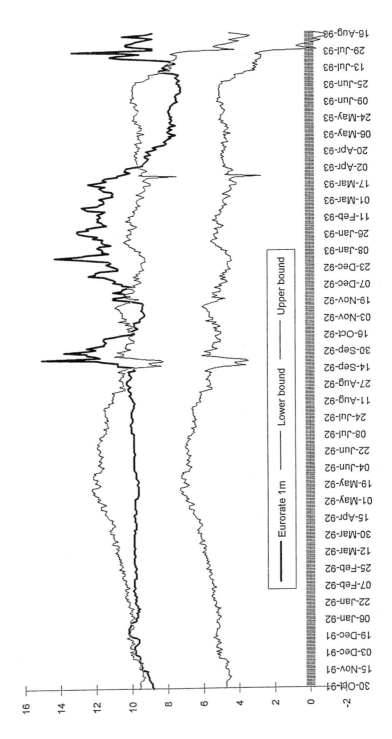

Figure 6.3: Svensson's Simple Measure of Credibility.

be estimated to get an operational measure of relative credibility. Once this estimated series is available we are in the position of deriving the exchange rate which would be perfectly consistent with the announcement, and hence of deriving the estimate of the relative credibility for the period under examination.

The chosen estimation strategy is by simulation in which, for a given set of parameters for the underlying fundamentals process, we can simulate paths of daily deviations from the central parity starting from the historical value on Oct. 30, 1991 where according to the AGS model at each period a new band-width is implicitly chosen by the policy maker through his actions and the market expectations are updated.

We then retain, from a large set of generated paths only those that show the need for a new announcement on or about Aug. 2, 1993 (a leeway of 7 business days prior or posterior to that date is allowed), because the cumulated political cost has passed the threshold which triggers such an announcement. For each replicated path we started at full relative credibility and at zero cumulated political cost. The estimator of the unobserved series is that which minimizes

$$(6) \quad \sum_{t=1}^{T} \left(s_t - g_w(k_t) \right)^2$$

i.e. the mean square error between the historical series and the simulated exchange rate as the outcome of the optimization process. From the optimal path we are able to invert the mapping onto the fundamentals $\hat{k}_t$ to estimate the implied fundamentals and hence retrieve the estimate for the exchange rate that would be consistent with the announced path $s_a(\hat{k}_t)$. The outcome is shown in Figure 6.4 where the historical and the announcement-consistent deviations from central parity are superimposed on each other. There are no extended periods of coincidence between the two paths, with days when the difference is positive (signalling that flexibility is exploited and political cost incurred) leading to a loss in relative credibility and periods of virtuous behaviour characterized by a negative difference and a gain in relative credibility.

For the estimated path, the relative credibility function can be computed for each day and is shown in Figure 6.5: we can observe various periods when it exceeds unity. In particular, we can see a big loss in relative credibility corresponding to the September 1992 crisis which is

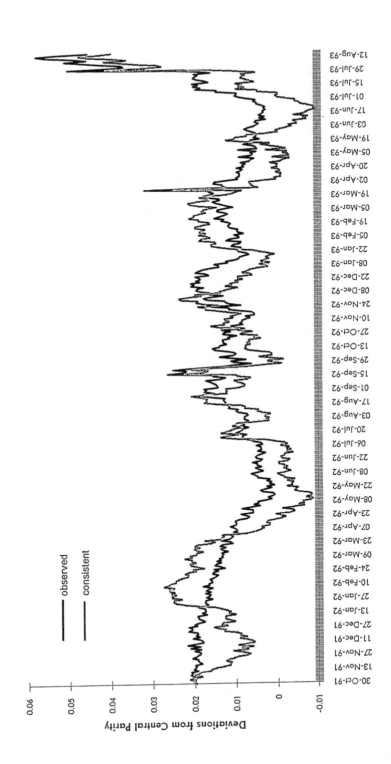

Figure 6.4: Observed and Consistent Deviations from Central Parity.

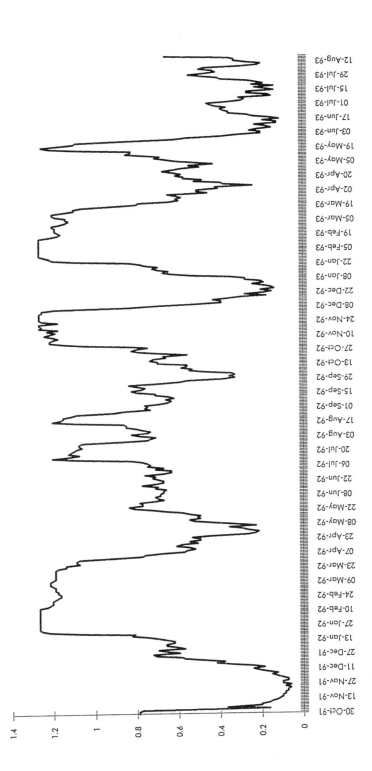

Figure 6.5: Relative Credibility.

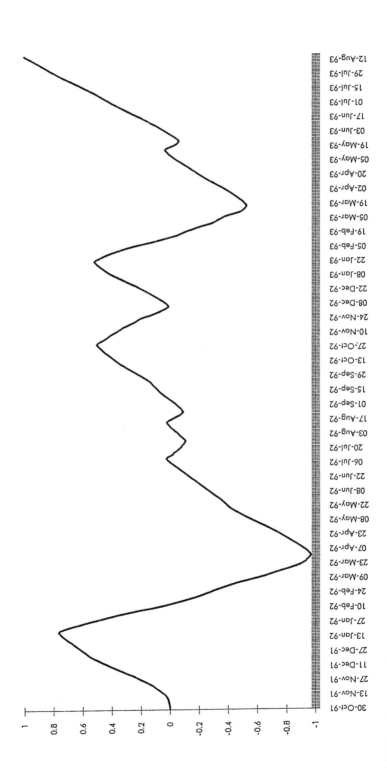

Figure 6.6: Cumulative Political Cost.

rapidly neutralised. The switching between gains and losses of credibility, mentioned above, at the end of 1992 and up to the spring of 1993 (which is in line with the press reports) and a rise in credibility from April '93 to the end of May or beginning of June is also consistent with the press evidence.

According to our estimates, then, one would notice a rapid loss in credibility in mid-June which corresponds to the French decision to lower the key intervention rate below the corresponding German rate, an episode which is detected also by Svensson's measure. The novelty is that relative credibility lingers (contrary to prior episodes) around low levels and corresponds to the accumulation of political cost. The widening of the band is triggered in our estimation by the political cost passing over the threshold as shown in the Figure 6.6.[5] When one looks at this last figure one realizes that the estimated cumulated political cost had been steadily growing since the beginning of March, and that the policy actions of April and May (cabinet formation, budget and reform plan for the BdF) had just temporarily held back that tendency. The level of perceived credibility at the point of crisis is estimated as $\hat{w} = 0.24$ and corresponds to a band-width of $\pm 7.9\%$ which would have been the optimal level suggested by our analysis as an expectation-compatible enlargement of the band (see Figure 6.2 to observe the behaviour of the exchange rate after the crisis). The institutionally chosen $\pm 15\%$ band corresponds in our calculations to $w = 0.06$, giving rise to a solution which thus places almost all weight on the free-float regime.

The results of the estimation process seem to be quite reassuring in that they show that optimizing behaviour in which flexibility is explicitly taken into account as in the AGS model appears to be consistent with the historical evidence for the French franc in the period leading up to the 1993 crisis in which the band-widths in the ERM were widened as predicted by the flexible target zone model. Previous crises are shown (cf. Figure 6.6) to have come close to the trigger point that would force a realignment but the cumulative political costs fell back (several times sizeably) corresponding to a recovery of relative credibility in the initial band-width announcement.

4 Conclusion

It would seem that the operation and structure of the ERM was eventually, if not initially, determined by motives other than simply stabilising currency fluctuations. The additional desire to impose convergence on the participating economies prior to European Monetary Union set a constraint on the system that it was eventually unable to bear and it was quite simply *not designed* to achieve these objectives. The policy coordination role explicitly recognised within the Maastricht Treaty appears to have taken a secondary role and the burden for achieving coordination and convergence was laid on the ERM. We have not considered in this paper how the equilibrium or central parity should be set which we see as being ultimately determined by these higher order issues relating to the international coordination of economic policy. Nevertheless we do feel that our analysis provides a clear explanation for the collapse of the ERM through its open loop commitment and suggests how it might be reformed by a more flexible *optimally* managed system within which policy coordination may be explicitly developed to achieve economic convergence should that be what is desired. It would seem inappropriate to attempt to achieve such an objective through an exchange rate target zone alone whether it be flexible or rigid.

The critical element of the AGS model lies in the incorporation of relative credibility into the policy formulation process of the monetary authorities. The nature of the commitment made by the policy maker then reflects both his clear intention to continuously maintain the exchange rate inside the announced band but also the reality of the need to respond to temporary shocks that may entail greater flexibility than originally permitted by the announced target zone. Pressure created by non-convergence in the fundamentals must be resolved by coordination and the appropriate adjustment of the central parity. The *flexible* target zone proposal can then be seen as the implementation of a reputation sustained feedback strategy rather than the open loop precommitment found in the ERM and Bretton Woods. Alternatively it represents a half way house between complete discretion or leaning against the wind, as discussed by Svensson (1992), and open loop strategies that are periodically forced through crises such as those that hit the ERM over 1992/3.

Notes

[1] This paper draws on and applies ideas from our earlier paper, *On the Evolution of Credibility and Flexible Target Zones,* that was presented, amongst other places, at the conference on "European Currency Crises

and After." We would like to thank Daniel Laskar for his detailed and very useful comments on both the original version of this paper and the present one.

[2] See also Williamson and Miller (1987).

[3] In this section we are only able to give a brief overview of Avesani, Gallo and Salmon (1994) and the full details can be found in that paper.

[4] There was even some talk of the need for the DM to devalue, or for adding or substituting the FF to the DM as an anchor for the system.

[5] In fact the cumulated political cost are shown as the ratio to the threshold and is thus set between the values (-1,1). When the value of 1 is reached then an enlargement of the band is required and a tightening is possible when the value of -1 is reached. Recall that the level at which the new band limits are established is determined by the market perceived level of absolute credibility.

References

Avesani, R., G.M. Gallo, and M. Salmon (1994), "On the Evolution of Credibility and Flexible Exchange Rate Target Zones," *Working Paper*, Economics Department, European University Institute, submitted for publication.

Bertola, G., and R. Caballero (1991), "Sustainable Intervention Policies and Exchange Rate Dynamics," in Krugman P., and M. Miller (eds), *Exchange Rate Targets and Currency Bands*, Cambridge University Press, pp. 186-205.

Bertola, G., and R. Caballero (1992), "Target Zones and Realignments," *American Economic Review*, 82, N° 3, pp. 520-536.

Krugman, P. (1991) "Target Zones and Exchange Rate Dynamics," *Quarterly Journal of Economics*, 106, pp. 311-325.

Krugman, P., and M. Miller (1993), "Why have a Target Zone?" *Carnegie Rochester Conference Series on Public Policy*, 38, pp. 279-314.

Pesenti, P. (1990), "Exchange Rate Stochastic Dynamics and Target Zones: an Introductory Survey," *Working Paper*, N° 9, Ente per gli Studi Monetari, Bancari e Finanziari L.Einaudi, Rome.

Svensson, L.E.O. (1991), "The Simplest Test of Target Zone Credibility," *IMF Staff Papers*, 38, N° 3, pp. 655-665.

Svensson, L.E.O. (1992), "Why Exchange Rate Bands? Monetary Independence in Spite of Fixed Exchange Rates," *CEPR Discussion Paper,* N° 742.

Williamson, J. (1983), *The Exchange Rate System,* revised edition (1985), Policy Analysis in International Economics, N° 5, Institute for International Economics, Washington D.C..

Williamson, J. (1986), "Target Zones and the Management of the Dollar," *Brookings Papers on Economic Activity,* 1: 165-74.

Williamson, J. (1987), "Exchange Rate Management: The Role of Target Zones," *American Economic Review,* Papers and Proceedings, May, 77, N° 2, 200-204.

Williamson, J. (1987), "Exchange Rate Flexibility, Target Zones, and Policy Coordination," *World Development,* 15, N° 12, 1437-1443.

Williamson, J. (1989), "The Case for Roughly Stabilising the Real Value of the Dollar," *American Economic Review,* Papers and Proceedings, May, 79, N° 2, 41-45.

Williamson, J., and M. Miller (1987), *Targets and Indicators: A Blueprint for the International Coordination of Economic Policy,* Policy Analysis in International Economics, N° 22, Washington, Institute for International Economics.

130-33   EU

F31

p106: **Discussion**

DANIEL LASKAR   F33

The paper contains two parts. The first one briefly presents the theoretical model. The second one applies this model to the 1993 ERM crisis. I will separetely comment on each of them.

1 The theoretical framework

This is a very interesting framework which incorporates into a formal analysis many aspects which have been neglected before in the literature on target zones. As in Williamson's proposal there are soft margins, which means that the exchange rate may stay for some time outside the announced band. This would of course imply some loss of credibility but the total stock of credibility could not be exhausted at once and could even be regained through some appropriate behaviour. The model also takes into account the fact that new exchange rate bands may be announced. It also emphasizes the role of sterilized interventions working through the manipulation of the beliefs of the private sector.

As the model is not fully exposed in the present paper I will only make a few brief comments on some underlying assumptions.

One of the important features of the model is that the monetary authorities are able to affect the exchange rate without changing the value of the fundamental. This is supposed to occur through "sterilized interventions". These interventions are actually equivalent to picking up a value for w, defined in equation (2), which is different from the announced value w^a. More explanations should be given on how this is done. For, in the model, sterilized interventions do not work through any asset portfolio, assets being implicitly considered as perfect substitutes, but through expectations, relying upon a different honeymoon effect (implicitly changing the expected band-width for the fundamental).

Furthermore, one of the reasons why sterilized interventions are introduced in the model is that they are more realistic. However, this may be the case only when such interventions tend to make the exchange rate get closer to the central rate. If on the contrary these interventions are needed to make the exchange rate go further away from the central rate, this may not be true. For, usually, sterilized interventions are not used in such a way. In the analysis of the paper, however, they are used both ways.

Concerning the private sector expectations, learning is assumed to be never switched off in order to be able to track the instability of the exchange-rate generating mechanism. But the choice of the implicit band-width, although constantly changing, is itself endogenous and depends on preferences and constraints of the model. The private sector may learn on these underlying parameters, which are not shifting over time. As a consequence, the way expectations are modelled in the paper may not give enough role to such a learning. The favourable aspects of flexibility, which are given by the possibilities of exchange rate surprises, may therefore be overestimated in the model.

2 The empirical analysis of the 1993 ERM crisis

The paper compares three ways to interpret the 1993 crisis. The first is based upon the press accounts, the second on the "simple measure" of target zone credibility proposed by Svensson, and the third applies the theoretical model previously developed. One of the conclusions is that the "relative credibility concept" of the theoretical model works better than the "simple measure" and is closer to the press accounts.

The application of the model to the ERM crisis tends to confirm the ability of the theoretical model to fit real events in the foreing exchange market. However its comparison with the "simple measure" and the interpretation given may need some qualifications.

First, the "simple measure" or "test", as its name suggests, is a rather crude way to test the credibility of a target zone. Svensson also developed a more sophisticated test, "the drift-adjustment method", which adjusts interest rate differentials by the estimated rate of depreciation within the band. An empirical analysis of Svensson which compares the two methods for the ERM concludes that the simple test has a relatively poor performance and that this is especially true for short horizons.[1] This is therefore likely to be the case in the present paper where a one-month maturity interest rate is considered. It is likely that the estimates found by the drift-adjustment method would have been closer to the press accounts.

Second, the simple measure, as well as the drift-adjustment method, give estimates of the expected rate of devaluation. If we take as given the amount of devaluation, we have an estimate of the probability of devaluation. The fact that no devaluation occurs when the interest rate is outside its band does not invalidate the test. On the contrary, because it is a more powerful test, the drift-adjustment method would have very likely given more episodes where the expected rate of devaluation would have been non zero while no devaluation would have occurred. For, the fact that this does not appear more often according to the simple test could be a consequence of the low power of that test which cannot reject the hypothesis of no expected realignment for some parts of the period.

Note

[1] See: Svensson, L.E.O. (1993), "Assessing target zone credibility - Mean reversion and devaluation expectations in the ERM, 1979-1992," *European Economic Review,* 37, pp. 763-802.

Modelling Credibility: An Application to the United Kingdom[1]

EU
UK
F31
E52
F33
F36

134-52

1 Introduction

There is now an extensive literature on "credibility," with the term given several different meanings and measured in various ways.[2] In some contexts, credibility is assumed to apply to the policymaker, in particular in models where policymakers attempt to signal their "type" for instance with respect to anti-inflationary credentials.[3] This is sometimes termed "reputation," especially when it is related to the past history of policy actions.[4] In other models, credibility is equated with an ability to precommit--that is, to convince the private sector that it will carry out policies that may be time inconsistent.[5] This permits the government to attain a higher level of welfare.

In the current paper, the concept of credibility is applied to the policies themselves, and is defined as the likelihood that policy commitments will in fact be carried out, as viewed by private agents. This concept of credibility is viewed as having two components: the private sector's assessment of the government's type, and also, given the type of government, an assessment of the probability that an optimising government will actually decide to carry out its announced policies in the face of adverse shocks. A formal model of policy choice and learning the type of government is developed, and it is then applied to the credibility of the U.K. commitment to its ERM parity (2.95 DM) during the October 1990-September 1992 period of ERM membership.

The September 1992 ERM crisis is an interesting testbed for models of credibility, partly because, as noted by other authors, the crisis followed five years of exchange rate stability, a period when it seemed increasingly as if the ERM could provide a smooth transition to monetary union. Correspondingly, most indicators of exchange market tension or lack of credibility did not, at least until a few weeks before the crisis, signal that things were likely to go wrong. The violence and suddenness of the crisis have naturally raised the issue of self-fulfilling speculation. Was the ERM crisis due to a speculative attack that took on a life of its own, rather than to fundamentals?[6] Of course, all the ERM currencies should not be put in the same boat; the pound sterling and the Italian lira, which were the first attacked and which were forced to leave the ERM, were currencies which were widely viewed as overvalued, while others which were also attacked were not in the same situation. The present paper, which examines data only for the United Kingdom, is not therefore intended to give a general answer to the question.

The model does allow for the possibility of multiple equilibria, and hence of self-fulfilling attacks. In particular, unemployment is assumed to depend on exchange rate surprises: an unexpected devaluation will tend to stimulate employment. Conversely, if private agents expect a devaluation, but the authorities do not change the parity, there are employment losses. Therefore, a "credibility crisis" in which, for instance, investors doubt that the government is committed to a particular parity or gives as much weight to inflation as it says it does, may make the costs of maintaining the parity very high, if the government also cares about unemployment, as is assumed.

Estimates of this model suggest that at least in the case of the United Kingdom, lack of credibility in the summer of 1992 was due not to doubts about the type of government, that is, its commitment to the ERM, but rather to concerns about the unemployment costs of maintaining the parity. Consequently, even a government committed to the ERM might not want to continue to bear those costs. In fact, continuing downward pressures on sterling and upward pressures on interest rates made the costs too high to bear, and sterling was floated on September 16, 1992. Though speculation made the defense of sterling more difficult, the model estimates suggest that speculation was linked to fundamentals, and hence was not purely self-fulfilling.

The paper first reviews the history of the United Kingdom's membership in the ERM in Section I. A theoretical model is presented in Section II, as are estimates derived from U.K. data. The implications of that model for the possibility of self-fulfilling crises are discussed in Section III, followed by some conclusions and topics for further research.

2 The Circumstances of the U.K.'s Brief Membership in the ERM

Britain joined the exchange rate mechanism of the European Monetary System on October 8, 1990, after a protracted debate on the merits of pegged exchange rates. Prime Minister Margaret Thatcher was widely known to be opposed to the idea--as were some of her advisors, most notably Sir Alan Walters--but she had committed Britain to join the ERM "when the time was right." In the fall of 1990 the United Kingdom was suffering from inflation rates of close to 10 percent, the result of over-expansionary monetary policies in the late 1980s, while inflation in Germany and France was 2-3 percent. Monetary policy had become more restrictive, and short-term interest rates were now 15 percent. It was felt that the ERM anchor would impart credibility to the disinflation process, and help to lower inflation at a smaller unemployment cost.

Sterling joined the wide band of the ERM, which allowed fluctuations of 6 percent around central parities with other currencies in the mechanism. In the weeks before joining, sterling had strengthened, and the parity chosen, an exchange rate of 2.95 Deutsche mark, was viewed generally as being somewhat over-valued. It has been argued (e.g., by Winckler, 1991) that the choice of parity was intended to signal anti-inflationary commitment; however, there were initial doubts about whether a realignment might be needed in a year or two to correct problems of competitiveness (related both to the initial level and to continued higher inflation than in partner countries), and about the commitment of the Thatcher government to the ERM.

Commitment to the ERM by the U.K. authorities was enhanced by the replacement of Margaret Thatcher as Prime Minister by John Major at the end of November, 1990. The latter, as Chancellor of the Exchequer, had urged for a more European policy, and had been an advocate of the ERM membership. He and the new chancellor, Norman Lamont, not only reiterated their commitment to the existing parity, but also committed themselves to joining the narrow ERM band ($\pm$ 2.25 percent around central parities) at that exchange rate.

Thus, after a year of ERM membership the credibility of the peg seemed to be established, since ERM membership had allowed a decline in retail price inflation to less than 5 percent and of short-term nominal interest rates to 10 percent, while the long-term interest differential with Germany had halved, from 2 to 1 percent (Figure 7.1). Indeed, the *Independent* could write (September 14, 1991):

"The broad conclusion is that the pound's membership of the ERM has worked: it has forced a rapid and painful adjustment on the country, but in less than a year that adjustment is secure, if not yet complete. There is now little talk of the pound having joined the ERM at too high a level. Instead, there is increasing confidence (within the Labour Party as well as the Government) that were the EC to move rapidly to a single currency, Britain would be strong enough to join the club."

The *Economist* (October 5, 1991) similarly argued that a year of ERM experience had proved Alan Walters wrong, and suggested that the time might be ripe for joining the narrow band. The agreement reached in Maastricht in December 1991 to proceed to economic and monetary union also added to the credibility of existing parities, though it included an opt-out clause for the United Kingdom.

The run-up to the general election, held on April 9, 1992, did little to alter confidence in sterling's ERM parity, since there was bipartisan support for ERM membership, if not for all aspects of economic policy. However, during the summer of 1992 it became clear that the recession was longer and more severe than had been expected; gross domestic product had declined by about 4 percent from 1990-Q2 to 1992-Q2. One indicator among many was the seemingly inexorable rise of the unemployment rate (Figure 7.1); labor shedding occurred at a rapid pace in the June-August period (*Bank of England Quarterly Bulletin*, November 1992).

Despite these strains, the Government publicly reasserted its determination not to devalue or leave the ERM. Even at this stage, it was generally felt that the disadvantages of withdrawing outweighed advantages:

"Many, even among those who had doubts about ERM entry, argued that once we had joined, we had to stick with it-toughing out periods of tension as necessary..." (Leigh-Pemberton, 1992, p.3).

The decision to leave the ERM, when it came on September 16, 1992, was at least to some extent forced on the authorities. Speculative pressures in the ERM had been rising since the Danish rejection of the Maastricht Treaty in a referendum in June; polls suggested that the September 20 French referendum might similarly produce a "no" vote.

Figure 7.1: United Kingdom - Unemployment Rate and Long-Term Interest Differential vs. Germany, October 1990 - August 1992 (In Percent).

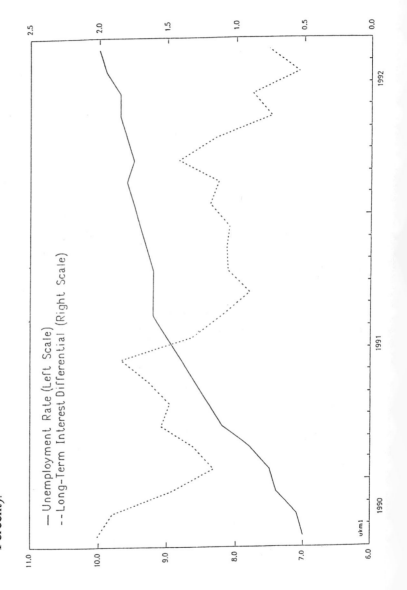

The U.K. monetary authorities, faced with a choice of raising interest rates to clearly unreasonable levels from a domestic perspective, given the weakness of the economy, chose instead to let the currency float outside the ERM. As the Governor of the Bank of England put it:

"... raising U.K. interest rates, when the economy was so weak and inflationary pressure so subdued... would have been regarded... as transparently perverse... [F]ar from adding to credibility, it was always likely to bring--indeed in the event it did bring--the latent pressure to a dramatic climax." (Leigh-Pemberton, 1992, p.7).

3 A Model of Credibility

The model of credibility described below contains two elements highlighted in the discussion of Britain's ERM experience: doubts about the commitment to the system, and concerns about the unemployment costs associated with maintaining the parity in the face of unexpected shocks. Key features of the model are: 1) the private sector does not know the true intentions of the authorities, in particular the weight they give to exchange rate stability; and 2) the effects of shocks to unemployment and of policy choices are persistent, so that the higher is the current level of unemployment, the more likely a further shock will make an optimizing government view the unemployment costs as being too great.

The model is developed and estimated in Masson (1994), and it will not be derived here. Instead, the main assumptions will be summarized.

The model is based on a simple relationship between devaluations and employment. Expected devaluations do not have a stimulative effect, but surprise devaluations do. A government therefore has the incentive to increase employment by devaluing; in the ERM context, the choice is assumed to involve maintaining the current parity or devaluing by a fixed amount d. There is also a stochastic shock u to unemployment; the private sector is assumed not to observe this shock when forming its expectations, while the government (or central bank) knows the value of the shock when deciding whether or not to devalue in the current period. Crucial to our purposes, shocks and government policies have persistent effects on unemployment that extend beyond the current period; this assumption explains why policy choices constrain the room for manoeuver in subsequent periods.

The model is written in terms of ur_t, the deviation of unemployment from the natural rate,

$$(1) \quad ur_t = \sqrt{a}\left[-(e_t - Ee_t) + u_t + \delta ur_{t-1}\right]$$

where e is the exchange rate and u is an unemployment shock. Private sector expectations Ee_t are conditional on information available prior to t, which excludes current and past shocks. The private sector knows that the government is one of two "types" (whose objective functions are known), but it does not know which, so it forms probability assessments of the government's type (described below).

The government is assumed for simplicity to minimize a loss function which depends on the squared deviations of unemployment from the natural rate and on the (squared) change in the exchange rate:

$$(2) \quad L_t = (ur_t)^2 + \theta(\Delta e_t)^2$$

The second term reflects both the cost of inflation and the policymaker's concern for exchange rate stability. A tough government has a larger value for θ than does a weak government: $\theta^T > \theta^W$. These values are known by the private sector, which updates its assessment π_t of the probability that a government is weak on the basis of observed behavior. Given the above assumptions, the government's optimal behavior can easily be characterized. It devalues when a shock u_t is large enough that the costs of maintaining the parity exceed those of incurring higher inflation. The private sector, knowing the behavior of each type of government, can formulate its expectations of devaluation--on the basis of the distribution of unemployment shocks and conditional on an assessment of the probability π_t that the government is weak. This gives expressions for the probability of devaluation by a weak or a tough government, ρ^W and ρ^T, respectively.

Next we consider how to formulate estimates of the probability that the government is of type W or T. Starting from a prior estimate π_{t-1}, suppose that the government does not devalue in period t-1. Then Bayesian updating would imply that

$$(3) \quad \pi_t = \frac{1 - \rho_{t-1}^W}{\left(1 - \rho_{t-1}^W\right)\pi_{t-1} + \left(1 - \rho_{t-1}^T\right)\left(1 - \pi_{t-1}\right)}\pi_{t-1}$$

Using expressions for ρ^W and ρ^T, linearizing, and adding an error term η_t we obtain

(4) $\quad \pi_t = \alpha \pi_{t-1} + \beta ur_{t-2} + \eta_t$

where α and $\beta \leq 0$ are parameters to be estimated. Higher unemployment lowers the probability assessment that the government is weak: the willingness to accept unemployment without devaluing reinforces the government's reputation for toughness.

Expected devaluation is not an observable variable. However, under specific circumstances, the long-term bond rate differential will be a good measure of expected devaluation, and it will be used here as the measure of (lack of) credibility. In particular, in the absence of risk premia and if movements within the ERM band can be ignored (they are increasingly insignificant, the longer the maturity of the bond), then the interest differential is equal to expected devaluation. In our framework, this reflects two components: the probability that the government is weak, and probabilities each type of government will devalue. The resulting expression for the long-term differential can be written as follows (see Masson, 1994):

(5) $\quad R_t^{(N)} = a_0 + a_1 \pi_t + \gamma ur_{t-1} + \varepsilon_t$

The model, in the form of equations (4) and (5), can be estimated using a Kalman filter.[7] The resulting coefficients and standard errors, taken from Masson (1994), are as follows:[8]

(6)
$$\pi_t = 0.509\,\pi_{t-1} - 0.064\,ur_{t-2}, \sigma_\eta^2 = .0035$$
$$\quad\quad (0.168) \quad\quad (0.040)$$

(7)
$$R_t^{(N)} = 1.196 + 3.407\,\pi_t + 0.263\,ur_{t-1}$$
$$\quad\quad (0.232)(2.237) \quad (0.470)$$

Except for α, the coefficients are not very well determined; however, parameter estimates seem sensible.

The model explains well movements in the interest differential with Germany. There is a downward trend in π_t over the period; this variable is

Figure 7.2: United Kingdom - Measures of Credibility. October 1990 - August 1992.

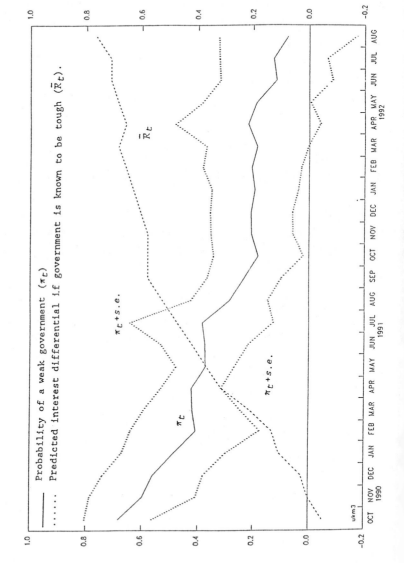

plotted in Figure 7.2, with bands around the one-step ahead estimates that correspond to plus or minus the state variable's standard error. The estimated value of π_t at the point of joining the ERM is 0.68, but by the fall of 1991, π_t is below 0.2. While there is a brief increase in π_t in April 1992, which may be explained by uncertainty in the run-up to the April general election (though, as mentioned above, neither the Conservatives nor Labour advocated devaluation), from April onward, the probability of a weak government declines once again, reaching 0.08 in August 1992, just before the crisis.

Despite this, the long-term interest differential remains high. The model explains this by the significant *positive* effect of lagged unemployment on the probabilities ρ^W and ρ^T that either a weak or a tough government will devalue, if further shocks to unemployment are sufficiently unfavorable-- as captured by the positive coefficient (γ) on ur_{t-1}. The importance of this effect can be gauged from the variable R_t which is plotted in Figure 7.2. This variable is defined as the interest differential that would have prevailed if there had been little doubt that the government was tough; i.e. equation (7) is evaluated at $\bar{\pi} = 0.08$, the value estimated for 1992:08. The chart suggests that the market attributed an increasing likelihood that either type of government would devalue, because of the magnitude of unemployment, which rose steadily throughout the period (see Figure 7.1).

4 Implications of the Model

4.1 *Dynamics*

It can be shown (see Appendix 7) that the model can be reduced to a system of two first-order difference equations in unemployment, ur_t and the probability that the government is weak, π_t. These equations can be written as follows (conditional on no devaluation occurring):

$$(8) \quad \pi_{t+1} = \frac{1 - \bar{\rho}^W - \dfrac{\delta ur_{t-1}}{2v - d} + (1 - \pi_t)\bar{\rho}^W \dfrac{d}{2v}}{1 - \dfrac{\delta ur_{t-1}}{2v - d} - \pi_t \bar{\rho}^W} + \eta_{t+1}$$

$$(9) \quad ur_t = \sqrt{a}\,\bar{\rho}^W\,d\pi_t + \sqrt{a}\,\delta\left(\frac{2v}{2v - d}\right)ur_{t-1} + \zeta_t$$

where a, δ and d are positive parameters as defined above, v is the upper bound of unemployment shocks, and $\bar{\rho}^W$ is the steady-state devaluation probability for a weak government.

The system of equations produces complicated non-linear dynamics, as a result of equation (8). Nevertheless, some interesting results can be derived.

In particular, it is easy to show that there are two fixed points in the absence of stochastic shocks. The first fixed point (labelled "L", for low unemployment),

(10) $\pi^L = 0$ and $ur^L = 0$,

corresponds to perfect credibility and unemployment at the natural rate. While the stability of the system is complicated to examine, numerical experimentation with plausible parameters suggests that for arbitrary initial values $\pi_0 \; \varepsilon \; (0, 1)$ and ur_0, the economy converges to this fixed point.

However, there is also another fixed point, with high unemployment:

(11) $\pi^H = 1$ and $ur^H = \dfrac{\sqrt{a}\,\bar{\rho}^W d}{1 - \sqrt{a}\,\delta\!\left(\dfrac{2v}{2v-d}\right)}$

where, for plausible parameters, $ur^H > 0$. It can also be shown that if $\pi_0 = 1$, lack of credibility persists. In particular, in this case, from equation (8),

(8') $\pi_{t=1} = \pi_t + \eta_{t+1}$

So, whatever the values taken on by unemployment, the government cannot (in the absence of favorable shocks) do anything to shake the conviction that it is weak. And, from (9), unemployment gradually converges to its level ur^H above the natural rate:

(9') $ur_t = \sqrt{a}\,\bar{\rho}^W d + \sqrt{a}\,\delta\!\left(\dfrac{2v}{2v-d}\right) ur_{t-1} + \zeta_t$

$= ur_{t-1} + \mu\left[ur^H - ur_{t-1}\right] + \zeta_t$

where $\mu = 1 - \sqrt{a}\,\delta\,2v/(2v-d)$

4.2 *Self-fulfilling crises*

The model described above puts the main emphasis on the role of shocks to fundamentals in explaining devaluations, and hence in explaining lack of complete credibility of a commitment to a particular exchange rate peg. However, the model also includes an important role for à priori judgments concerning the intentions of the authorities - i.e., the type of government. This opens the door for self-fulfilling crises. If speculators doubt the word of the authorities, then they raise the costs of maintaining the peg, making it more likely that an unfavorable shock to fundamentals will make them decide to devalue.

The mechanism can be understood by considering equation (1) above. It is exchange rate surprises that affect unemployment: if the authorities maintain the peg when they are expected to devalue, unemployment rises. Expected devaluation has two components, the assessment of the type of government (π_t) and the probability that either type of government will devalue (ρ_t^W and ρ_t^T for weak and strong governments, respectively):

$$(12) \quad Ee_t - e_{t-1} = \left[\pi_t \rho_t^W + (1-\pi_t)\rho_t^T\right]d$$

In general, a weak government (i.e., one which assigns a lower weight to inflation or exchange rate changes) will be more likely to devalue: $\rho_t^W > \rho_t^T$. Therefore, if private agents place a greater likelihood on the government being weak, then this raises their expectations of devaluation.

Figure 7.3 illustrates the effect of different values of π_t (for convenience, time subscripts are omitted). As shown in Masson (1994), a government of type i (i = W or T) will devalue when the unemployment shock plus expected devaluation is larger than a certain value b^i, related to its preferences and to the effect of devaluation on unemployment; that is, when

$$(13) \quad u > b^i - (Ee - e_{-1})$$

Suppose the government is thought to be tough ($\pi = 0$) ; then the situation is as depicted in panel a. The critical value of the shock u for a tough government to devalue will be

$$(14) \quad u > b^T - \rho^T d$$

Figure 7.3: Probability of Devaluation with Different Degrees of
Credibility.

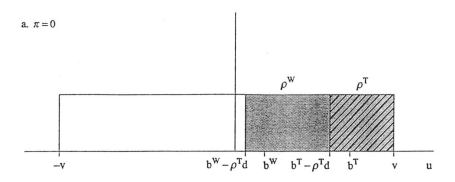

a. $\pi = 0$

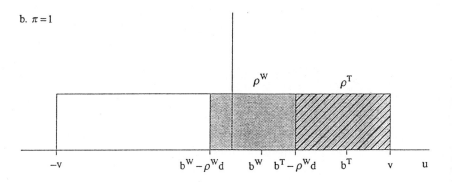

b. $\pi = 1$

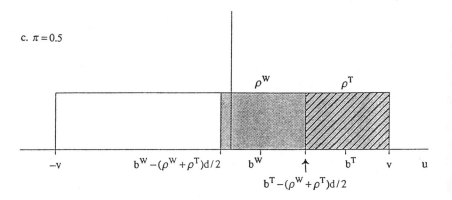

c. $\pi = 0.5$

Since ρ^T is simply the probability that the shock u will take on such values, i.e.,

(15) $\rho^T = \text{prob } (u > b^T - \rho^T d)$

and ρ^T is assumed uniformly distributed in the interval [-v, v] then

(16) $\rho^T = \dfrac{v - b^T + \rho^T d}{2v}$

and solving for ρ^T

(17) $\rho^T = \dfrac{v - b^T}{2v - d}$

The devaluation size is assumed to have an effect that is less than twice the maximum unemployment shock, so the denominator is positive. In panel a., ρ^T is consistent with the above relationships, and the trigger point for a weak government is also displaced by an amount $\rho^T d$.

In panel b., in contrast, private agents are convinced that the government is of a weak type. In this case,

(18) $\rho^W = \dfrac{v - b^W}{2v - d}$

and ρ^T instead of being given by equation (17) above, is given by

(19)
$$\rho^T = \dfrac{v - b^T + \rho^W d}{2v}$$
$$= \dfrac{v - b^T + \left(b^T - b^W\right)d / 2v}{2v - d}$$

Therefore, in this case the devaluation probabilities for both types of government are higher. As drawn, even a zero shock to unemployment would trigger a devaluation if the government is weak. It is clear therefore that a crisis of confidence in the government could produce a self-fulfilling exchange rate adjustment.

An intermediate case, with equal probabilities assigned to the two types of government, is illustrated in panel c. In this case, the threshold levels for unemployment shocks beyond which devaluation is triggered reflect the preferences of both governments. In general,

$$(20) \quad \rho^T = \frac{v - b^T + \left(b^T - b^W\right)\pi d / 2v}{2v - d}$$

$$(21) \quad \rho^W = \frac{v - b^W - \left(b^T - b^W\right)(1 - \pi)d / 2v}{2v - d}$$

so that the devaluation probability of a tough government is raised relative to its value if its type were known, and that of a weak government is lowered.

5 Conclusions and Directions for Further Research

The ERM crisis of September 1992 has generated considerable controversy over the respective roles of economic fundamentals and speculation in causing the crisis. The model discussed in the paper includes among those fundamentals unemployment, and highlights the role of shocks to that variable in affecting the costs and benefits of sticking to an exchange rate peg. If unemployment exhibits persistence, so that the higher is current unemployment, the more likely a new shock will take it to unacceptable levels, then expectations of devaluation will depend on that unemployment level.

The model also allows for uncertainty concerning the government's type. It is assumed that assessments of type are updated in a Bayesian fashion, through comparing the probabilities that either a tough or a weak government would have maintained the peg, given the observed level of unemployment. A Kalman filter is used to estimate the Bayesian updating, along with an observation equation that relates the long-term interest rate differential with Germany to the factors that the model implies should explain devaluation expectations.

The model, when estimated using two years of monthly data taken from the period of ERM membership of the United Kingdom, suggests that unemployment fundamentals explain the persistence of a sizable long-term interest differential with Germany. In contrast, lack of confidence in the government's commitment to the ERM - that is, its "toughness" - seems to have declined steadily over the October 1990 - August 1992 period. Thus, the estimation results do not support the hypothesis of a self-fulfilling speculative crisis due to lack of confidence in the authorities.

The conclusions are necessarily tentative. The model could be extended in a number of directions and tested using data for other countries. A more complicated model would allow for a multi-period objective function and thereby give a larger role to the government's desire to signal its type through its policy actions. A two-period horizon is considered in Drazen and Masson (1993), for instance; unfortunately, closed-form solutions for estimation in a dynamic context are not easily developed for general models. The model could also be extended by considering shocks to other fundamental variables, such as output, inflation, or the balance of payments, and other channels, including interest rates and public debt accumulation. Differences across countries in the size of public debt and the relative importance of short-term and long-term interest rates might emerge from cross-country estimation. Finally, the Kalman filter could be generalized to ensure that calculated probabilities are bounded between zero and unity (perhaps along the lines of Hamilton (1988, 1989, 1990)) and imposing the same distribution on the errors as was used to derive the model.

Notes

[1] The author is grateful to participants at the conference "European Currency Crises and After," for helpful comments on an earlier paper on the same subject. The present paper was in part written at the University of Warwick's Summer Research Workshop, which is supported by the Economic and Social Research Council (U.K.) and the Human Capital and Mobility Programme of the European Community. The views expressed here are personal to the author and do not represent those of the International Monetary Fund.

[2] See, for instance, Andersen and Risager (1988), Blanchard (1985), Horn and Persson (1988), and Weber (1991, 1992).

[3] Vickers (1986).

[4] Backus and Driffill (1985 a, b).

[5] Cukierman and Liviatan (1991).

[6] Obstfeld (1994). Some empirical support for this view is given in Eichengreen, Rose, and Wyplosz (1994).

[7] See Harvey (1989).

[8] Only the updating equation has a non-zero error variance.

Appendix 7
Derivation of Dynamics

Expected depreciation is decomposed into the probability of a weak government (π_t) and the probability weak and tough governments will devalue next period (ρ_t^W and ρ_t^T, respectively):

(A1) $\quad Ee_t - e_{t-1} = \left[\pi_t \rho_t^W + (1 - \pi_t) \rho_t^T \right] d$

In Masson (1994), it is shown that ρ_t^W and ρ_t^T can be written as follows:[1]

(A2) $\quad \rho_t^W = \overline{\rho}^W + \dfrac{\delta ur_{t-1}}{2v - d} + (1 - \pi_t)\left(\overline{\rho}^T - \overline{\rho}^W \right) d / 2v$

(A3) $\quad \rho_t^T = \overline{\rho}^T + \dfrac{\delta ur_{t-1}}{2v - d} - \pi_t \left(\overline{\rho}^T - \overline{\rho}^W \right) d / 2v$

where $\overline{\rho}^T$ and $\overline{\rho}^W$ are constant "steady state" devaluation probabilities for the two types of government, and shocks to unemployment are distributed uniformly in the interval $[-v, v]$. Substituting (A2) and (A3) into (A1) yields

(A4) $\quad Ee_t - e_{t-1} = \left[\overline{\rho}^T + \dfrac{\delta ur_{t-1}}{2v - d} + \pi_t \left(\overline{\rho}^W - \overline{\rho}^T \right) \right] d$

Further substituting into (1) in the text above gives, in the case of no devaluation (so $e_t = e_{t-1}$):

(A5) $\quad ur_t = \sqrt{a}\left[\overline{\rho}^T d + \dfrac{2v\delta}{2v - d} ur_{t-1} + \left(\overline{\rho}^W - \overline{\rho}^T \right) d\pi_t + u_t \right]$

Imposing $\overline{\rho}^T = 0$, and letting $\zeta_t = \sqrt{a}\, u_t$, gives equation (9) in the text.

Equation (8) results from the updating equation (3) in the text, with all variables led one period, after substituting equations (A2) and (A3) and adding an error term η_{t+1}.

References

Andersen, T., and O. Risager (1988), "Stabilization Policies, Credibility, and Interest Rate Determination in a Small Open Economy," *European Economic Review,* 32 (March), pp. 669-79.

Backus, D., and E.J. Driffill (1985a), "Inflation and Reputation," *American Economic Reviews,* 75 (June), pp. 530-538.

Backus, D., and E.J. Driffill (1985b), "Rational Expectations and Policy Credibility Following a Change in Regime," *Review of Economic Studies,* 52 (April), pp. 211-221.

Blanchard, O.J. (1985), "Credibility, Disinflation, and Gradualism," *Economics Letters,* 17, pp. 211-17.

Cukierman, A., and N. Liviatan (1991), "Optimal Accommodation by Strong Policymakers Under Incomplete Information," *Journal of Monetary Economics,* 27 (February), pp. 99-127.

Eichengreen, B., A.K. Rose, and C. Wyplosz (1994), "Speculative Attacks on Pegged Exchange Rates: An Empirical Exploration with Special Reference to the European Monetary System," *CEPR Discussion Paper,* N° 1060, November.

Drazen, A., and P.R. Masson (1993), "Credibility of Policies versus Credibility of Policymakers," *NBER Working Paper,* N° 4448.

Hamilton, J.D. (1988), "Rational-Expectations Econometric Analysis of Changes in Regime: An Investigation of the Term Structure of Interest Rates," *Journal of Economic Dynamics and Control,* 12, pp. 385-423.

Hamilton, J.D. (1989), "A New Approach to the Economic Analysis of Nonstationary Time Series and the Business Cycle," *Econometrica,* 57 (March), pp. 357-84.

Hamilton, J.D. (1990), "Analysis of Time Series Subject to Changes in Regime," *Journal of Econometrics,* 45 (July/August), pp. 39-70.

Harvey, A.C. (1989), *Forecasting, Structural Time Series Models and the Kalman Filter,* Cambridge University Press.

Horn, H., and T. Persson (1988), "Exchange Rate Policy, Wage Formation and Credibility," *European Economic Review,* 32 (October), pp. 1621-36.

Leigh-Pemberton, R. (1992), "Speech Given by the Governor of the Bank of England at the CBI Eastern Region Annual Dinner in Cambridge on 8/10/92," *BIS Review,* N° 197, October 15.

Masson, P.R. (1994), "Gaining and Losing ERM Credibility: The Case of the United Kingdom," paper presented at the conference "European Currency Crises and After," University of Bordeaux I, July 11-12, 1994 (revised, August 1994 ; forthcoming in the *Economic Journal,* May 1995).

Obstfeld, M. (1994), "The Logic of Currency Crises," in Mouvements de capitaux et marchés des changes, *Cahiers économiques et monétaires,* Banque de France, N° 43, pp. 189-214.

Vickers, J. (1986), "Signalling in a Model of Monetary Policy with Incomplete Information," *Oxford Economic Papers,* 38 (November), pp. 443-55.

Weber, A. (1991), "Reputation and Credibility in the European Monetary System," *Economic Policy,* N° 12 (April), pp. 57-102.

Weber, A. (1992), "The Role of Policymakers' Reputation in the EMS Disinflations: An Empirical Evaluation," *European Economic Review,* 36, pp. 1473-92.

Winckler, G. (1991), "Exchange Rate Appreciation as a Signal of a New Policy Stance," *IMF Working Paper,* WP/91/32 (March).

Discussion

BENOIT COEURE

I am very glad to comment upon this paper by P. Masson and I shall first stress that it is both stimulating and useful. People talk a lot about "credibility" in the conduct of monetary policy but they do seldom attempt to measure it. This paper is stimulating first on a theoretical ground because it offers a complete model of exchange rate credibility that is at the same time fairly realistic, explicitly dynamic (describing how the market learns) and rational, with no ad-hoc assumptions about the government's choices. Indeed, most models of currency crises are theoretically appealing but hard to confront with the facts: this one is also to be praised for presenting both theoretical and empirical arguments.

This is valuable for researchers as well as for policymakers, in a field which is of such a political and social importance.

1 The Model

Paul Masson proposes us a model where the government decides on a rational basis whether it will devalue or not weighting the gains from an improved competitiveness on the one hand, a moderate inflation on the other hand. The government can be *weak* or *tough* (in British words, one would say "wet" or "dry") depending on its willingness to fight inflation. The market learns about the government's type and bad news from the real economy, say a rise in unemployment, will have two opposite effects on devaluation expectations:

- unemployment is persistent, thus a temporary rise increases the likelihood that further shocks in the near future will force the government to devalue.

- a higher level of unemployment signals that the government is willing to accept sacrifices to bring inflation down. Thus it is presumably of the *tough* type and it will not devalue.

I find this basic idea very appealing and I will not discuss the algebra it involves but rather compare it with other models. Part of the theoretical debate following the 1992 and 1993 exchange rate crises has contrasted two broad classes of models. In the "traditional" model of balance of payments crises in the line of Krugman (1979), a speculative attack occurs because a drift in the fundamental of the exchange rate (say, the growth rate of domestic credit) makes the fixed parity unsustainable given that there is only a finite amount of central bank's reserves. An important feature is that the market will eventually trigger the crisis before the reserves are depleted. A more recent - one could say, more fashionable - type of model promoted by Obstfeld (1986, 1994) makes use of multiple equilibria. If the monetary policy is expected to loosen after a crisis has occurred, then two regimes are equally likely: a fixed exchange rate with no inflation or a floating exchange rate with inflation. The market can force the government out of the first equilibrium, in which case its expectations will be self fulfilled. The former models can be criticized because they rely on a specific structural model of exchange rate determination, e.g. the monetary model, and because they give a crucial role to foreign exchange reserves, which perhaps do not deserve it. The latter models can be criticized because of their ad-hoc assumptions on the behaviour of the government after the crisis, and because nothing explains how and why the market should coordinate and make the crisis happen unless some exogenous, coordinating signals are invoked (sunspots).

Paul Masson builds on the so-called exchange rates escape clauses literature (see Obstfeld, 1991, Drazen and Masson, 1993) to account, as in the first story, for the dynamics of the domestic economy, at the same time reshaping the second story into a repeated game between a rational government and a rational market. If it is true that the economists like to consider that the policymakers are fools while the market is wise, then the view advocated here seems somewhat more balanced.

A common feature of models of exchange rate crises is that expectations play a role through the financial market. By contrast, expectations appear in this model through the labor market, the real wage being identified with unexpected changes in the parity. This is certainly a convenient way to present the credibility mechanism because it is basically the Barro-Gordon model, which everyone knows how to understand. However, one may wonder whether the mechanisms embodied in equation (1), including wage bargaining, could really play a role in such a short period. Indeed, there are many other candidates to the status of "fundamental of credibility" here attributed solely to unemployment. Suppose for instance that the real activity depends negatively on nominal interest rates - then the whole model could presumably be written with cumulated past interest rates as a measure of credibility. This is to highlight the fact that a richer "real sector" in the model would generalize its conclusions and widen its applications.

2 The Results

To describe the credibility problem, Paul Masson asks if skipping the breakfast should increase the likelihood that you are not going to have lunch. On the one hand, it signals how tough you are: $\beta<0$ in equation (4). On the other hand, it makes it more likely that you will be too hungry to resist temptation: $\gamma>0$ in equation (5). It turns out that $\hat{\beta}$ is significantly different from zero while $\hat{\gamma}$ is not: thus people should be convinced that you will not have lunch. Note that this is at odds with the evolution of the credibility measure shown in Figure 7.2. Till mid-1992, credibility ($-\pi$) had been rising steadily and the implied probability that a "tough" government would devalue, though slightly increasing, was still very low. Surely, this provides convincing evidence on one of the *lieu commun* of the literature on exchange rates systems: that a country can build a reputation provided that it has accepted to tie its hands, in this case, by joining the ERM. But it also shows that "credibility" in the sense of the model is not enough. In other words, these results suggest that the British government and the Bank of England had successfully proven that they were "tough" and committed to the ERM ... but that this revealed of little help to save the pound. Thus the crisis remains a mystery.

3 The Model and the British Case

In this model, the decision problem is repeated in the same terms each period given the current levels of the state variables. Following a devaluation, business resumes as usual with a fixed exchange rate, and other devaluations may occur at some time in the future. Is this *stationary*, state-dependent decision rule well fitted to such a dramatic event as Britain leaving the ERM, which occurred once? The very words "Black Monday" that were coined at that time suggest that the decision to leave was not mere routine for both agents, the government and the market. Another modelling strategy could have considered the irreversible switch from a fixed rate to a free-float. This is closer to what actually happened in september 1992, and the anatomy of the crisis is different in this setting. It was believed then that a free-float would be associated with a higher inflation rate and could even (still now) prevent the UK from joining the stages of EMU. Such expectations could have been self-validating. This is the simple multiple equilibria story, that has been strongly advocated in the case of the UK (Eichengreen and Wyplosz, 1993). Certainly, such an explanation cannot be fully convincing as long as what triggered the crisis itself remains unexplained - but this is not so clear in the model presented here as well. Moreover, many other explanations have been proposed in the case of the UK: as in all other European countries, the depressive effects of high interest rates on the real economy, a downward trend in competitiveness due to the ongoing weakening of the US dollar (more than to high labor costs), widespread concerns about future public debts due to the expansionary fiscal policy, the overall political weakness of the commitment to ERM...

As a conclusion, I wonder if one can model credibility as being only related to unemployment, particularly in the British case. I am confident that one could use the same model and introduce other fundamentals, possibly different across countries if the model is to be applied to other currency crises. Besides, a striking feature of this model is that it stresses the role of history, being very much backward-looking (through the cumulative measure of credibility) though it has at its heart the market's expectations of future policies. This captures the fact that the market too has a memory. It must be possible to reconciliate this approach with the traditional, forward-looking models of exchange rates crises, which may well describe the short-run dynamics and the timing of the crisis. But let me insist that this paper, as it is now, is very impressive - and I look forward to seeing it applied to the French case.

References

Drazen, A., and P. Masson (1993), "Credibility of Policies vs. Credibility of Policymakers," *NBER Working Paper,* N° 4448.

Eichengreen, B., and Ch. Wyplosz (1993), "The Unstable EMS," *Brookings Papers on Economic Activity,* N° 1, pp. 51-143.

Krugman, P. (1979), "A Theory of Balance of Payments Crises," *Journal of Money, Credit and Banking,* N° 11, pp. 311-325.

Obstfeld, M. (1986), "Rational and Self-Fulfilling Balance of Payments Crises," *American Economic Review,* N° 76, pp. 72-81.

Obstfeld, M. (1991), "Destabilizing Effects of Exchange Rates Escape Clauses," *NBER Working Paper,* N° 3603.

Obstfeld, M. (1994), "The Logic of Currency Crises," *Cahiers Economiques et Monétaires,* Banque de France, N° 43, pp. 189-214.

Exchange Rate Risk Under a Peso Problem: The Case of the Peseta in the ERM[1]

EU $157- 74$

$Spain$

$F31$

$F33$

$F36$

1 Introduction

Between 1987 and the summer of 1992, the exchange rates of the currencies in the Exchange Rate Mechanism (ERM) of the European Monetary System (EMS) showed a high degree of stability. After that, however, the system was hit by the worst crisis it had ever faced. This crisis gave rise to a reform of the ERM that entailed the temporary widening of the maximum fluctuation limits for bilateral rates to ± 15%.

One of the main concerns prompted by the widening of ERM bands refers to the possibility that the wider margin of fluctuation available may jeopardise the goal of exchange rate stability and, by heightening the exchange rate risk perceived by agents, may undermine the benefits and even the feasibility of the process of economic integration in Europe.

However, all too frequently, this concern arises from the reading of measures of exchange rate volatility which, in general, provide poor estimates of the concept of exchange rate risk that is relevant to the decisions of market agents. Following the study of Ungerer et al. (1986) on the effects of EMS membership on exchange rate and interest rate volatility, numerous papers have underscored the importance of using statistics that measure the conditional variance of the series rather than the unconditional variance. To this end, by estimating processes that model the predictable component of volatility, efforts have focused on obtaining an indicator for the volatility perceived or anticipated by agents. Thus, Artis and Taylor (1988) and Fratianni and Von Hagen (1990), for example, model the conditional variance of the exchange rates using the ARCH methodology introduced by Engle (1982).

Nonetheless, even measures of the conditional variance of exchange rates can prove inadequate for measuring the perceived exchange rate risk, if they focus solely on historical data, as in the ARCH models. Those measures fail to take into account the possibility that agents may consider that the exchange rate regime is likely to change, even though this might not be later confirmed. If, for instance, agents expect a devaluation of the currency, the subjective distribution of the exchange rate incorporates this event in its first and second order moment. If the devaluation does not occur, the volatility estimated on the basis of observed data will tend to underestimate the risk perceived by agents when they carry out transactions in a foreign currency. The effect of those unobservable events on the conditional mean is known in the literature as the "peso problem" (see e.g. Krasker, 1980) and has been the subject of a number of analyses in different contexts. This contrasts with the dearth of studies that extend the analysis to second order conditional moments, as the study of exchange risk requires.

The importance of using exchange risk indicators which incorporate the degree of credibility of the fluctuation regime is even greater if we consider that, in general, those who have expressed concern over the increase of exchange rate variances have also acknowledged that the widening of fluctuation bands has made the ERM more sustainable. Naturally, this gain in the System's credibility-which is evident by simple inspection of the usual indicators (see e.g. Svensson, 1993)-, was also favoured by the corrections made on exchange rates during the crisis and by the observed easing of economic policy dilemmas.

This opposite evolution of exchange rate volatility and exchange rate credibility is particularly evident in the case of the peseta. From june 1989 until its first devaluation in september, 1992, the peseta was steadily appreciated with respect to its central parity with the D-mark, being during that period one of the most stable currencies in the ERM. At the same time, interest rate differentials were never below three percentage points (on annual basis) at all maturities, signalling significant devaluation expectations. After the widening of the ERM fluctuation bands, exchange rate volatility increased threefold, but interest rate differentials decreased substantially, reflecting greater credibility of the (new) exchange-rate regime.

Therefore, an analysis of exchange rate risk for currencies under a peso problem, requires an indicator that is capable of reflecting both the observed volatility and the perceived sustainability of the exchange rate regime. This indicator is used to evaluate the exchange rate risk associated to the peseta since its entry into the ERM in June, 1989, paying special attention to the changes observed after the widening of the bands.

The rest of the paper is structured as follows: Section 2 obtains the conditional variance of the exchange rate when it is subject to a system with imperfect credibility and proposes a method for its estimation. Section 3 uses this indicator to study the risk associated to the peseta/D-mark exchange rate. Section 4 presents the main conclusions of the analysis.

2 Exchange rate risk under imperfect credibility

In line with the financial literature, this paper measures the risk associated to the exchange rate variation at moment t at term τ as the variance of the exchange rate at $t+\tau$, conditioned to all information available at t. This conditional variance is defined as

$$V_t s_{t+\tau} \equiv E_t \left(s_{t+\tau} - E_t s_{t+\tau} \right)^2,$$

where E_t is the conditional expectation operator at t, and s_t is the (log) market exchange rate. Thus, the exchange risk at t is defined as the expected value of the volatility of the unanticipated component of the exchange rate at $t+\tau$.

This definition is justified on two fronts. First, even though it is true that greater fluctuations generally imply greater risk, not all the volatility of a series can be considered risk, since part of these fluctuations can be anticipated by the market, and the risk indicator should evaluate the degree of unpredictablity in the exchange rates. Second, the measure of relevant exchange risk should be based on the expected or anticipated component of volatility in the series, because this is the component that determines agents' decisions.

2.1. *Conditional variance under regimes which are not perfectly credible*
Assume that the (log) exchange rate s, follows at period t a process (R1) characterized by a conditional mean μ_t^1 and a conditional variance h_t^1. However, agents assign at that period, a probability p_t to the next period

exchange rate being a realization of a different stochastic process (R2) with conditional mean μ_t^2 and conditional variance h_t^2.

Therefore, the conditional mean at period t of the (log) exchange rate is

(1) $E_t s_{t+1} = (1 - p_t) E_t [s_{t+1} | R1] + p_t E_t [s_{t+1} | R2]$

Likewise, the conditional variance is

$$V_t s_{t+1} = E_t (s_{t+1} - E_t s_{t+1})^2 = (1 - p_t) E_t \left[(s_{t+1} - E_t s_{t+1})^2 | R1 \right]$$

(2)
$$+ p_t E_t \left[(s_{t+1} - E_t s_{t+1})^2 | R2 \right]$$

Substituting equation (1) into equation (2) yields

$$V_t s_{t+1} = (1 - p_t) E_t \left[\left(s_{t+1} - \mu_t^1 \right) - p_t \left(\mu_t^2 - \mu_t^1 \right) | R1 \right]^2$$

(3)
$$+ p_t E_t \left[\left(s_{t+1} - \mu_t^2 \right) + (1 - p_t) \left(\mu_t^2 - \mu_t^1 \right) | R2 \right]^2$$

$$= \left[(1 - p_t) h_t^1 + p_t h_t^2 \right] + p_t (1 - p_t) \left(\mu_t^2 - \mu_t^1 \right)^2$$

Thus, the conditional variance of the exchange rate has two components. The first one is the mean of the *within the regime* conditional variances of both regimes. The second component measures the effect on the conditional variance of the expected change in the conditional mean of the process.

In order to illustrate the meaning of equation (3), consider a currency subject to a regime characterised by a zero-width band. Assume also that the probability of devaluation is not zero. In this case, the *within the regime* conditional variance would be zero under both regimes. However, since there exists a risk of devaluation ($0 < p_t < 1$), the conditional variance will be positive. Thus, even though the observed market rate does not fluctuate, the foreign exchange risk measured by the conditional variance can be high if the observed parity is not sufficiently credible.

Similarly, for regimes characterized by target zones-like the ERM, equation (3) suggests a method to correct the traditional GARCH-type volatility indicators. Thus, equation (3) can be rewritten as

(4) $\quad V_t s_{t+1} = h_t^1 + C_t$,

where

(5) $\quad C_t = p_t \left(h_t^2 - h_t^1 \right) + p_t (1 - p_t) \left(\mu_t^2 - \mu_t^1 \right)^2$

Since the standard indicators only take into account the history of the series, they only estimate the *within the regime* component $\left(h_t^1 \right)$ of the conditional variance. Therefore, when estimating risk, the usual indicators ignore the correction term C_t which measures the impact of the imperfect credibility of the official bands (or of the target zone within those bands).

Note first that if $h_t^1 \approx h_t^2$, imperfect credibility ($p_t > 0$) implies that the standard GARCH approach understimates unambiguously the conditional variance of the exchange rate. Second, the higher the *within the regime* volatility of the alternative regime and the higher the absolute variation of the conditional mean, the higher the correction term. Third, the second term of equation (5) is independant of the alternative regime implying a currency depreciation or a currency appreciation. Finally, the correction term is not a monotonic function of the switching probability p_t. In fact, $p_t = 5$ maximizes the second term of equation (5) for given μ_t^1 and μ_t^2.

2.2. Measuring foreign exchange risk

In order to measure foreign exchange risk we must specify two alternative processes for the exchange rate. Using a common practice in the literature, we only consider univariate processes. In particular, we assume that the exchange rate is the realization of one of the following stochastic processes

(6) $\quad$ R1: $\quad s_{t+1} = c + \phi s_t + \varepsilon_{t+1}$
(7) $\quad$ R2: $\quad s_{t+1} = c + d_t + \phi s_t + \omega_{t+1}$

where d_t is the difference between the conditional mean of the two processes (a jump) and ε_t and ω_t are innovations with zero mean and common conditional variance[2] (h_t). We also assume that agents assign at every period t a probability p_t to the current regime switching from R1 to R2. Thus at every period t, an exchange rate jump of size d_t is expected with probability p_t.

From equations (6) and (7), we can rewrite equation (3) as

(8) $V_t s_{t+1} = h_t + p_t d_t (d_t - p_t d_t)$

Thus, measuring exchange risk requires computing the switching probability p_t, the expected jump size d_t and the conditional variance *within the regime* h_t.

Assuming that Uncovered Interest Rate Parity (UIP) holds, the expected rate of exchange rate jump $(p_t d_t)$ can be easily calculated since

(9) $i_t - i_t^* = E_t s_{t+1} - s_t = p_t d_t + c - (1-\phi)s_t$

where i_t and i_t^* are the domestic and foreign one-period interest rate respectively.[3]

Naturally, splitting the expected rate of the exchange rate jump into probability and size is less straightforward. The approach taken is the usual one in the related literature (see Lindberg, Svensson and Söderlind, 1993 and Drazen and Masson, 1992). Thus, we fix exogenously the expected jump size, taking into account real exchange rate appreciations and the jumps observed after devaluations and other regime variations (free floating and band narrowing and widening). Once the expected jump size (d_t) has been determined, the probability p_t is obtained by dividing the interest rate differential over d_t.

The conditional variance within the regime is estimated using the GARCH methodology proposed by Bollerslev (1986). Thus, we assume

$$\varepsilon_{t+1|t} \approx D_\varepsilon(0, h_t) \quad \text{and} \quad \omega_{t+1|t} \approx D_\omega(0, h_t)$$

where

$$h_t = \alpha_0 + \sum_{i=1}^{p} \alpha_i \varepsilon_{t+1-i}^2 + \sum_{j=1}^{q} \beta_j h_{t-j}$$

In the empirical work we use daily data. However, since we are interested in estimating the foreign exchange risk associated to horizons longer than one day, we must deal with interest rates which correspond to maturities longer than the frequency of the data. In order to handle this problem, we assume that there is only one possible jump within the considered horizon τ and rewrite equations (6) and (7) in the following way

(10)   R1': $s_{t+\tau} = k + \phi^\tau s_t + v_{t+\tau}$
(11)   R2': $s_{t+\tau} = k + d_t + \phi^\tau s_t + \eta_{t+\tau}$

where

$$k = \frac{c\left(1 - \phi^\tau\right)}{1 - \phi}, \quad v_{t+\tau} = \sum_{i=1}^{\tau} \phi^{\tau-i} \varepsilon_{t+i}, \quad \eta_{t+\tau} = \sum_{i=1}^{\tau} \phi^{\tau-i} \omega_{t+i}$$

and

$$V_t \upsilon_{t+\tau} = V_t \eta_{t+\tau} = \sum_{i=1}^{\tau} \phi^{2(\tau-i)} V_t \varepsilon_{t+i}$$

Therefore, p_t and d_t should be reinterpreted as the probability and the expected size of an exchange rate jump between t and $t + \tau$ respectively. Taking advantage of the linear form of the GARCH model it is straightforward to compute the τ-period conditional variance $V_t v_{t+\tau}$. For example, for the standard GARCH (1, 1) model, it holds that

$$V_t \varepsilon_{t+1} = h_t$$

(12)
$$V_t \varepsilon_{t+j} = \alpha_0 \left[\frac{1 - (\alpha_1 + \beta_1)^{j-1}}{1 - (\alpha_1 + \beta_1)} \right] + (\alpha_1 + \beta_1)^{j-1} h_t, \quad j = 2, \cdots, \tau$$

3   The exchange rate risk of the Spanish peseta

In this section, we use the methodology described in section 2 to analyse the risk associated to the peseta/D-mark exchange rate since the entry of the peseta into the ERM.

In order to calculate the conditional variance of the exchange rate we chose a maturity of 1 month, since this is the term habitually used in the descriptive studies of exchange rate volatility in the ERM. Thus, the (daily) interest rates used correspond to 1-month deposits in the euromarket, denominated in pesetas and D-marks, respectively.

Juan Ayuso, Maria Pérez-Jurado & Fernando Restoy

Figure 8.1: (LOG) Exchange rate Peseta/DM.

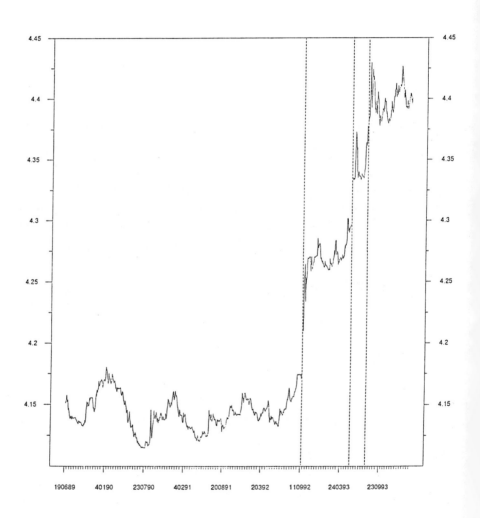

We distinguish four subperiods (see Figure 8.1). The first subperiod begins with the peseta's entry into the ERM, ends at the time of the September 1992 devaluation and coincides with the period of greatest stability in the system. The second subperiod ends with the devaluation of May 1993, and the third concludes few days before the widening of the bands on August 2, 1993 (concretely, July 22). Hence the second and third subperiods can be taken as the stages of greatest tension in the ERM, while the fourth subperiod can be used to illustrate the behaviour of the exchange rate within the framework of the new ERM following the widening of fluctuation bands.

For all four subperiods the parameters of the equations (6) and (7) were fixed such that $c = 0$ and $\phi = 1$. These values of the parameters imply that the exchange rate follows a random walk process without drift within each regime. Although the empirical evidence is not very favourable to this hypothesis for ERM currencies[4], we use it as a simplification that facilitates the subsequent analysis and allows isolating the proposed measure of risk from the possible effects caused by the changes in the mean reversion process throughout the four subperiods studied.[5]

As regards the estimation of the GARCH processes, Table 8.1 shows the results for the subperiods considered. As can be observed, with the exception of the third subperiod (characterised by a constant variance), the model that best explains the conditional variances is a GARCH (1, 1).

In the breakdown of the expected rate of exchange rate jump by the probability of the jump and its expected size, the size corresponding to each of the four subperiods was obtained under the criteria described forthwith. If the average value in the year 1988 is fixed as a reference, at the time of the peseta's entry into the ERM the Spanish economy had accumulated losses in competitiveness ranging between 3% (production prices) and 10% (unit labour costs in the manufacturing sector). In addition, one month after the devaluation of September 1992, the peseta/D-mark exchange rate was depreciated by approximately 13%. Taking these data as a reference, we imposed linearly increasing size from 5% to 13% for the first subperiod. As for the second and third subperiods, we use constant sizes of 7% and 5% respectively. Those sizes correspond approximately to the observed market depreciations one month after the third devaluation and the band widening respectively. Lastly, for the fourth subperiod we used the minimum constant size compatible with the observed interest rate differentials.[6] This assumption is justified by the

Table 8.1: GARCH estimates: Peseta/DM.

$$s_{t+1} - s_t = \varepsilon_{t+1} \, , \, \varepsilon_{t+1|t} \sim D(0, h_t)$$
$$h_t = \alpha_0 + \alpha_1 \varepsilon_t^2 + \beta_1 h_{t-1}$$

Subsample	α_0	α_1	β_1	$\chi^2(5)$	N
22.06.89-15.09.92	• 91E-6	• 28	• 55	2.99	782
	(• 22E-6)	(• 05)	(• 07)		
18.09.92-12.05.93	• 66E-5	• 33	• 35	7.64	155
	(• 24E-5)	(• 18)	(• 19)		
15.05.93-22.07.93	• 70E-3	--	--	1.83	47
	(--)				
26.07.93-25.02.94	• 11E-5	• 14	• 80	5.44	146
	(• 73E-6)	(• 07)	(• 08)		

Notes:

– standard errors in parenthesis.

– N stands for the number of observations.

– χ^2 (5) stands for the LM test on residual heteroskedasticity up to order 5.

absence of devaluations in the period and by the elimination of the currency real overvaluation as a consequence of the three devaluations experienced by the peseta.[7]

Figure 8.2 shows the expected rate of jump of the exchange rate and its breakdown in the expected size and the probability of the jump. As can be observed, the product $(p_t d_t)$ tended to move downwards from the peseta's entry into the ERM until approximately the Danish referendum of June 1992. It then headed on a generally upward course, albeit with significant falls after each devaluation. Following the upturn in July 1993 and the widening of the bands on August 2 of that year, the rate slipped again and, by the end of February 1994, reached values close to those of June 1992.

With respect to the probability and expected size of the jump, the pronounced difference observed between the periods prior and subsequent to the widening of the bands is congruent with the interpretation occasionally made of the difference between a system of pegged exchange rates and a system of more flexible rates (Edison and Melvin, 1990): characteristically, in a pegged exchange rate system, the probability is small (less than 15% in this case) that a large jump will occur (up to 13%) whereas, in a system of more flexible rates, there is a large probability (nearly 50%) of a small jump (less than 1%).

Lastly, the *within the regime* conditional variance $(V_t v_{t+\tau} = V_t \eta_{t+\tau})$ can be obtained by using expression (12) and the GARCH estimates of Table 8.1.

After obtaining the probability of a change of regime (p_t), the expected jump in the peseta/D-mark exchange rate (d_t) and the *within the regime* conditional variance $(V_t v_{t+\tau})$, the exchange rate risk associated with the peseta/D-mark exchange rate is estimated by computing equation (8).

Figure 8.3 compares the *within the regime* (uncorrected) conditional variance to the (corrected) conditional variance of the exchange rate.

The key finding derived from the analysis of Figure 8.3 is the enormous quantitative importance of the correction arising from the possibility of a jump in the market exchange rate. In fact, it can be observed that, due to this correction, the exchange rate risk that characterised the period between June 1989 and August 1992 is approximately four times greater than what would be deduced from the simple estimation of the *within the regime* volatility. During the crisis period (September 1992-July 1993), the exchange rate risk is still substantially higher than what would be

Figure 8.2: Expected rate of the Peseta/DM exchange rate jump.

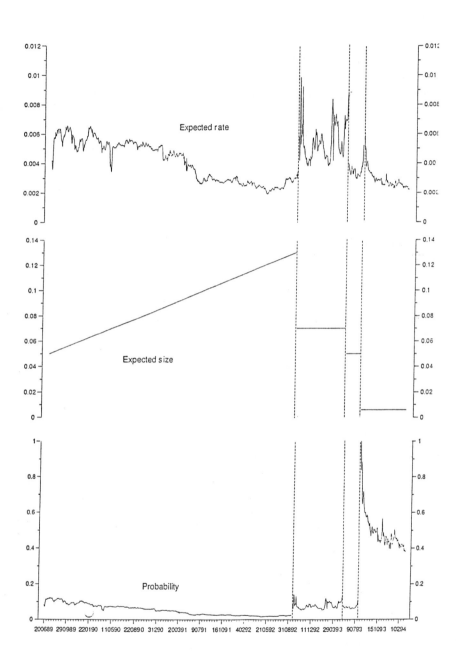

Figure 8.3: Conditional variance Peseta/DM.

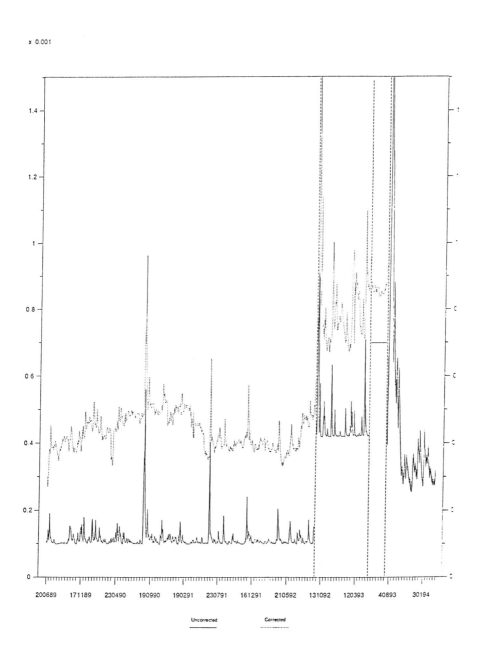

Figure 8.4: Conditional variance Peseta/DM ($\phi = .97$).

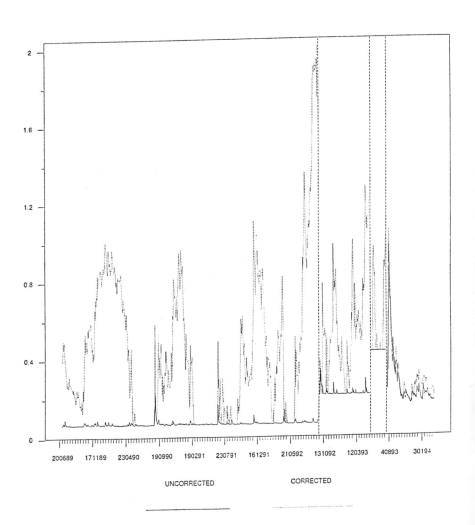

UNCORRECTED   CORRECTED

reflected in the standard analysis of observed exchange rate volatility. However, after the widening of fluctuation bands, the narrowing of the interest rate differential with Germany makes the discrepancy between the proposed measure of risk and the standard volatility estimates much less relevant.[8]

The importance of the correction of the conventional volatility indicator is also evident if we compare the levels of the peseta's exchange rate risk before and after fluctuation bands were widened (August 2, 1993). In this sense, the performance of the standard volatility (uncorrected conditional variance) suggests that the volatility of exchange rates following the widening of the bands is practically three times greater than the level observed in the period prior to September 1992 and only 25% lower than in the crisis period. However, the analysis of the corrected conditional variance shows that, after an initial bout of high volatity, the risk characterising the wide-band period is 60% lower than in the crisis period and 25% lower than during the three-year period that preceded the first devaluation of the peseta in the ERM.

These findings signal that, as expected, the larger margin of fluctuation available has translated into more volatile exchange rates. However, the observed gain in credibility of the fluctuation regime has a greater impact on the conditional variance of the exchange rate than the rise in observed volatility. Thus, contrary to what conventional estimators suggest, the proposed indicator shows that the exchange rate risk of the peseta has subsided since the widening of the bands.

4 Conclusion

In this paper, we questioned the general pratice of measuring exchange rate risk by applying the standard models of conditional heteroskedasticity to the observed exchange rate data. This practice fails to take into account much of the risk assumed by agents when they operate with currencies of scant volatility but which fluctuate around parities perceived to be fairly unsustainable. To surmount this problem, we propose an indicator of exchange rate risk that explicitly reflects the possible lack of credibility of the fluctuation regime.

This indicator was applied to the peseta in order to evaluate the evolution of its exchange rate risk. The following conclusions were drawn:

– The conventional measures of volatility considerably underestimate the exchange rate risk in practically the entire period prior to the ERM crisis.

– The proposed indicator signals a pattern of exchange rate risk for the peseta very different from that suggested by conventional volatility yardsticks. Within months from the widening of the bands, the prevailing exchange rate risk is not only substantially lower than during the crisis period; it is also milder than during the period prior to the signing of the Maastricht Treaty and comparable to the levels observed during the period of greatest stability in the narrow-band ERM.

The results obtained for the peseta suggest that, even in the absence of speculative attacks, exchange rate regimes that severely limit the exchange rate fluctuations can have negative effects on the perceived exchange risk, if those regimes require economic policies that the market considers fairly unsustainable. Naturally, the gain in credibility of the peseta exchange rate regime, which explains much of the evidence presented, cannot be attributed solely to the System's reform. Thus, the positive effect of the exchange rate adjustments made during the crisis is also at play. In any case, the results presented raise the question of whether minimizing foreign exchange risk requires exchange rate commitments that are flexible enough to warrant an acceptable degree of credibility, even though they may imply some exchange rate volatility.

Lastly, a note of caution. The empirical implementation of the indicator involves assumptions -difficult to test- regarding the expected size of the exchange rate jumps associated with the changes of regime. Since the quantitative results inevitably depend on these assumptions, we used conservative criteria which are, in any event, consistent with those habitually applied in the literature. Nevertheless, additional work on this issue together with the analysis of other currencies seem to be natural extensions of this paper.

Notes

[1] We are grateful to Santiago Fernandez de Liz, Eric Girardin, and José Viñals for helpful comments. We should also like to thank Francisco Alonso and Juan J. Pacheco for outstanding research assistance. The views expressed in this paper are the authors' and they do not necessarily correspond to those of the Banco de España.

[2] This assumption implies that both regimes only differ in their conditional mean. Although this assumption might not be verified ex-post, it avoids making additional arbitrary assumptions on the expected change of the conditional variances. In any case, the ex-post estimates of h_t for the different regimes show that this assumption is, at best, biasing downwards the correction term in equation (5).

[3] Svensson (1992) and Ayuso and Restoy (1992) provide theoretical and empirical arguments in favour of using UIP as an approximate measure of expected exchange rates within the ERM. Notice also that under UIP, $i_t - i_t^* - c + (1-\phi)s_t$ is the expected rate of devaluation defined in Svensson (1993).

[4] See Frankel and Phillips (1991), Holden and Vikoren (1992), Ayuso, Pérez-Jurado and Restoy (1993), Svensson (1993) and Alberola, Humberto and Orts (1994).

[5] In any case, all quantitative results proved to be robust to an alternative specification where the exchange rates were allowed to follow unrestricted stationary AR(1) processes (compare Figures 8.3 and 8.4).

[6] Note that, since probability is bounded by 0 and 1, the maximum (positive) value for the observed interest differential is the lower limit for a (constant) size of the expected jum.

[7] In Ayuso, Pérez-Jurado and Restoy (1994) we present some preliminary work where the exchange rate risk indicator is applied to other ERM currencies. In that paper we evaluate an alternative method to split the expected rate of devaluation (jump) into probability and expected size, using simultaneously UIP and a Tobit model.

[8] This result does not decisively depend on imposing a relatively small jump in the last subperiod. It holds also for reasonably higher sizes (e.g. 3%).

References

Alberola, E., J. Humberto, and V. Orts (1994), "An Application of the Kalman Filter to the Spanish Experience in a Target Zone (1989-1992)," forthcoming in *Revista Espanola de Economia*.

Artis, M.J., and M.P. Taylor (1988), "Exchange Rates, Capital Controls and the European Monetary System: Assessing the Track Record," in Giavazzi, F., S. Micossi, and M. Miller (eds), *The European Monetary System,* Cambridge University Press.

Ayuso, J., M. Pérez-Jurado, and F. Restoy (1993), "Indicadores de Credibilidad de un régimen cambiario: el caso de la peseta en el SME," *Cuadernos Economicos de ICE,* 53.

Ayuso J., M. Pérez-Jurado, and F. Restoy (1994), "Is Exchange Rate Risk Higher in the ERM after the Widening of Fluctuation Bands?" Mimeo, Banco de Espana.

Ayuso, J., and F. Restoy (1992), "Efficiency and Risk Premia in Foreign Exchange Markets," Banco de Espana, *Working Paper,* N° 9225.

Bollerslev, T. (1986), "Generalised Autoregressive Conditional Hetero-skedasticity," *Journal of Econometrics,* 38.

Edison, H., and M. Melvin (1990), "The Determinants and Implications of the Choice of an Exchange Rate System," in Haraf, W., and T. Willet, (eds), *Monetary Policy for a Volatile Global Economy,* American Enterprise Institute, Washington D.C..

Engle, R.F. (1982), "Autoregressive Conditional Heteroskedasticity with Estimates of the Variance of UK Inflation," *Econometrica,* 50.

Frankel, J., and S. Phillips (1991), "The European Monetary System: Credible at Last?" *NBER Working Paper,* N° 3819.

Fratianni, M., and J. Von Hagen (1990), "The European Monetary System Ten Years After," *Carnegie Rochester Conference Series,* 32.

Holden, S., and B. Vikoren (1992), "Have Interest Rates in the Nordic Countries Been Too High? A Test Based on Devaluation Expectations," Norges Bank, Arbeids Notad 1992/6.

Krasker, W.S. (1980), "The 'Peso Problem' in Testing the Efficiency of Forward Exchange Markets," *Journal of Monetary Economics,* 6.

Krugman, P. (1990), "Target Zones and Exchange Rate Dynamics," *Quarterly Journal of Economics,* 106.

Lindberg, H., L.E.O. Svensson, and P. Söderling (1993), "Devaluation Expectations: The Swedish Krona 195-1992," *Economic Journal,* 103.

Svensson, L.E.O. (1992), "The Foreign Exchange Risk Premium in a Target Zone with Devaluation Risk," *Journal of International Economics,* 33.

Svensson, L.E.O. (1993), "Assessing Target Zone Credibility: Mean Reversion and Devaluation Expectations in the EMS," *European Economic Review,* 37.

Ungerer, H., O. Evans, T. Mayer, and P. Young (1986), "The European Monetary System: Recent Developments," *IMF Occasional Paper,* N° 48.

Discussion

ERIC GIRARDIN

This paper provides a very welcome contribution to the study of exchange rate risk in and out of narrow-band exchange rate target zones. This contribution is twofold. First it is methodological and intends to improve upon standard measures of exchange rate risk conceived for floating exchange rate regimes. Second the results obtained on the evolution of exchange rate risk for the peseta between the pre and post ERM crisis period are particularly interesting and informative. However, it seems to me that the implementation of the new method involves a number of postulates or simplifications which should be lifted before the robustness of the results obtained can be confirmed.

It is undeniable that the presence of heteroscedasticity in exchange rate series is a major problem. Thus the modelling of time varying volatility or changing uncertainty has become common practice for currencies in a floating exchange rate regime. Even in a target zone, in absolute value, clusters of large observations are followed by clusters of smaller ones.

The methodological contribution of the authors consists in arguing that in a target zone the conditionnal variance of the exchange rate has two components :

(1) the within regime conditionnal variance, which is what traditionnal GARCH estimates à la Bollerslev endeavour to do for floating exchange rates;

(2) a correcting factor specific to target zones or to fixed exchange rates which stems from the possible change in regime, i.e. a devaluation or a switch to floating/widening of the bands.

	Fixed exchange rates	Floating	Target zone
Components of the conditionnal variance			
(1)	0	> 0	> 0
(2)	> or < 0	0	> or < 0

(1) Within Regime.
(2) Correcting factor.

The measures of the two components both raise some problems. The correcting factor specific to fixed exchange rate regimes is made up of the product of the probability of devaluation by the expected size of the latter. As far as the size of expected devaluation is concerned, Ayuso et alii make rather strong assumptions i.e., for periods prior to the recent currency crises, the expected size of the jump in the exchange rate of the peseta is set equal to the average variation that actually arose after the crises. In other words, this is an assumption of perfect foresight.

The estimation of the within regime conditionnal variance, using the traditionnal GARCH method is quite similar to the one pioneered by Baillie and Bollerslev (1989) for floating exchange rates. However there are two differences which raise a number of problems.

First Ayuso et alii do not introduce any daily dummies, even though they were shown by Baillie and Bollerslev to play a very important role for currencies vis a vis the dollar. Why would this not also be the case for exchanges rates vis a vis the Deutche mark in the EMS? Such dummy variables for day of the week effects would allow daily seasonal variation to effect the conditional variance equation (1) :

$$(1) \quad h_t = \alpha_0 + \alpha_1 \, \varepsilon^2_{t-1} + \beta_1 h_{t-1} + \sum_{j=1}^{6} q_j D_{jt}$$

Indeed, while conditional mean dummies are generally not significant jointly, dummies in the conditional variance part are generally significant.

For all subperiods Ayuso et alii assume that the exchange rate of the peseta follows a random walk without drift. They acknowledge that such an assumption is in conflict with the results of available empirical works on intra-ERM exchange rates. The rationale for using it consists in a wish to separate the measurement of the evolution of risk from the evaluation of the effects of changes in the mean reversion process. At least some unit-root tests would have been welcome here, not to speak of tests of the degree of differentiation.

It is asserted in the paper that in light of the results reported in table 8.1 a GARCH (1,1) model is the one which "best explains the conditional variance". It would be useful to know which is the criterion which leads the authors to such an assertion. Indeed, an interesting aspect of the results contained in this table concerning the parameters of the GARCH (1,1) process, is the closeness of the sum of two parameters α_1 and β_1 to unity. Indeed, this sum is equal to 0.83 and 0.94 respectively for the first and the last subperiods (see table 8.1). This indicates in many cases the probable existence of an integrated GARCH process, what Engle and Bollerslev (1986) call IGARCH, such as:

$$(1.3) \quad \Delta h_t = \alpha_0 + \alpha_1 \varepsilon^2{}_{t-1} + \sum_{j=1}^{6} q_j D_{jt}$$

We can recall here that for the GARCH (p, q) model, the unconditional variance is given by $[\alpha_0 / (1 - \alpha_1 - \beta_1)]$. This implies that in a GARCH (1, 1) model, when the sum $(\alpha_1 + \beta_1) = 1$, the unconditional distribution for Δs_t has an infinite variance.

The infinite persistence of shocks to the IGARCH volatility is particularly unattractive as a description of exchange rate behaviour. However, we know first that IGARCH properties in high frequency data can be the product of the empirical approximation of continous-time diffusions or semi-martingale processes (Nelson and Foster, 1994); second that regime shifts in the unconditional variance may be easily mistaken for IGARCH type behaviour (Hamilton and Susmel, 1994); third that apparent IGARCH behaviour may well be due to the existence of a process with long memory fractionally IGARCH volatility (see Baillie, Bollerslev and Mikkelsen, 1994). All these possibilities would deserve to be examined.

An interesting and challenging result of this paper is the rather surprising ability of the statistical models to explain exchange rate changes. It would of course be useful to conceive of an economically based model to explain the nature of this time dependent heteroskedasticity.

Besides, in the context of the analysis of European currency crises presented in this book, it may seem advisable to try and extend this methodology by not limiting oneself to univariate processes. Thus, the jump variable, which is the difference between the unconditional mean of the two processes may depend on one or several of the following variables: the domestic unemployment rate, the foreign interest rate...

Thus in equation (7), d_t could be replaced by μZ_t, with Z_t a vector of variables driving expectations of jumps in the exchange rate :

$$(7') \quad S_{t+1} = c + \mu Z_t + \phi S_t + \omega_{t+1}$$

A multivariate extension of the model could also involve having a Z_t term in the specification of the conditional variance equation.

Moreover the results are obtained by estimating the GARCH process for the Spanish peseta in isolation. But can we consider that conditional volatilities of ERM currencies vis a vis the DM are independent of each other? Another multivariate extension would thus involve replacing S_t by a vector of ERM exchange rates in order to be able to take into account relationships between them.

Finally, as far as the results are concerned, the paper does not comment on the comparison of the values of the GARCH coefficients obtained for different periods. Thus the estimates contained in table 8.1 apparently imply shifts in these coefficients. This table could usefully contain tests of the significance of these shifts with a likelihood ratio statistic.

Besides, the main result of the paper is that exchange rate risk increased after the September 1992 crisis until the August 1993 one. It is worth recalling here that by estimating a standard ARCH process for the pre-1979 and the EMS periods, Artis and Taylor (1988) had found a significant reduction in the conditional variance of exchange rate innovations over the EMS period. It would thus be interesting to know whether the apparent symmetry in entering and leaving the narrow-band ERM could be confirmed by using the corrected GARCH technique developed by Ayuso et alii for the overall ERM period.

References

Baillie, R., and T. Bollerslev (1989), "The Message in Daily Exchange Rates: A Conditional Variance Tale," *Journal of Business and Economic Statistics*.

Baillie, R., T. Bollerslev, and H.O.E. Mikkelsen (1994), "Fractionally Integrated Generalized Autoregressive Conditional Heteroskedasticity," *Journal of Econometrics*, forthcoming.

Engle, R.F., and T. Bollerslev (1986), "Modelling the Persistence of Conditional Variances," *Econometric Review*, 5, pp. 1-50.

Hamilton, J.D., and R. Susmel (1994), "Autoregressive Conditional Heteroskedasticity and Changes in Regime," *Journal of Econometrics*, forthcoming.

Nelson, D.B., and D.P. Foster (1994), "Asymptotic Filtering Theory for Univariate ARCH Models," *Econometrica*, 62, pp. 1-41.

The Effect of Misalignment on Desired Equilibrium Exchange Rates: Some Analytical and Applied Results[1]

179- 99 USA
          Japan
          UK
F31   France
F33   Germany

1 Introduction

The shape of future arrangements in the European Monetary System is still unclear. However, attention has increasingly been drawn to the possibility of a 'two tier' approach to European Monetary Union. In such an approach, a core group of countries would form a monetary union first, leaving others to join at a later date. One issue this prospect immediately raises is the nature of the relationship between the 'outer fringe' and the 'inner core' countries. There would, presumably, be some kind of exchange rate union between the two. But, by definition, this would need to be sufficiently flexible to accommodate the (initially) 'non-convergent' characteristics of the outer fringe economies. In light of the need to maintain a stable level of competitiveness, one plausible suggestion is that the outer fringe countries should target their real exchange rates, maintaining these at, or close to, their desired equilibrium values. To make such an objective fully operational, it would need to be clear that problems of hysteresis in the equilibrium rate can be taken care of. Our objective in this paper is to investigate the effects of hysteresis--operating through shifting international net asset stocks during periods of misalignment--on the desired equilibrium exchange rate.

The concept of the equilibrium exchange rate is not unique. As noted by Frenkel and Goldstein (1986), there are at least three approaches to determining the equilibrium exchange rate--corresponding to structural exchange rate models such as the monetary model or the portfolio balance model of exchange rate determination, the purchasing power parity approach, and the "underlying balance" approach.[2] In this paper, we are concerned with the underlying balance approach. According to this approach, the equilibrium exchange rate is defined as the real effective exchange rate that is consistent with medium-term internal and external macroeconomic balance. This definition is discussed further below.

The former of these two conditions can be identified with equilibrium employment and output, which would be typically taken to be the non-accelerating inflation rate unemployment level (or NAIRU), the latter with current account balance or, in the presence of sustainable medium-term capital inflow or outflow, a corresponding deficit or surplus. In any case, the current account should incorporate the flow of debt service payments or receipts (and other investment income) corresponding to the underlying net foreign asset position of the economy. These definitions are explored further below.

The underlying balance approach to the equilibrium exchange rate was developed by Fund staff during the early 1970s (see International Monetary Fund (1984)).[3] More recently, the equilibrium rate associated with underlying balance has been labeled the "fundamental equilibrium exchange rate" (FEER) (Williamson (1985)). The concept of "fundamental" equilibrium would be more applicable, however, to a *long-term* situation where all underlying economic forces had worked themselves out. Moreover, we wish to stress that the concept of the equilibrium real exchange rate consistent with underlying macroeconomic balance is essentially normative, as it is contingent upon a set of desired macroeconomic objectives. In this paper, therefore, we shall use the term "desired equilibrium exchange rate" (DEER) to refer to this concept. The DEER has been used as an analytical device by a number of authors to assess exchange rate misalignment (Williamson (1985, 1990), Barrell and Wren-Lewis (1984)), as well as in the context of discussions of "blueprints" for international policy coordination (Williamson and Miller (1987)), Frenkel and Goldstein (1986), Currie and Wren-Lewis (1989)), and in discussions of the "appropriate level" at which to join a pegged exchange rate system such as the European Monetary System (EMS) (Wren-Lewis, et al. (1991)).

This paper addresses an issue concerning DEER computations which, although it has not been entirely overlooked in the literature, has been given relatively little attention, namely: How sensitive is the DEER to the path chosen for convergence towards it? A given DEER trajectory has associated with it a particular path for the current account and debt service flows; a deviation of the actual rate from the DEER immediately implies a different current account and correspondingly a change in debt service flows compared to the original. The level of the real exchange rate consistent with medium-term external balance must therefore change. Thus, the final DEER arrived at will not be independent of the path chosen towards it.

Where equilibrium values turn out to be dependent on the dynamic path of adjustment, the situation is generally termed one of "hysteresis" (Cross (1992)). Contemporary economic analysis is turning up a number of instances in which it appears that hysteresis effects may be important, for example, in the determination of the NAIRU (Lindbeck and Snower (1986)), and in the analysis of trade responses to exchange rate variation, taking account of the sunk costs of setting up in overseas markets (Baldwin and Krugman (1986)). For economists trained in the neoclassical tradition, hysteresis is a troublesome feature since its presence renders inapplicable the method of comparative statics upon which much of modern economic analysis is founded.[4] The implicit use of something at least approximating the comparative static method is common in analyses involving the DEER. For example, enumerating the attractions of the DEER apparatus, Wren-Lewis et alii (1991), note: "First and foremost, it provides a fixed point for a variable that is notoriously difficult to forecast and analyze empirically."[5]

In the remainder of this paper we evaluate the importance of hysteresis effects on the DEER as they arise through the debt service consequences of misalignment.[6] That there are hysteresis effects of this kind is not in dispute; our aim is to provide a sense of their empirical significance. In particular, we provide broad rules of thumb by which to judge the importance of such effects for any given degree of perceived exchange rate misalignment and desired period of monotonic adjustment towards the DEER.

We begin in Section II by discussing the issue of hysteresis in the DEER in more detail and by showing analytically that the DEER is not independent of the path chosen to achieve it. In Section III we derive the full set of dynamic solutions to the problem when the real exchange rate adjusts by a proportion of its deviation from the DEER. In particular, we derive restrictions--which turn out to be quite intuitive--on the partial adjustment process, which are necessary in order to ensure eventual convergence on the DEER. In Section IV we attempt to gauge how important hysteresis effects have been by examining the historical path of real exchange rates for the G-5 countries over an eleven-year period. A final section concludes.

2 Debt Accumulation and Misalignment

The DEER is defined as that value of the real exchange rate that will reconcile internal and external equilibrium "in the medium term." As already explained, external equilibrium is defined in terms of a desired value of the current account balance; this value may be non-zero if there is a presumption about a "normal" rate of capital inflow or outflow. Otherwise a zero value seems a plausible objective, corresponding as it does to a constant level of net foreign assets. Internal balance is usually defined as potential full employment output; in most computations (e.g., those of Williamson (1985, 1990)) this appears to be assumed to be independently computed and to be independent of the real exchange rate itself and we shall follow that tradition here. This is illustrated in Figure 9.1; the NAIRU schedule is drawn as a vertical line in real exchange rate (S) and utilization (u) space. In a very open economy, the NAIRU may be modelled as a function of the real exchange rate. An appreciation of the real exchange rate allows a higher real wage (markup of wages over prices) for a given rate of utilization, since holding the current account constant in volume terms, the improvement in the terms of trade implies an increase in real revenues which may be passed on to workers. This view, which is represented analytically in the Layard-Nickell (1985) "Battle of the Markups" view of inflation is reflected in the econometric modelling work of Wren-Lewis et al (1991). In terms of the diagram, the NAIRU schedule would be positively sloped from left to right. The current account (CA) schedule is drawn for a given level of the current account balance and slopes down from left to right for well-known (net import propensity) reasons: as utilization increases, (net) imports tend to rise, requiring a devaluation of the real exchange rate as an offset. The solution for S^*, u^* gives the DEER and the internal balance or utilization rate.[7]

For given assumed values of the target current account and internal balance, then, the corresponding "fundamental equilibrium exchange rate" (DEER) can be computed. It should be clear that the DEER needs to be computed as a trajectory if there is evolution in the values of the current account and internal balance targets, (or predictable change in the structure of the economy for given values of those targets), even if we set on one side all issues of hysteresis. (An example of a step change in an otherwise flat DEER trajectory is introduced below in Section IV.)

It is easy to see from considering Figure 9.1 how hysteresis in the DEER can arise. Suppose that the actual exchange rate happens to correspond initially to its DEER value and that internal balance is at the optimal level--in

Figure 9.1: Internal and External Balance.

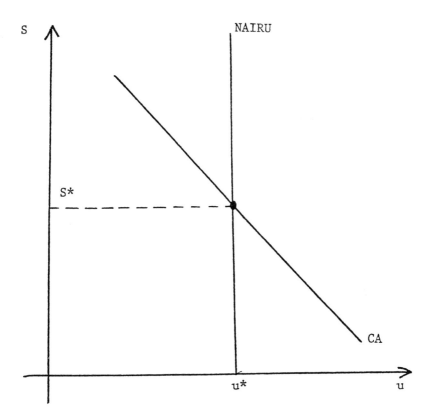

other words, that there is no problem of the starting point or transition period. In terms of the figure, we are at (u^*, S^*). Now suppose that in the next period the actual real exchange rate departs from its DEER value--specifically that it appreciates--whilst utilization remains at u^*. The appreciation causes the current account to deteriorate relative to the initial equilibrium target positions, which is assumed to be zero. Then the DEER calculation must be performed afresh. The deficit increases net foreign indebtedness and creates an obligation to service debt interest. Even disregarding any desire to rectify the increase in indebtedness, the obligation to service more debt must cause the CA schedule to move in to the left: the real exchange rate which would have been consistent with the current account target in the absence of the increased debt service will now produce a deficit due to the increased debt-service obligation. More precisely, the *trade* account target has changed to provide a surplus sufficient to cover the increased debt service obligation. The current account target remains the same since debt service is incorporated in it, but the "structure" of the economy has changed, forcing CA to shift inward.

The departure of the actual exchange rate from its DEER value (trajectory) thus forces a revision of the DEER. A "hysteresis loop" (Cross (1992)) would ensue if the previous DEER were to be re-established. The exchange rate would need to "overdepreciate" in order to reinstate the previous schedule (Figure 9.2). A displacement of the actual real rate of exchange from its DEER value--say, to point A--involves a real appreciation and a current account deficit (relative to the current account balance underlying CA). This requires a re-evaluation of the CA schedule, to CA', and a devaluation of the DEER from S^* to $S^{*'}$. For the DEER to be re-established at S^*, an overdepreciation would be needed to reduce the stock of debt to the original level, resulting in the "hysteresis loop" shown.[8]

How large a revision of the DEER is required as a result of misalignment? To derive an answer to this question, imagine again that starting from a favorable position, (i.e., where the current real exchange rate is at its DEER value and internal balance is realized), the current exchange rate departs from its DEER value by, say, x percent. For concreteness, suppose this is an appreciation. Then a deficit in the current account will appear of $x(m+t)X$ where m and t are, respectively, the import and export elasticities and X is the volume of exports (or imports--we suppose the two to be approximately equal). If this is a one-off deviation of "one-year" duration, then the DEER will have to be devalued to the extent necessary to service the additional debt incurred. It is convenient to assume that the DEER adjustment depends on

Figure 9.2: Hysteresis Effects.

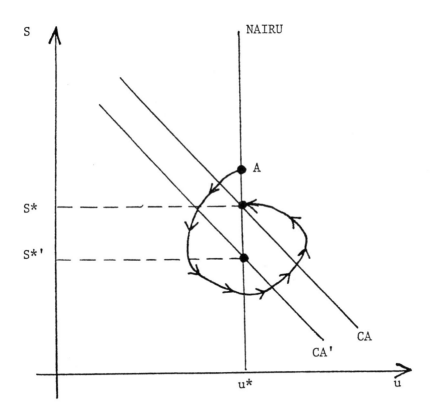

the same elasticities,[9] but the adjustment need only be large enough to service the cost of the debt incurred; then it is easy to see that, if the interest rate is r, the adjustment required is d = rx. (The DEER devaluation, d, must yield rx(m+t)X to cover the debt service, or d(m+t)X = rx(m+t)X.) If the deviation is sustained for two "years," the total adjustment required will be twice as large. Thus, each initial x percent deviation of the actual from the fundamental equilibrium exchange rate will require a DEER adjustment of rx percent in the opposite direction if DEERs are adjusted annually.[10]

Notice that this makes no allowance for what might logically be seen as the need to reverse the increment in debt acquired in this example through the appreciation of the current exchange rate over its DEER value. The reason this might seem logical is that the DEER external balance criterion is typically for a zero net foreign asset accumulation (or for a particular baseline growth in net foreign assets). Thus, an event that causes a departure from this initial desired condition should lead to an action calculated to offset it. In this case every x percent appreciation of the actual rate over its DEER value should lead to a reduction big enough to pay back the debt over a defined period of time. The size of hysteresis effects will clearly be potentially much larger if the DEER adjustment is required to be big enough to repay the debt incurred rather than simply to service the additional interest obligation. In what follows, however, we calculate DEER adjustments on the more modest of the two possible criteria, looking therefore for a DEER adjustment sufficient only to cover the cost of the additional interest burdens arising from misalignment. This case is clearly the most conservative one to take and sets a natural "lower band" to the size of the hysteresis problem. Had we chosen to assume that debt repayment objectives were involved, we should also have been obliged to specify--quite arbitrarily--the speed with which debt repayments were to occur. We now proceed to derive a formula for the DEER adjustment process. The result expresses formally the hysteresis effect--the dependence of the DEER on the path of the actual exchange rate.

Suppose that initially, in year 0, the actual real exchange rate is at its DEER value, which has a flat (stationary) trajectory at that point in time. Internal balance is assumed to be maintained at its optimal level throughout. Then any deviation of the actual rate from the DEER value implies a deviation from current account balance and requires a recomputation of the DEER on the lines indicated above.

Approximately, then:

(1) $F_n = F_{n-1} - r(S_{n-1} - F_{n-1})$

or

(2) $F_n = (1 + r)F_{n-1} - rS_{n-1}$

where F_n is the logarithmic value of the DEER in year n, S_n is the logarithm of the actual exchange rate in year n, and r is the rate of interest.

Equation (2) implies that

(3) $F_{n-1} = (1 + r)F_{n-2} - Rs_{n-2}$
(4) $F_{n-2} = (1 + r)F_{n-3} - rS_{n-3}$

Recursive substitution (of (4) and (3) into (2) etc.,) yields

$$(5) \quad F_n = (1+r)^n F_0 - r\sum_{i=1}^{n}(1 + r)^{i-1} S_{n-i}$$

Equation (5) shows how the initial stationary trajectory for F, F_0, will require updating in the light of the evolution of the actual real exchange rate. Thus, the DEER is not independent of the history of exchange rate movements. In particular, if the authorities wished to move the current exchange rate to the DEER, at the end of n periods, they would need to choose a path for the real exchange rate $(S_1, S_2 ... S_n)$ such that $S_n = F_n$ with F_n as defined in (5). Thus, given a deviation of the actual rate from the DEER and a desire ultimately to equate the two, the DEER arrived at when the actual rate again coincides with it will not be independent of the path taken by the exchange rate towards this goal. Indeed, as equation (1) makes clear, if S deviates from F, F will actually move *away* from S at speed r per period. Intuitively, therefore, we should expect eventual convergence of F and S to require a movement of S towards F at a speed greater than r in the following period. This intuition turns out to be correct when we analyze the dynamics of adjustment more rigorously.

3   Catching a Moving Bus: The Dynamics of Adjustment

In the previous section we derived a dynamic equation for the DEER (equation (1)). We now examine the problem of adjustment to the DEER, in the framework of a general partial adjustment equation:

(6) $S_n = S_{n-1} - q(S_{n-1} - F_{n-1})$,

with $q > 0$.

The questions we pose are the following: given (1) and (6), what restrictions must be placed on q to ensure eventual convergence and what does q imply about the nature of convergence? These are interesting questions since, at the normative level, policy makers may have a plan for converging on the rate they calculate as the DEER. In this case answers to the question posed are directly relevant to the choice of speed of adjustment towards the DEER (of course, this assumes that the authorities have the means to influence S in the right direction). Thus, although (6) may be a simplification in the sense that we make no attempt to reconcile it with any theoretical model of exchange rate movements, it is useful because it allows us to derive sharp analytic conclusions concerning the speed of adjustment towards the DEER which are likely to apply, at least qualitatively, within a more elaborate framework.

We define the absolute deviation of the actual real exchange rate from the DEER in period n as:

(7) $d_n \equiv |S_n - F_n|$

Then convergence on the DEER may be formally defined as:

(8) $\lim_{n \to \infty} d_n = 0$

Now a sufficient condition for (8) is that the series of absolute deviations be convergent (Widder (1961)):

(9) $\lim_{n \to \infty} \sum_{i=1}^{n} d_n = L$

where L is finite. Thus, we can apply results on the convergence of positive series to answer our questions. In particular, D'Alembert's ratio test (Widder (1961)) implies that (8) is satisfied if

(10) $d_n / d_{n-1} < 1$

which is merely the requirement that successive deviations from the DEER should decrease in absolute magnitude. Using (1) and (6) and the definition of d_n, equation (7), inequality (10) becomes:

(11) $|1 - \theta + r| < 1$

From inspection of (11), and for given r, it is possible to deduce information about the behavior of the system for any value of q on the real line:

(a) $q < r$: *monotonic divergence:* F_n and S_n move steadily away from one another.

(b) $q = r$: *bounded monotonic divergence.* F_n and S_n move on parallel trajectories.

(c) $r < q < 1 + r$: *monotonic convergence.* F_n and S_n converge monotonically over more than one period.

(d) $q = 1 + r$: *one-period convergence.* F_n and S_n are equal after exactly one period.

(e) $1 + r < q < 2 + r$: *oscillating convergence.* S_n moves alternately above and below F_n as the two converge.

(f) $q = 2 + r$: *bounded oscillating divergence.* S_n moves alternately above and below F_n but the absolute deviation, d_n, remains constant.

(g) $q > 2 + r$: *oscillating divergence.* S_n moves alternately above and below F_n and d_n grows over time.

The phase portrait of the system in (S_n, F_n)-space, for cases (a)-(g), is given in Figure 9.3.

Michael Artis & Mark Taylor

Figure 9.3: The Phase Portrait for Given Initial Misalignment.

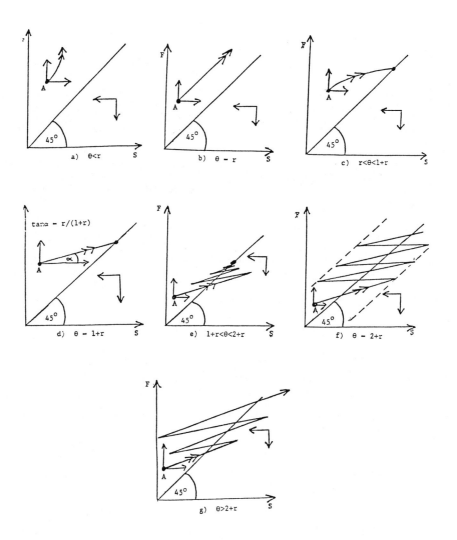

For values of q in the open interval (r, 1+r), the speed of adjustment of S_n towards the DEER is sufficiently greater than the speed at which the DEER is moving away for the two to eventually coincide--a little like running for a moving bus.[11]

If, on the other hand, q lies in the closed-open interval (1+r, 2+r), the exchange rate continually overshoots the DEER but by smaller and smaller absolute amounts, so that convergence is eventually achieved but the adjustment path is not monotonic.

In the case where q = 1+r, convergence is achieved in one period with the DEER revised upward by r times the initial divergence and S higher by (1+r) times the initial divergence.

Given the range of values of q for which the system is convergent--the open interval (r, 2+r)--it would seem, prima facie, that eventual convergence on the DEER is quite likely. Note, however, that equation (6) is in effect an *assumption* that S will tend to move towards F. In fact, it is not immediately obvious that this will be the case, since the DEER is a normative rather than a positive concept.[12]

Given, then, that the issue of convergence is largely empirical, we need to turn to the data to examine whether the hysteresis effects are likely to be important. This is the subject of the next section.

4 How Important Has Hysteresis Been?

Our approach to the question "How important has hysteresis been?" involves applying the measures developed in Section II to a historical data set. The approach is illustrative and, given its purpose, allows us to make simplifying assumptions. In this spirit we shall assume--purely for illustrative purposes and without any presumption that this was actually the case--that at the starting point, DEERs coincide with actual real exchange rates for all the countries in the sample; and, with an exception to be discussed below, that the initial DEER trajectories are flat throughout the period under examination. However, we are obliged to take account of a feature of real world experience from which we abstracted in the earlier sections. There, deviations of the actual exchange rate from the DEER were treated as if they were deviations at a constant level of utilization, hence implying a deviation from the current account target, with attendant consequences for debt service obligations. A glance at Figure 9.1, however, serves as a reminder that deviations of actual exchange rates from DEER values need not necessarily imply movement off the CA schedule. An appreciation of the exchange rate and a simultaneous fall in utilization, for example, could imply that the economy has moved left along the CA schedule, with no consequences for debt service or DEER revision. When using historical data therefore it is necessary to purge movements in actual real exchange rates of that part which can be held to reflect changes in utilization. In essence, this involves estimating the slope of the CA schedule. Empirically, one can use medium-term elasticities derived from an econometric macro model to do this. In this paper, we employ elasticities derived from the IMF's multi-country macroeconometric model, MULTIMOD (Masson, Symansky, and Meredith (1990)).

Given values for changes in the rate of capacity utilization, output elasticities yield the implied change in the current account. The real exchange rate elasticities then yield the change in the real exchange rate that would eliminate this. That is, if e_y is the output elasticity of net imports and Δu the percentage change in utilization, the corresponding real exchange rate change, ΔS, can be found from

$$\varepsilon_y \ \Delta u \ X = X(\mu + \tau) \ \Delta S \ (12)$$

or

$$\Delta S = \frac{\varepsilon_y \ \Delta u}{\mu + \tau} \ (13)$$

where m + t is the sum of import and export elasticities with respect to the real exchange rate and X is the level of exports (or imports).

The exercise described was conducted on data for the G-5 countries over the period 1979-90. Our simplifying assumptions thus equate the actual real exchange rates (effective rates) with DEERs for those countries at the outset (1979) of the period and project a flat trajectory for the DEERs throughout the period with the exception of a small modification for the effect of OPEC II. The steep increase in oil prices at the end of 1979 is assumed to have raised the U.K. DEER by 10 percent in 1980 and later years, with corresponding adjustments to the DEERs for other G-5 member countries.[13] An annual interest rate of 5 percent was assumed. As noted above, we used medium-term elasticity estimates derived from MULTIMOD. We also used IMF data on the estimated level of capacity utilization, which is derived using the Hodrick-Prescott filter.[14]

Assuming, then, misalignment of zero for each of the G-5 countries in 1979,[15] Figure 9.4 depicts actual movements in the real exchange rate,[16]

Figure 9.4: Illustrative DEER Trajectories for the G5.

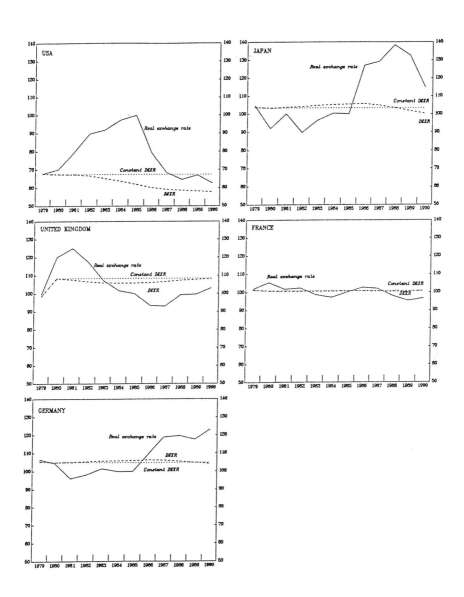

movements in the DEER and a "constant" DEER trajectory adjusted only for the OPEC II shock as discussed above.[17]

As Figure 9.4 shows, the DEER trajectory is distorted away from the constant path in each case. It appears most significantly, however, in the cases where there are large sustained deviations of the real exchange rate from the DEER in one direction. In the case of the U.S., most strikingly, the chronic overvaluation of the dollar leads to an increasing deviation of the DEER trajectory away from the constant path reaching some 14 percent by 1990 and averaging 7 1/2 percent per year (Table 9.1). In cases where the exchange rate is alternately over- and undervalued--most notably France--however, the DEER trajectory is kept approximately flat, so that the loss to assuming a constant DEER trajectory may be slight (Table 9.1). As we might expect, then, we see that exchange rate volatility (defined as relatively high-frequency oscillations in the exchange rate) is less damaging than sustained misalignment (defined as sustained deviation from the DEER).

Table 9.1: Percentage Deviation of Illustrative G-5 DEER
Trajectories from Constant DEERs[1]

Year	United States	Japan	United Kingdom	France	Germany
1980	0.00	0.00	0.00	0.00	0.00
1981	0.27	0.57	0.61	0.21	0.07
1982	1.23	0.76	1.55	0.29	0.50
1983	3.20	1.46	2.19	0.38	0.79
1984	5.38	1.84	2.32	0.31	0.96
1985	7.94	2.07	2.23	0.19	1.24
1986	10.82	2.35	2.05	0.22	1.53
1987	12.35	1.44	1.53	0.35	1.36
1988	13.13	0.22	0.93	0.47	0.71
1989	13.61	1.45	0.54	0.36	0.01
1990	14.30	2.94	0.15	0.08	0.61
Sum	82.22	15.11	14.09	2.87	7.78
Mean	7.47	1.37	1.28	0.26	0.71

[1] The "Constant DEER" paths incorporates an adjustment for OPEC II--see text.

Overall, therefore, the results of this section demonstrate that hysteresis effects on the DEER, operating through the effects of debt accumulation or decumulation, may have been significant historically, particularly for countries whose real exchange rate has moved predominantly in one direction over a sustained period of time--such as the U.S. dollar during the 1980s.

5 Conclusions

The efficient conduct of policy on matters relating to the international monetary system requires some basis for the evaluation of market-determined exchange rates. One such basis can be found in the concept of the fundamental equilibrium exchange rate (DEER) to which Williamson has appealed in his advocacy of exchange rate target zones. The fundamental rate appeals to the notion that in the medium term it is desirable to obtain both internal balance and external balance. The DEER is simply that rate of exchange which fulfills this condition. It is reasonably straightforward, given estimates of the relevant elasticities, to compute values for the fundamental rate on "medium-term" assumptions, that is to say, ignoring the dynamics of adjustment.

However, it appears that the true value of the DEER must depend on the path taken towards it. The reason is that, while the actual exchange rate deviates from its DEER value, so in general will the current account realizations deviate from those implicit in the initial calculation of the DEER trajectory. For this reason debt service obligations will differ from those assumed in the initial computation of the trajectory. The DEER will change and a recomputation is called for. The DEER is thus not independent of the path taken towards it, and suffers from hysteresis.

In this paper we were able to show that this problem could be formalized in a fairly straightforward manner, enabling us to obtain a formal representation of the hysteresis effect on the DEER. Using this formalization we were then able to demonstrate the properties required for convergence of the actual exchange rate on the DEER. Since the existence of hysteresis operating through misalignment and debt stocks is not in doubt the important question is its empirical significance. We thus investigated whether, over a particular historical time period, misalignment would have contributed significantly to recomputations of the DEER; it appeared that it could. However, the orders of magnitude involved appear to be manageable, and, it would appear that they should not obstruct the successful operation of a real exchange rate targeting system. It is arguable that such a system may be what would be needed to hold together a future European Monetary System which comprises a "core" of fully convergent countries and an "outer fringe" of less convergent economies.

Notes

[1] The research reported in this paper was begun while Mark Taylor was a Senior Economist and Michael Artis a visiting scholar in the Research Department of the International Monetary Fund, Washington D.C., although any view expressed are entirely these of the authors and are not necessarily these of the International Monetary Fund.

[2] See Taylor (1995) for a recent survey relating to the first two of these approaches. Frenkel and Goldstein (1986) discuss the relative merits of the three approaches.

[3] See also Nurske (1945) and International Monetary Fund (1970) for precursors of this approach.

[4] The locus classicus on the method of comparative statics is Samuelson (1947). Cuthbertson and Taylor (1987, chapter 1) provide a textbook discussion.

[5] It should be noted, however, that in the same paper, Wren-Lewis critically analyzes many of the assumptions of the DEER approach and explicitly mentions the hysteresis effects which are the topic of this paper.

[6] Note that we specifically do not address hysteresis effects that might arise in other ways, e.g., through shifts in the NAIRU or on account of the presence of set-up costs in international trade.

[7] In some computations, a desired value of the fiscal deficit is also involved, but the assumption here is that there is no additional effect of fiscal policy to be allowed for on top of its effect on u--i.e., that changes in fiscal policy will not shift the schedules. To a good first approximation, this seems a reasonable assumption.

[8] To some extent, this problem may be mitigated by adjustment of the market exchange rate towards the equilibrium level brought about by the effects on domestic absorption of changes in net foreign asset holdings - see Masson, Kremers and Horne (1994).

[9] It might be objected that the short-run elasticities differ from the medium-run elasticities used in constructing the DEER. A further adjustment could be made for any such differences.

[10] It may be worthwhile noting in this connection that market exchange rate instability may ensue when a country becomes a net foreign debtor - see Masson (1981) and Buiter (1984).

[11] The authors have in mind a London bus of traditional type, which allows passengers to leap on at the rear while the bus is moving. A North American alternative would be a San Francisco cable car.

[12] Indeed, given the widespread use of nonfundamental or "chartist" analysis in foreign exchange markets (Taylor and Allen (1992)), and given that a high proportion of the chartist techniques which are used are in some way extrapolative (ibid.), one might expect there to be substantial divergences between actual exchange rates and DEERs over time since the use of such extrapolative advice by the market would tend to push the nominal and hence the real exchange rate in the opposite direction to the DEER.

[13] Adjustment to other exchange rates was based on sterling's weight in the relevant index, using MERM weights.

[14] See Prescott (1986) or King and Rebelo (1989) for a discussion of the Hodrick-Prescott filter.

[15] Note that this is for purely illustrative purposes, with no presumption that any of these real exchange rates actually *did* coincide with the FEER in 1979.

[16] From the IMF's International Financial Statistics (IFS) data tape; 1985=100.

[17] Clearly, each of the G5 exchange rates is treated in 'ceteris paribus' terms in this illustrative analysis, rather than being treated together as a system.

References

Artis, M.J., and M.P. Taylor (1986), "DEER Hunting: Misalignment, Debt Accumulation and Desired Equilibrium Exchange Rates," National Institute of Economic and Social Research, *Review*, forthcoming 1995.

Baldwin, R., and P. Krugman (1986), "Persistent Trade Effects of Large Exchange Rate Shocks," *NBER Working Paper*, N° 2167.

Barrell, R., and S. Wren-Lewis (1989), "Equilibrium Exchange Rates for the G7," *CEPR Discussion Paper*, N° 323.

Buiter, W.H. (1984), "Exchange Rate Policy after a Decade of 'Floating': Comment," in Bilson, J.F.O., and R.C. Marston (eds), *Exchange Rate Theory and Practice*, University of Chicago press, pp. 108-12.

Cross, R. (1992), "On the Foundations of Hysteresis in Economic Systems," International Centre for Macroeconomic Modelling, University of Strathclyde, *Discussion Paper*, N° 4.

Currie, D., and S. Wren-Lewis (1989), "Evaluating Blueprints for the Conduct of International Macropolicy," *American Economic Review*, 79, pp. 264-69.

Cuthbertson, K., and M.P. Taylor (1987), *Macroeconomic Systems*, Oxford: Blackwell.

Frenkel, J.A., and M. Goldstein (1986), "A Guide to Target Zones," International Monetary Fund (Washington), *Staff Papers*, 33, pp. 633-73.

International Monetary Fund (1970), *The Role of Exchange Rates in the Adjustment of International Payments: A Report by the Executive Directors*, Washington: International Monetary Fund.

International Monetary Fund (1984), "Issues in the Assessment of the Exchange Rates of Industrial Countries," *Occasional Paper*, N° 29, Washington: International Monetary Fund.

King, R., and S. Rebelo (1989), "Low-Frequency Filtering and Real Business Cycles," *Working Paper*, Rochester Center for Economic Research, N° 205.

Layard, R., and S. Nickell (1985), "The Causes of British Unemployment," *National Institute Economic Review*, N° 111, pp. 62-85.

Lindbeck, A., and D. Snower (1986), "Wage Setting, Unemployment and Insider-Outsider Relations," *American Economic Review*, 76, pp. 235-39.

Masson, P.R. (1981), "Dynamic Stability of Portfolio Balance Models of the Exchange Rate," *Journal of International Economics*, 11, pp. 467-77.

Masson, P.R., J. Kremers, and J. Horne (1994), "Net Foreign Assets and international Adjustment: The United States, Japan and Germany," *Journal of International Money and Finance*, 13, pp. 27-40.

Masson, P.R., S. Symansky, and G. Meredith (1990), "MULTIMOD Mark II: A Revised and Extended Model," *Occasional Paper*, International Monetary Fund, N° 71, Washington.

Nurske, R. (1945), *Conditions of International Monetary Equilibrium*, Essays in International Finance, N° 4, Princeton University Press.

Prescott, E.C. (1986), "Theory Ahead of Business Cycle Measurement," *Federal Reserve Bank of Minneapolis Quarterly Review*, Fall, pp. 9-22.

Samuelson, P.A. (1947), *Foundations of Economic Analysis,* Cambridge, Massachusetts: Harvard University Press.

Taylor, M.P. (1995), "The Economics of Exchange Rates," *Journal of Economic Literature,* forthcoming.

Taylor, M.P., and H.L. Allen (1992), "The Use of Technical Analysis in the Foreign Exchange Market," *Journal of International Money and Finance,* 11, pp. 304-14.

Widder, D. (1961), *Advanced Calculus,* Englewood Cliffs, N.J.: Prentice-Hall.

Williamson, J. (1985), *The Exchange Rate System,* Institute for International Economics, Washington.

Williamson, J. (1990), "Equilibrium Exchange Rates: An Update," unpublished paper, Institute for International Economics, Washington, October.

Williamson, J., and M. Miller (1987), *Target Zones and Indicators: A Blueprint for the International Coordination of Economic Policy,* Washington, D.C.: Institute for International Economics.

Wren-Lewis, S., P. Westaway, S. Soteri, and R. Barrell (1991), "Evaluating the United Kingdom's Choice of Entry Rate Into the ERM," *Manchester School,* 59, Supplement, pp. 1-22.

Discussion

AGNES BENASSY

The concept of Fundamental Equilibrium Exchange Rate (FEER), which was developed by Williamson in the mid-1980s, refers to real exchange rates that are consistent with both internal and external balance. In fact, these equilibrium exchange rates are essentially normative: the aim is to provide a reference for international co-ordination on exchange rates. Thus the terminology of Desired Equilibrium Exchange Rate (DEER) appears more convenient, as suggested by Artis and Taylor, as well as Bayoumi et al. (1994).

The main result of Artis and Taylor's paper is to show that the DEER is not a constant reference: when external deficits accumulate, the DEER depreciates in order to restore the current account balance in spite of increased debt payments. The longer the real exchange rate stays away from the DEER, the larger will be the required depreciation, because of greater debt accumulation. Conversely, the DEER appreciates in case of current account surpluses. An important implication of this result is that there is an infinity of DEERs, depending on the path of the exchange rate. This is of great importance for foreign exchange markets. It justifies changes in expectations even when the internal and external disequilibria do not change.

The purpose of the paper is not to give DEER estimates, but to explain its dynamics. Thus it is more a complement than a substitute for DEER computations made for instance by Williamson (1994) with the help of various multicountry macroeconomic modelling teams. Restricting the study to the dynamics avoids the problem of choosing the right current account target. While Williamson tries to take fundamental capital flows into account, Artis and Taylor consider the current account balance both as a starting point for 1979 and as a reference. This can be interpreted as a long run target as it entails a constant net foreign asset position.

Like Williamson, Artis and Taylor define the internal equilibrium as the highest level of activity consistent with the control of inflation. Here it is proxied by the level of capacity utilization, which is not perfectly consistent with the long run approach of the external equilibrium, as it depends on capital accumulation. In other words, a steady rise in unemployment is consistent with a stable rate of capacity utilization provided firms adjust their capital stock: the DEER does not depreciate. This could explain why the French franc appears to be undervalued in 1990 compared to 1979. In fact the French DEER might need a devaluation as a consequence of the steady rise in unemployment. This could be interpreted in the model as a rise in the NAIRU (a move of the NAIRU schedule in figure 9.2).

More generally, the internal and external equilibria do not receive the same treatment in the study. The distance between the actual exchange rate and the DEER is corrected for changes in capacity utilization. For example, in the case of a simultaneous appreciation of the observed exchange rate and fall in capacity utilization, the appreciation is not interpreted as a departure from the DEER but as a consequence of the fall in utilization. But the DEER itself stays constant since in figure 9.1 neither the NAIRU nor the CA schedule move, and the way towards the internal equilibrium is not specified: the DEER adjusts to achieve current account balance provided internal equilibrium is achieved, no matter in what way it is achieved. The model explains the over-shooting of the exchange rate along the NAIRU schedule in figure 9.2, but not the loop which involves the rate of capacity utilisation. Nevertheless, this figure is instructive since it justifies large movements in the real exchange rate in order to come back to the initial DEER. It also explains unstable paths when the CA schedule moves quicker than the actual exchange rate.

In the last section, Artis and Taylor give, for five countries, the evolution of the DEER provided the real exchange rate was at its DEER level in 1979. According to these computations, the large misalignment of the dollar since 1979 resulted in a depreciation of the DEER averaging 7.5% per year. But the interpretation of the computations is not easy since there is no international consistency: the only DEER that appreciates is the UK one because of the exogenous oil shock. The actual appreciation of the mark and the yen since 1985 have triggered a DEER depreciation for both currencies, although this could also be interpreted as the end of the DEER appreciation, depending on the starting point. Nevertheless, the DEER depreciation is much larger for the dollar. It is interesting to compare this evolution to the implicit target of the G-7 as recorded by official reports. It can be assessed that the target Deutsche mark-dollar exchange rate of G-7 ministers was devalued by around 7% in 1990-1991 (see Bénassy and Pisani-Ferry, 1993). A similar devaluation occurred for the yen-dollar exchange rate over the same period. Although much smaller, these movements are in line with the depreciation of the US DEER.

References

Bénassy, A., and J. Pisani-Ferry (1993), "Taux de change: les sept ans du G-7," *La Lettre du CEPII,* N° 112, avril.

Bayoumi, T., P. Clark, S. Symansky, and M. Taylor (1994), "The Robustness of Equilibrium Exchange Rate Calculations to Alternative Assumptions and Methodologies," *Estimating Equilibrium Exchange Rate,* in Williamson, J. (ed.), Institute for International Economics, September.

Williamson, J. (1994), "Estimates of FEERs," *Estimating Equilibrium Exchange Rate,* in Williamson, J. (ed.), Institute for International Economics, September.

Exchange Rates and the Effectiveness of Central Bank
Intervention: New Evidence for the G-3 and the EMS

202 - 35

EU
USA
Japan
Germany

E58
F31
F33

1 Introduction

The present paper deals with the issue of whether or not central bank's
foreign exchange intervention is effective in stabilizing exchange rates.
The aim of the paper is to question the validity of commonly held views
about intervention within the framework of the G-3 consultations
(between the United States, Japan and Germany) and the European
Monetary System (EMS), and to provide new empirical evidence on how
intervention within these systems was conducted and why it may have
failed in maintaining stable exchange rates in the long run.

The paper first regards G-3, in particular transatlantic exchange rate
management and foreign exchange intervention. After a period of benign
neglect for the exchange rate prior to 1985, the United States reportedly
changed its attitude towards exchange rate policies with the Plaza-Louvre
agreement in 1985. Following an initial period aimed at driving down the
value of the dollar, the G-3 countries switched towards a policy of
targeting their dollar exchange rates within wide unofficial bands of ±12
percent (see Funabashi (1988) or McKinnon (1993)). The collapse of the
narrow exchange rate target zones of the EMS in August 1993 has also
resulted in a system of wide exchange rate bands of ±15 percent around
the unchanged old parities. Both systems may therefore currently operate
in a quite similar fashion, and it is thus interesting to analyse whether the
past experience of G-3 countries with exchange rate management and
central bank intervention in the framework of wide exchange rate bands

holds any lessons for the future of the EMS. In order to pass such judgement, a quantitative evaluation and comparison of both the G-3 and the EMS experience is in order.

The key issue to be discussed in the present paper is how the G-3 and EMS countries have conducted central bank intervention, and whether such intervention was coordinated, sterilized and effective. It is found that G-3 intervention during the Plaza-Louvre period appears to have displayed three main characteristics: first, as postulated by McKinnon (1993), intervention was coordinated between the Bundesbank and the Federal Reserve, but there is much less evidence of coordination between these two central banks and the Bank of Japan. Second, G-3 intervention was apparently sterilized, both in its immediate impact and in its long-run consequences. Third, intervention by G-3 countries was ineffective in the long-run in the sense that it did not significantly reverse the trend of bilateral exchange rates. The present study thus confirms results reported previously by Obstfeld (1988), Bordo and Schwartz (1991), Klein and Rosengren (1991), Ghosh (1992), Kaminsky and Lewis (1992), and Lewis (1992) that sterilized intervention has had no lasting exchange rate effects.

Similar evidence is obtained for the EMS. It is shown that intervention by all EMS countries was sterilized in its effect on the monetary base. Furthermore, such sterilized intervention is found to have been ineffective in stabilizing EMS exchange rates. It is argued that ultimately the predominant use of sterilized intervention, which represents the most ineffective means for stabilizing exchange rates, must be seen as the prime cause for the collapse of the narrow exchange rate bands of the EMS.

The paper is organized as follows: section 2 presents a summary of commonly held views about G-3 intervention and exchange rate management, and confronts these views with the data. Section 3 provides similar evidence for the EMS. Section 4 concludes the paper with a summary of the main findings and an outlook onto the future of European monetary and economic integration.

2 G-3 intervention and exchange rate management

In a recent paper McKinnon (1993) summarizes a number of distinctive characteristics of the international monetary order. McKinnon's (1993) view of the "rules of the game" is derived from economists' interpretation of G-3, G-5 or G-7 declarations and Funabashi's (1988) transcripts of interviews with policy-makers involved in these events.[1] McKinnon

(1993) thereby differentiates between the pre-1985 *"floating rate dollar standard"* and the post-1985 *"Plaza-Louvre intervention accords for the dollar exchange rate"* primarily on the basis of issues related to exchange rate management and foreign exchange intervention. For example, McKinnon (1993) postulates that the United States remained passive in the foreign exchanges prior to 1985, but became more active thereafter. Germany and Japan, on the other hand, are supposed to have used the dollar as an intervention currency in order to smooth near-term fluctuations in dollar exchange rates without committing to a par value or to long-term exchange rate stability prior to 1985. In the Plaza-Louvre accord of 1985 the G-3 central banks then agreed to set broad target zones for the mark/dollar and yen/dollar exchange rate (of approximately ±12 percent), but they did not announce the agreed-on central rates, and left the zonal boundaries flexible. In case of substantial disparities in economic fundamentals among the G-3 an adjustment of the implicit central rates occurred, but otherwise infrequent concerted intervention was supposed to reverse short-run trends in the dollar exchange rate. The G-3 central banks thereby signalled their collective intentions by not disguising these concerted interventions. McKinnon (1993) further states that G-3 central banks agreed to sterilized the immediate monetary impact of intervention by not adjusting short-term interest rates, whilst in the long-run each country aimed its monetary policy towards stabilizing the national price level of traded goods — thus indirectly anchoring the world price level and limiting the drift of the (unannounced) exchange rate target zones.

An obvious question is whether or not the above propositions are consistent with the stylized facts reported about intervention in the literature. This issue is discussed in the following section, whereby special attention will be paid to the objectives governing foreign exchange intervention, their degree of domestic sterilization and international coordination as well as their effectiveness in influencing the exchange rate. In addition to reviewing the literature, the present paper also report some new empirical evidence.

2.1. *Stylized facts about G-3 interventions*
Catte, Galli and Rebecchini (1992) report that G-3 intervention was rare and concentrated in time, and that during 1985-92 each of the G-3 central banks was on the market for less than one out of six trading days. Figure 10.1, which displays the U.S. $/DM market interventions by the

Bundesbank (BBK) and the Federal Reserve (FED), shows that this fact only holds for the post-1985 intervention.[2] Unilateral intervention by the Bundesbank in the pre-1985 period occurred regularly and not sporadically: the Bundesbank was on the market for the majority of trading days, and frequently with substantial amounts. Also, the Federal Reserve intervened frequently prior to 1981, but completely abstained from intervention during the early Reagan years (1981-1985).

Catte, Galli and Rebecchini (1992) also report that the G-3 countries never pursued conflicting intervention. Panel (a) of Figure 10.2 clearly supports this statement for the U.S. $/DM market. When the Federal Reserve was on the market to support the dollar, the Bundesbank was either absent from the market or was doing the same thing, and *vice versa*. Panel (b) of Figure 10.2 further shows that the Fed never pursued inconsistent intervention. When the Federal Reserve was on the U.S. $/Yen market to support the dollar, it was either absent from the U.S. $/DM market or was also intervening in support of the dollar there, and *vice versa*. Catte, Galli and Rebecchini (1992) further report that the timing of G-3 intervention clusters almost always coincides for at least two of the three countries, which strongly suggests that the bulk of the post-1985 intervention was coordinated amongst pairs of G-3 central banks.[3]

The effectiveness of foreign exchange intervention is also discussed by Catte, Galli and Rebecchini (1992). The authors identify 19 non-sporadic, prolonged and concerted intervention episodes between 1985 and 1991, 18 of which they classify as aimed at countering the trend of the dollar ('leaning-against-the-wind'). The authors report the following stylized facts about the effectiveness of coordinated central bank intervention: (i) all episodes were successful in temporarily inverting the trend of the dollar, and in 9 out of 19 cases intervention was definitely successful in the sense that the next concerted intervention took place in the opposite direction; (ii) all major turning points of the dollar coincided with concerted intervention; (iii) in the majority of the intervention episodes the very short-term interest rate differentials moved according to the exchange rate objective pursued by the authorities, that is, helped the intervention.

The problem with this evidence is that it is purely descriptive and not based on any formal testing. Also, as Truman (1992) points out, adopting a slightly different criterion for the evaluation of the effectiveness of intervention leads to the conclusion that at the best 5 out of 19 episodes were partially successful. Figure 10.3 reproduces the graphical evidence from Catte, Galli and Rebecchini (1992) for the U.S. $/DM exchange rate. Whilst it is true that intervention occurred at many turning points of the exchange rate, there also exist many turning points at which no intervention at all occurred. This strongly supports Truman's (1992) scepticism with respect to the claim of Catte, Galli and Rebecchini (1992) that coordinated intervention was definitely effective in influencing the exchange rate in the short run.

A more differentiated view with respect to the effectiveness of central bank intervention is suggested by Figure 10.4, which displays the U.S. $/DM exchange rate jointly with a coding of foreign exchange trading days with sales (panels a and b) and purchases (panels c and d) of foreign exchange by the Bundesbank and the Federal Reserve. The most obvious fact from Figure 10.4 is the difference in the Bundesbank's intervention behaviour prior to 1985 and thereafter. Prior to 1985 the Bundesbank pursued frequent unilateral leaning-against-the-wind intervention by selling dollars when the $/DM rate rose (1977-81) and buying dollars when it declined (1981-85). After 1985 the Bundesbank appears to have intervened much less frequently by buying dollars when the level of the exchange rate was relatively high and selling dollars when it was relatively low. This suggests that the Bundesbank may have switched from a first difference to a level target for the exchange rate. Figure 10.4 also points out that the link between intervention policy and exchange rate movements must be studied carefully, since it may simultaneously reflect both the central bank's reaction function as well as measuring the effectiveness of intervention.

This brings me to the question of what objectives govern central bank intervention. Figure 10.5 looks at a number of potential arguments which are frequently referred to in studies of central bank reaction functions. Panel (a) of Figure 10.5 reveals that for the post 1977 period the Bundesbank on average bought dollars when the exchange rate was below a value of 0.45 $/DM and sold dollars when it was above. Furthermore, massive intervention occurred when the exchange rate took extreme values. In terms of a level target this would suggest that during the post-1977 sample period the Bundesbank aimed at a target zone with a 0.45 $/DM (=2.22DM/$) parity and fluctuation bands of ±33 percent on either side of the parity. Such a level target is, however, only a poor description of the Bundesbank's intervention pattern in the $/DM market. Similar poor representations of a Bundesbank intervention objective are obtained when average intervention is displayed against short-term and medium term interest rate differentials (panels b and d) or expected exchange rate movements, as reflected by the forward premium (panel c).

The best explanation of Bundesbank and Federal Reserve intervention in the $/DM market is obtained when short-term leaning-against-the-wind behaviour is postulated, as is shown in Figure 10.6. Panel (a) displays the Bundesbank's average intervention against the change of the $/DM exchange rate over an eight week period. The Bundesbank purchased dollars when the $/DM rate was falling and sold dollars when the DM/$ rate was rising. The average intervention amounts increased as the short-term drift in the exchange rate accelerated, suggesting that leaning-against-the-wind intervention was stronger the more exchange rates changed. The same intervention pattern is revealed in panel (c) for the Federal Reserve in the post-1985 period. Both results strongly suggest that intervention by G-3 central banks was governed by attempts to smooth near-term fluctuations in the dollar exchange rate without committing to a par value or long-term level target for the exchange rate.

So far it was established that G-3 intervention was largely coordinated and likely to have been aimed at stabilizing near-term exchange rate movements by leaning-against-the-wind. In order to judge the effectiveness of intervention it is further important to establish whether or not intervention was sterilized, since theoretical arguments in favour of the effectiveness of sterilized intervention are weak, as will be discussed in more detail below. Sterilization is typically judged by comparing intervention or the corresponding changes in central bank's net foreign assets with corresponding movements in the domestic credit component of the monetary base. Complete sterilization implies that the intervention leaves the monetary base unaltered and is offset by a corresponding contraction in domestic credit. Two issues have to be discussed here. First, balance sheet data on changes in the net foreign asset component of the monetary base are typically used as a proxy measure for central bank intervention. The validity of this approximation has to be questioned. Second, the degree of sterilization has to be assessed.

Figure 10.7 shows that for the United States and Germany, the two countries where daily intervention data are publicly available, the approximation of central bank intervention by changes in the balance sheet data on net foreign assets works quite well: between 1977 and 1992 the correlation between intervention and changes in net foreign assets is 58.9 percent for the United States, and 42.1 percent for Germany. Thus, in order to obtain comparative international evidence, the remainder of the study is based on the monthly proxy of intervention.

Figure 10.8 shows that for the United States and Germany some weak evidence of sterilization exists, as measured by a negative correlation between changes in the domestic credit and net foreign asset components of the monetary base. This link is, however, far from being contemporaneously complete.

2.2. *Empirical evidence about G-3 intervention*

Before reporting any empirical results about the effectiveness of intervention, it is important to highlight some problems faced by any empirical study of this issue. In my view the key problem is that the effectiveness of intervention, the degree of sterilization and the degree of coordination of intervention must not be viewed as separate issue, as will be discussed in more detail below.

One potential link exists between the coordination and the effectiveness of intervention. For example, Catte, Galli and Rebecchini (1992) argue that coordinated intervention is likely to have more substantial effects than non-coordinated intervention. A second and more important link exists between the sterilization of intervention and its effectiveness. For example, the Jurgensen (1983) report did not view sterilized intervention as an effective policy instrument. According to the Jurgensen (1983) report, the effect of unsterilized intervention, which directly affects a country's monetary base, has to be considered to be much larger than that of sterilized intervention. Funabashi (1989) also reports that the Bank of Japan at times conducted unsterilized intervention in order to maximize its effectiveness. In general, whilst the effectiveness of unsterilized central bank intervention is unquestioned in the theoretical literature, there exists considerable controversy over the effectiveness of sterilized intervention. To date only two channels have been identified through which sterilized intervention may affect the exchange rate: the expectations or signalling channel and the portfolio channel.

The signalling channel has first been formulated by Mussa (1981), who points out that if uncovered interest rate parity holds, then sterilized intervention which leaves interest rates unaltered can have an indirect effect on the spot exchange rate by changing the expected future exchange rate. This may be the case if current intervention is perceived by market participants as a signal of future changes in monetary policy and hence future exchange rate changes. However, the empirical evidence in support of this expectations or signalling channel is weak, and most empirical studies, such as Klein and Rosengren (1991), Ghosh (1992), Kaminsky and Lewis (1992), and Lewis (1992) provide rather unfavourable results.

The portfolio channel literature postulates that due to foreign exchange risks domestic and foreign assets are imperfect substitutes. Risk averse agents then have to be compensated for the higher risk of holding foreign bonds by being paid a risk premium. Sterilized intervention, that is a change in the supply of domestic relative to foreign assets then requires a change in the risk premium for portfolio investors to maintain asset market equilibrium. This risk premium is typically measured as the deviation from uncovered interest rate parity. Thus, for given exchange rate expectations and a given interest rate differential the change in the risk premium requires a corresponding change in the spot exchange rate. The exchange rate effects of sterilized intervention thus depend critically on the imperfect substitutability of domestic and foreign assets. Whilst Dominguez and Frankel (1992, 1993) report some empirical evidence in favour of the portfolio channel by using survey data on exchange rate expectations, most of the empirical literature finds little or no evidence in its support, as Rogoff (1984), Obstfeld (1988) and Bordo and Schwartz (1991) point out.

To summarize, the existing literature strongly questions the effectiveness of sterilized central bank intervention, both on theoretical and empirical grounds. The following section reconsiders this evidence by first evaluating the effectiveness of intervention and then testing whether or not intervention was sterilized.

2.2.1. The effectiveness of G-3 intervention

The problem with the proposed empirical study is that in order to judge the effectiveness of intervention it is necessary to relate central bank intervention to its ultimate objective. To be more precise, the discussion of the daily intervention data above has revealed that intervention by the Bundesbank and the Federal Reserve may best be explained in terms of a leaning-against-the-wind objective: in the event that the Bundesbank buys U.S. dollars through sales of German marks ($\Delta f > 0$) in order to support the dollar, such stabilizing intervention should be negatively correlated with present or past changes in the \$/DM exchange rate ($\Delta e < 0$). If such intervention ($\Delta f > 0$) were effective, it should further cause current and/or future exchange rate changes in the opposite direction ($\Delta e > 0$). Thus, in order to capture both aspects of intervention, the present paper reports empirical results obtained by estimating the simultaneous two equation system

$$(1) \quad \Delta e_t = \lambda_{e,f} \Delta f_t + \sum_{j=1}^{p} \alpha_{e,e}^j \Delta e_{t-j} + \sum_{j=1}^{p} \alpha_{e,f}^j \Delta f_{t-j} + \varepsilon_t^v,$$

$$(2) \quad \Delta f_t = \lambda_{f,e} \Delta e_t + \sum_{j=1}^{p} \alpha_{f,f}^j \Delta f_{t-j} + \sum_{j=1}^{p} \alpha_{f,e}^j \Delta e_{t-j} + \varepsilon_t^\eta,$$

whereby Δf and Δe represent the changes in the net foreign assets component of the monetary base and changes of the exchange rate (measured as the ratio of foreign to domestic currency units) respectively. The above two equation system clearly points out the simultaneity problem between the causes and the effects of intervention. This problem has been completely disregarded in the previous literature, but will be the prime focus of the analysis below.

In order to estimate the coefficients in this vector autoregressive system the 2SLS instrumental variable techniques developed in King and Watson (1992) and discussed in more detail in Weber (1994a,b) is used. This simultaneous equation approach has two major advantages over the previous empirical literature: first, the estimates explicitly allow intervention to be both predetermined ($\lambda_{fe}=0$) and/or exogenous in the long-run [$\gamma_{fe}=\alpha_{fe}(1)/\alpha_{ff}(1)=0$ with $\alpha_{fe}(L)=\lambda_{fe}+\sum_{j=1}^{p}\alpha_{fe}^j L^j$ and $\alpha_{ff}(L)=1-\sum_{j=1}^{p}\alpha_{ff}^j L^j$] without necessarily imposing these restrictions onto the data. Second, equations (1) and (2) provide a natural framework within which the concept of immediate effectiveness ($\lambda_{ef}=0$) versus long-run effectiveness [$\gamma_{ef}=\alpha_{ef}(1)/\alpha_{ee}(1)=0$ with $\alpha_{ef}(L)=\lambda_{ef}+\sum_{j=1}^{p}\alpha_{ef}^j L^j$ and $\alpha_{ee}(L)=1-\sum_{j=1}^{p}\alpha_{ee}^j L^j$] can be formalized and tested empirically. In the discussion below the long-run effectiveness of intervention will be of prime interest.

The simultaneous equation system (1) and (2) is econometrically unidentified. In the present context this implies that the effectiveness of intervention is no longer testable when intervention is endogenous. Thus, even if the hypothesis that the shocks ε_t^r and ε_t^η are uncorrelated is maintained, one additional restriction is required in order to identify the linear simultaneous equation model. In the literature only one identifying restriction is to be found: it is common practice to assume that intervention is exogenous, so that $\gamma_{fe}=(\lambda_{fe}+\Sigma_{j=1}^{P}\alpha_{fe}^{j})/(1-\Sigma_{j=1}^{P}\alpha_{ff}^{j})=0$, which holds, for instance, if one imposes $\lambda_{fm}=\alpha_{fm}^{1}=\alpha_{fm}^{2}=...=\alpha_{fm}^{P}=0$. Another, less restrictive approach is to assume that the model is recursive, so that either $\lambda_{mf}=0$ or $\lambda_{fm}=0$ applies. Finally, long-run ineffectiveness of intervention with $\gamma_{mf}=(\lambda_{mf}+\Sigma_{j=1}^{P}\alpha_{mf}^{j})/(1-\Sigma_{j=1}^{P}\alpha_{mm}^{j})=0$ may be assumed in order to identify the system and estimate the remaining parameters. In principle it is possible to identify the above simultaneous equation model by specifying a value of any one of the four parameters λ_{ef}, λ_{fe}, γ_{ef}, or γ_{fe} and then finding the implied estimates for the other three parameters. This is in fact the approach taken by King and Watson (1992) and Weber (1994a,b), but rather than focusing on a single identifying restriction, the authors report results for a wide range of identifying restrictions by iterating each of the four reaction coefficients (λ_{ef}, λ_{fe}, γ_{ef}, and γ_{fe}) within a reasonable range, obtaining each time estimates of the remaining three parameters and their standard errors.

The empirical evidence about the effectiveness of G-3 intervention uncovered by this approach may best be discussed by referring to Figure 10.9, which displays the estimates for the effectiveness of Bundesbank interventions in the pre-1985 period (panel a) and the post-1985 period (panel b). Long-run ineffectiveness of Bundesbank intervention is consistent with the pre-1985 data only within a narrow range of identifying parameter restrictions, whilst it cannot be rejected over the entire range of possible identifications in the post-1985 sample. Figure 10.9 thus clearly suggests that Bundesbank intervention in the post-1985 period has been ineffective in altering the dollar exchange rate in the long-run, irrespective of the possible identifying restrictions on the coefficients λ_{fe}, γ_{fe} and λ_{ef}. Imposing long-run ineffectiveness ($\gamma_{ef}=0$) reveals no significant short-run effects ($\lambda_{ef}\neq0$) of predetermined intervention ($\lambda_{fe}=0$), as is indicated by the fact that the origin lies within the 95% confidence ellipse for the long-run ineffectiveness hypothesis. In contrast, a rather different result is obtained for the pre-1985 period. Although predetermined and long-run exogenous intervention ($\lambda_{fe}=0$, $\gamma_{fe}=0$) are again found to be ineffective in the long-run, modestly leaning-against-the-wind intervention ($\lambda_{fe}<-0.1$ and $\gamma_{fe}<0.09$) is found to have significant long-run exchange rate effects. Moreover, imposing long-run ineffectiveness ($\gamma_{ef}=0$) reveals significant short-run effects ($\lambda_{ef}>0$) of predetermined intervention ($\lambda_{fe}=0$) since the origin lies outside the 95%

confidence ellipse for parameters satisfying the long-run ineffectiveness restriction.

Table 10.1 shows the results for all combinations of G-3 exchange rates and intervention policies. The long-run effectiveness of intervention is rejected by all the data for the post-1985 period, and imposing long-run exchange rate neutrality of intervention reveals no significant short-run effects. For the pre-1985 period the long-run effectiveness of intervention is not rejected over such a wide range of identifying restrictions. Predetermined ($\lambda_{fe}=0$) or leaning-against-the-wind intervention ($\lambda_{fe}<0$) typically has significant positive long-run effects ($\gamma_{ef}>0$). Furthermore, intervention by the Bank of Japan in the DM/¥ market and by the Federal Reserve in the DM/$ market has significant short-run effects even if long-run ineffectiveness is imposed upon the data.

2.2.2. The degree of sterilization of G-3 intervention

The degree of sterilization of intervention is analyzed in Weber (1994b) by using the methodology outlined above. Weber (1994b) estimates the *simultaneous* two equation system

$$(3) \quad \Delta m_t = \lambda_{mf}\Delta f_t + \sum_{j=1}^{p}\alpha_{mm}^j\Delta m_{t-j} + \sum_{j=1}^{p}\alpha_{mf}^j\Delta f_{t-j} + \varepsilon_t^m$$

$$(4) \quad \Delta f_t = \lambda_{fm}\Delta m_t + \sum_{j=1}^{p}\alpha_{ff}^j\Delta f_{t-j} + \sum_{j=1}^{p}\alpha_{fm}^j\Delta m_{t-j} + \varepsilon_t^{\eta}$$

with Δf and Δm as changes in net foreign assets and changes in the monetary base respectively. As above, intervention or changes in net foreign assets are allowed to be both predetermined ($\lambda_{fm}=0$) and/or exogenous in the long-run [$\gamma_{fm}=\alpha_{fm}(1)/\alpha_{ff}(1)=0$ with $\alpha_{fm}(L)=\lambda_{fm}+\Sigma_{j=1}^{p}\alpha_{fm}^j L^j$ and $\alpha_{ff}(L)=1-\Sigma_{j=1}^{p}\alpha_{ff}^j L^j$] without necessarily imposing these restrictions onto the data. Equations (3) and (4) may then be used to test degree of immediate sterilization ($\lambda_{mf}=0$) versus long-run sterilization [$\gamma_{mf}=\alpha_{mf}(1)/\alpha_{mm}(1)=0$ with $\alpha_{mf}(L)=\lambda_{mf}+\Sigma_{j=1}^{p}\alpha_{mf}^j L^j$ and $\alpha_{mm}(L)=1-\Sigma_{j=1}^{p}\alpha_{mm}^j L^j$].

The sterilization issue has been estimated in a large number of studies before. The evidence from these studies is somewhat mixed. Some early studies find that the Bundesbank completely sterilized its interventions (Herring and Marston (1977a) (1977b), Obstfeld (1983), Mastropasqua,

Micossi and Rinaldi (1988)), whilst others find that sterilization was less than complete (Neumann (1984), Gaiotti, Giucca and Micossi (1989)), in particular in its long-run effects on base money growth (von Hagen (1989), Neumann and von Hagen (1991)). Empirical studies for Japanese data, on the other hand, largely reveal complete contemporary sterilization (Gaiotti, Giucca and Micossi (1989), Takagi (1991)).

The empirical evidence on the degree of sterilization derived in Weber (1994b) is reported in Figure 10.10, which displays the estimates for the Bundesbank's sterilization attempts for the pre-1985 period (panel a) and the post-1985 period (panel b). Long-term sterilization of Bundesbank intervention is consistent with the pre-1985 data only within a narrow range of identifying parameter restrictions, whilst it cannot be rejected over the entire range of possible identifications in the post-1985 sample. For the case of predetermined ($\lambda_{fm} = 0$) or long-run exogenous ($\gamma_{fm} = 0$) intervention, which is typically analysed in the literature, the data reject long-run sterilization in the pre-1985 period, but not in the post-1985 sample. Furthermore, in the first sub-sample short-run sterilization ($\lambda_{mf} = 0$) does not guarantee long-run sterilization ($\gamma_{fm} = 0$), and *vice versa*. Rather, the estimates suggest that in order to achieve long-term sterilization the Bundesbank would have had to overcompensate the effects of intervention by a more than proportional reduction of the domestic credit component. I view this as evidence against the long-run sterilization hypothesis for Bundesbank intervention prior to 1985. Given its very frequent and in part substantial daily intervention activities in the first sub-sample, it is scarcely surprising that the Bundesbank was unable to safeguard the domestic money supply completely from the long-run consequences of its foreign exchange operations, even if sterilization of any immediate impact was possible at times.

Table 10.2, which displays the results for the entire post-1973 period and the two sub-periods postulated in McKinnon (1993), further reveals that for the United States and Japan both predetermined and long-run exogenous intervention are compatible with long-run sterilization in both sub-samples. The point estimates under long-run sterilization of intervention suggest that the Federal Reserve in both sub-samples has tended to reduce the foreign component when the monetary base increased ($\lambda_{fm} < 0$), whilst for Japan and Germany positive but insignificant coefficients ($\lambda_{fm} > 0$) are found for the post-1985 period.

The above findings of long-term non-sterilized intervention by Germany in the pre-1985 period and sterilized intervention otherwise is broadly consistent with the results reported in the previous literature. As in the papers by Gaiotti, Giucca and Micossi (1989) and Takagi (1991), the data suggest complete sterilization for Japan. The pre-1985 result for Germany further explains why long-run sterilization ($\gamma_{mf} = 0$) is frequently rejected in single equation studies, such as von Hagen (1989) and Neumann and von Hagen (1991), which imply $\gamma_{fm} = 0$. Finally the present study also shows that failure to sterilize the long-run impact of intervention does not rule out that the immediate impact of intervention may have been sterilized, as has been suggested by Herring and Marston (1977a,b) and Obstfeld (1983).

To summarize, G-3 intervention during the Plaza-Louvre period appears to have displayed the following two main characteristics: first, as postulated by McKinnon (1993), G-3 intervention was apparently sterilized, both in its immediate impact and in its long-run consequences. Second, intervention by G-3 countries was ineffective in the long-run in the sense that it did not significantly reverse the trend of bilateral exchange rates. A major finding of the present paper therefore is that sterilized G-3 intervention has had no lasting exchange rate effects. The evidence on the effectiveness of central bank intervention obtained by the simultaneous equation approach of the present paper is therefore also consistent with previous results reported in Obstfeld (1988), Bordo and Schwartz (1991), Klein and Rosengren (1991), Ghosh (1992), Kaminsky and Lewis (1992), and Lewis (1992) for the post-1985 period. Furthermore, the present paper reveals a striking parallel between the degree of sterilization of intervention and their ineffectiveness in influencing the exchange rate. This strongly supports the results pointed out by the Jurgensen (1983) report, which views sterilized intervention as an ineffective policy instrument for influencing the exchange rate.

3 EMS intervention and exchange rate management

In order to compare the EMS and the G-3 experience with foreign exchange intervention, the tests reported in the previous section were also conducted for the original EMS member countries, Germany, France, Italy, the Netherlands, Belgium, Denmark and Ireland, and in addition for the United Kingdom.

3.1. *The effectiveness of EMS intervention*

The evidence about the effectiveness of intervention in EMS foreign exchange markets is displayed in Table 10.3. EMS intervention during the post-1985 period is found to have been ineffective in stabilizing DM exchange rates in the long-run, regardless of the possible identifying restrictions on the coefficients λ_{fe}, γ_{fe} and λ_{ef}. The only exception is the Bundesbank's intervention with respect to the Italian lira exchange rate, where significant positive long-run effects are obtained no matter what identifying restrictions were placed on λ_{fe}, γ_{fe} and λ_{ef}. The positive sign thereby suggests that Bundesbank intervention has without doubt been unsuccessful, as it appears to have destabilized ($\lambda_{ef} > 0$) rather than stabilized ($\lambda_{ef} < 0$) the Lira exchange rate.

3.2. *The degree of sterilization of EMS intervention*

Table 10.4 reports the estimation results for the sterilization issue. As for the G-3 countries above, there is little evidence about long-run non-sterilized intervention in the post-1985 period. Except for Germany and France in the pre-1985 period and the Netherlands and Ireland in the post-1985 period, predetermined intervention ($\lambda_{fm}=0$) and long-run exogenous intervention ($\gamma_{fm}=0$) are found to have been sterilized in the long-run ($\gamma_{mf} \neq 0$). Also, short-run sterilization ($\lambda_{mf}=0$) does not guarantee long-run sterilization ($\gamma_{mf}=0$) for France in either sub-sample. Finally, the point estimates under long-run sterilization of intervention suggest that most European central banks in the post-1985 period have tended to increase the foreign component when the monetary base increased ($\lambda_{fm}>0$), although the coefficient λ_{fm} is only statistically significant for Ireland.

To summarize, central bank intervention in the EMS exhibited the following two characteristics: first, intervention by all EMS countries, and not only German intervention as postulated by McKinnon (1993), has been sterilized in both its immediate impact and in its long-run consequences for national money supplies. Second, intervention by EMS central banks was ineffective in the long-run in the sense that it did not significantly stabilize bilateral exchange rates. This finding is consistent with the non-formal evidence reported in Weber (1994b) that the Bundesbank only participated in mandatory intervention at the margins of the bands. The fact that such marginal intervention typically occurred prior to EMS realignments in itself suggests that it was unsuccessful in defending the pre-realignment exchange rate target zone. The key point is that the predominant use of sterilized intervention by all EMS member countries may have strongly undermined any potential disciplinary effects arising from quasi-fixed exchange rates. This long-run ineffectiveness result for the EMS is furthermore consistent with the evidence reported for intervention in the G-3 context: sterilized intervention is unlikely to be an effective means for stabilizing exchange rates.

4 **Summary and policy conclusions with respect to the future of EMU**

In this paper I have examined the degree to which intervention policies differ between G-3 countries and the EMS. Foreign exchange intervention activities are found to have been very similar within the G-3 and the EMS context. Two sets of issues have been discussed: first, intervention was shown to have typically been sterilized. Second, such sterilized intervention was not found to have had significant long-run exchange rate stabilization effects. This is not surprising, given that sterilization aims at delaying or avoiding precisely those domestic monetary policy adjustments which would be necessary for guaranteeing long-run exchange rate stability.

In my view the sterilization of intervention by all EMS countries and not just by Germany is in part responsible for the collapse of the exchange rate mechanism of the EMS. Sterilized intervention signals a non-credible commitment to long-run exchange rate stability. Foreign exchange markets understood this signal perfectly well and hence have launched a speculative attack. These speculative attacks were successful for two reasons: first, it was commonly known that the German Bundesbank preferred to sterilize the effects of its foreign exchange intervention. Under sterilized intervention any accumulation of foreign assets in support of the Italian lira and British pound would have had to be offset by a corresponding decline in German domestic credit. Such a tightening of German domestic credit in the face of the huge private and public investment demand in the aftermath of German unification would have been very unpopular, and may have further driven up German domestic interest rates. The other option was not to sterilize the intervention in support of the Italian lira and British pound. However, this would have driven German domestic interest rates down and may ultimately have added to German inflation, which for the Bundesbank at the time was an even less appealing option. Against this background the reluctance of the Bundesbank to intervene at all in support of the Italian lira and the British pound was well understandable. The second reason for the success of the speculative attacks is that the evidence reported in the present paper suggests that EMS intervention was not able to stabilize exchange rates in the long-run or even in the short-run. This empirical finding holds for both the rare German obligatory marginal intervention and the intramarginal intervention by the remaining EMS central banks. The evidence of the present paper further reveals an apparent correlation between the ineffectiveness of inframarginal intervention and the fact that the bulk of EMS intervention was sterilized. For the Bundesbank the sterilization of intervention was a necessary prerequisite for the pursuit of an independent monetary policy aimed at anchoring the price level. For the remaining EMS countries sterilization clearly violates the *implicit* rules of the EMS as a "DM-zone", as portrayed by McKinnon (1993). The use of sterilized intramarginal intervention is motivated by the desire of the non-German EMS central banks to maintain some degree of monetary independence from Germany. Ultimately this signals a non-credible commitment to long-term exchange rate stability, and markets fully understood this signal.

The failure of the EMS may best be understood in terms of violations of *implicit* "rules of the game" on both sides. The Bundesbank is to blame in part for not having intervened sufficiently at the margins of the bands in support of the weak EMS currencies, but such intervention was undesirable at the time. The central banks of the weak EMS currency countries are to blame in part because they did not aim at stabilizing exchange rates intramarginally by their most effective means, the use of non-sterilized intervention. Ultimately the collapse of the EMS was caused by the fact that neither the Bundesbank nor the central banks in the remaining EMS countries were prepared to give up some monetary autonomy for the sake of exchange rate stability. This clearly points out the failure to co-ordinate monetary policy within the EMS.

In my view the key to future successful exchange rate targeting lies alone in international policy coordination, which needs to be re-enforced in the EMS. Economic and Monetary Union differs from the old EMS primarily in the degree to which monetary policy is coordinated and subject to joint decision making. Stage 2 of the transition to EMU should therefore strengthen the policy coordination and consultation process within the EMS. The new Community institutions, such as the European Monetary Institute, will greatly enhance this process. In my view the old EMS has placed too much emphasis on exchange rate stability as a means for enforcing policy coordination and convergence. But exchange rate stability must be viewed as the outcome of a process of policy coordination and convergence in Europe, and not *vice versa.* The current wide-band EMS therefore exemplifies the need for increased policy coordination much more clearly than the old EMS system ever did.

5 Time series and data sources

The paper uses both daily and monthly data. The econometric evidence is based on monthly data. Whenever original data were not seasonally adjusted, seasonal adjustment was carried out using the multiplicative adjustment procedure in MicroTSP 7.0. The time series and data sources used were

Monthly data
Base money: IMF, *International Financial Statistics*, various issues, line 14.
Net foreign assets: IMF, *International Financial Statistics*, various issues, calculated as the difference between foreign assets (line 11) and foreign liabilities (line 16c).

Daily Data
Intervention: Bundesbank intervention in the DM/$ market and in the EMS, Deutsche Bundesbank, *unpublished data.*
Federal Reserve intervention in the DM/$ and Yen/$ market, Federal Reserve Board of Governors, *unpublished data.*
Interest rates: Bank for International Settlements, *unpublished data.*
Exchange rates: Bank for International Settlements, *unpublished data.*
Forward premia: Bank for International Settlements, *unpublished data.*

Notes

[1] The G-3 countries are the United States, Japan and Germany, the G-5 countries consist of the G-3 plus the United Kingdom and France, and the G-7 additionally include Canada and Italy.

[2] See the Appendix 10 for figures and tables.

[3] Due to the lack of Japanese intervention data this proposition cannot be re-confirmed here and is merely reported as it stands.

Appendix 10
Figures and Tables

Figure 10.1: Bundesbank and Fed interventions (billions of U.S. dollars).

(a) Bundesbank intervention, sales (-) and purchases (+) of dollars for DM, 1977-1992

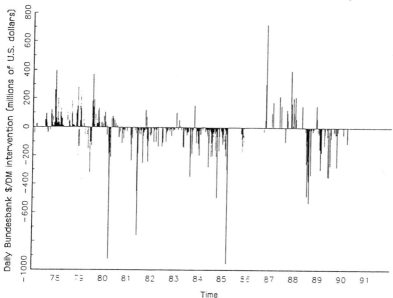

(b) Fed intervention, sales (-) and purchases (+) of dollars for DM, 1985-1992

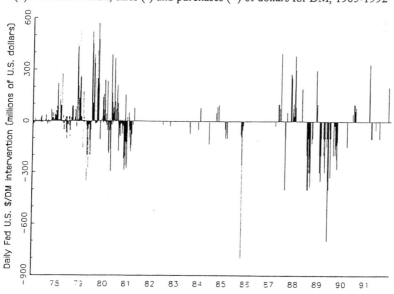

Figure 10.2: Bundesbank and Fed intervention coordination, 1985-1992.

(a) Coordination between the Bundesbank's and the Fed's $/DM interventions

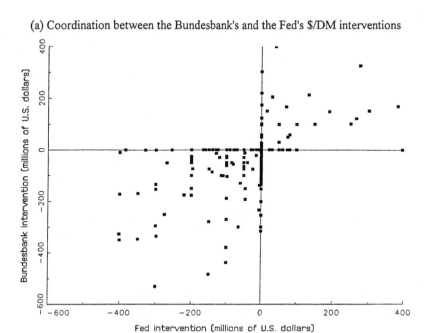

(b) Coordination between the Fed's $/DM and $/Yen interventions

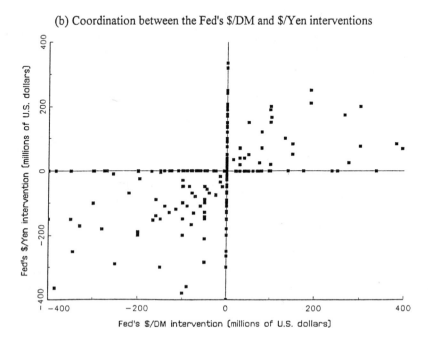

Figure 10.3: Coordinated daily central bank intervention and the U.S. $/DM exchange rate, second sub-sample (01/01/1985 - 31/12/1991).

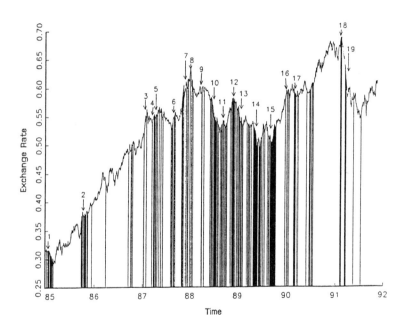

Figure 10.4: U.S. $/DM exchange rate and Bundesbank's and Fed's interventions.

(a) Bundesbank's dollar sales for DM, 1977-1992

(b) Fed's dollar sales for DM, 1977-1992

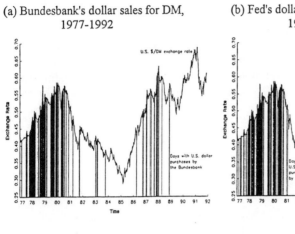

(c) Bundesbank's dollar purchases for DM, 1977-1992

(d) Fed's dollar purchases for DM, 1977-1992

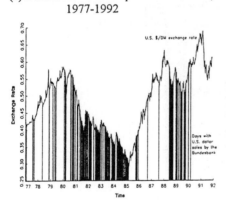

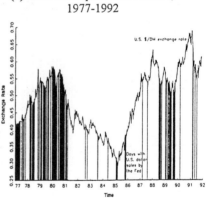

Figure 10.5: The relationship between Bundesbank interventions and exchange rates, interest rate differentials and forward premia/discounts, 1977-1992.

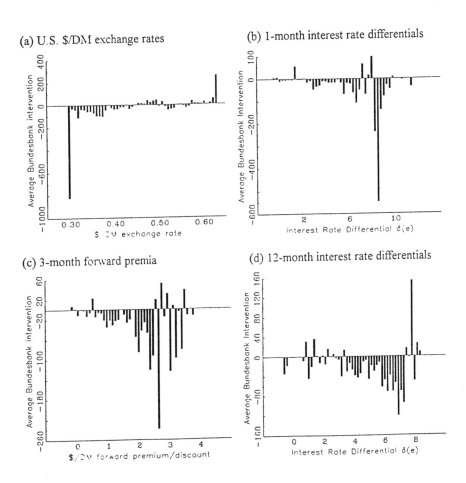

(a) U.S. $/DM exchange rates

(b) 1-month interest rate differentials

(c) 3-month forward premia

(d) 12-month interest rate differentials

Figure 10.6: The relationship between Bundesbank and Fed interventions
and U.S. $/DM exchange rates changes (over 8 week interval, in % p.a.).

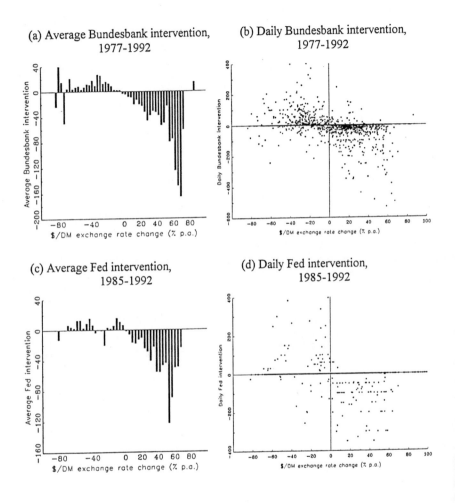

(a) Average Bundesbank intervention,
1977-1992

(b) Daily Bundesbank intervention,
1977-1992

(c) Average Fed intervention,
1985-1992

(d) Daily Fed intervention,
1985-1992

Figure 10.7: Monthly sums of daily interventions and monthy changes in
the net foreign assets of the Federeal Reserve and the Bundesbank.

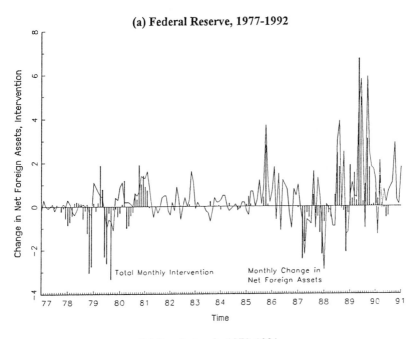

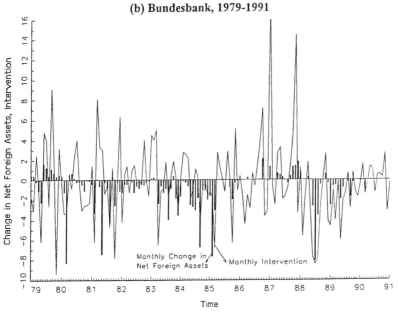

Figure 10.8: The relationship between changes in the net foreign assets and the domestic credit component of the monetary base.

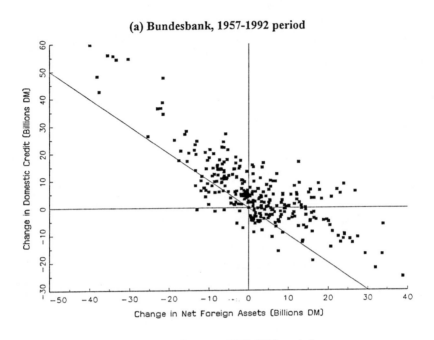

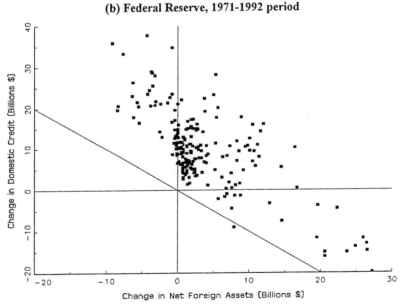

Figure 10.9: Long-run ineffectiveness of the Bundesbank's $/DM interventions.

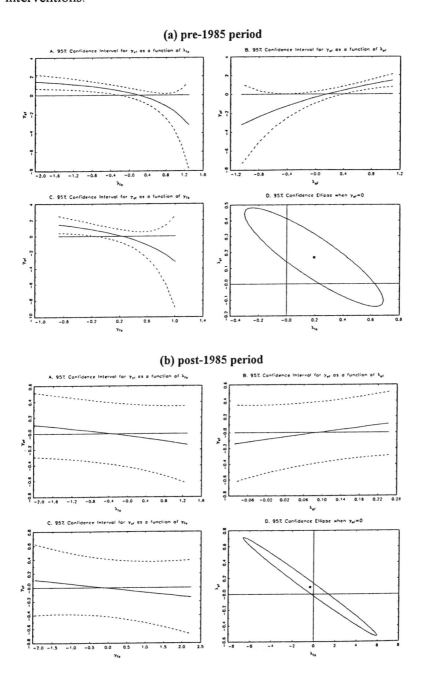

Figure 10.10: Long-run sterilization of Bundesbank interventions.

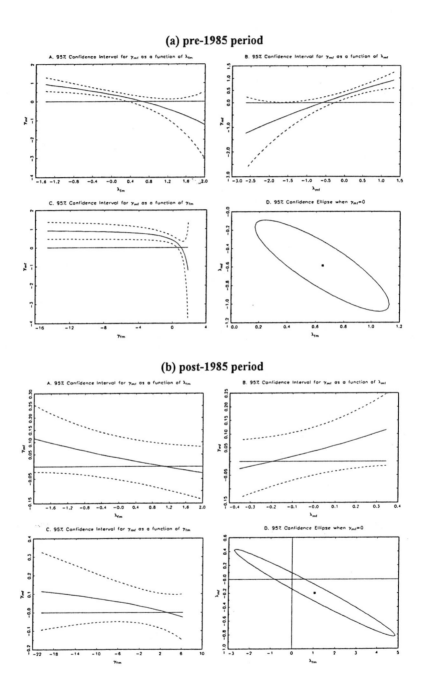

(a) pre-1985 period

(b) post-1985 period

Table 10.1: The long-run ineffectiveness of foreign exchange interventions in G-3 countries, two sub-periods (1973:1-1084:12, 1985:1-1992:12).

Bank, rate	Period	VAR Estimates			Structural Model Estimates			$\gamma_{ef}=0$ in 95% confidence interval			Estimates imposing $\gamma_{ef}=0$		
		σ^2_e	σ^2_i	cor_{ef}	σ^2_e	σ^2_f	cor_{gf}	λ_{if}	λ_{cf}	γ_{fe}	λ_{if}	λ_{cf}	γ_{fe}
BBK, $/DM	73:1-84:12	37.91	32.28	0.35	26.23	38.06	0.33	>-0.1	<0.35	>-0.09	0.19 (0.20)	0.17 (0.13)	0.23 (0.17)
FED, DM/$	73:1-84:12	17.92	31.45	0.02	28.46	37.92	0.52	>0.2	<-0.59	>0.08	**0.27 (0.13)**	**0.82 (0.36)**	**-0.39 (0.17)**
BOJ, $/¥	73:1-84:12	62.23	29.26	0.29	74.65	38.46	0.55	>-1,<-0.1	<0.1,>3.5	-	**1.18 (0.49)**	-0.15 (0.13)	**1.06 (0.48)**
FED, ¥/$	73:1-84:12	18.20	29.04	-0.03	27.76	39.55	0.06	>0.4	<0.04	>-0.04	0.04 (0.12)	0.15 (0.28)	-0.04 (0.20)
BOJ, DM/¥	73:1-84:12	65.27	27.47	0.13	89.39	52.36	0.77	>0.45	<-0.06	<0.84	**1.29 (0.54)**	**0.19 (0.10)**	**-1.31 (0.36)**
BBK, ¥/DM	73:1-84:12	38.75	27.09	0.24	25.40	48.72	0.03	>-0.1,<1.3	<0.86	-	0.46 (0.25)	-0.07 (0.12)	0.01 (0.16)
BBK, $/DM	85:1-92:12	99.04	32.36	0.17	189.1	46.21	-0.03	-	-	-	-0.33 (2.59)	0.09 (0.26)	-0.13 (3.47)
FED, DM/$	85:1-92:12	56.58	31.72	-0.15	71.65	46.98	-0.33	<0.4,>1	>-0.4,<-0.1	-	-1.48 (0.95)	0.43 (0.37)	-0.50 (0.66)
BOJ, $/¥	85:1-92:12	57.18	31.74	-0.08	74.50	46.27	0.20	-	-	-	-0.09 (0.67)	-0.02 (0.20)	0.33 (0.73)
FED, ¥/$	85:1-92:12	87.01	31.85	0.19	127.4	44.72	0.04	-	-	-	-0.34 (1.08)	0.11 (0.13)	0.11 (1.28)
BOJ, DM/¥	85:1-92:12	98.94	25.78	0.00	121.1	36.33	-0.23	-	-	-	-3.16 (2.91)	0.21 (0.19)	-0.76 (1.76)
BBK, ¥/DM	85:1-92:12	92.34	26.36	-0.02	129.4	37.21	-0.16	-	-	-	0.30 (1.19)	-0.03 (0.09)	-0.55 (1.49)

Key to Table: All results for the second moments are based on VAR's with six lags. σ^2_i denotes the variance estimate for variable i, cor_{ij} indicates the correlation between variables i and j. Variances and correlations are calculated for the residuals of the unrestricted VAR's and the shocks implied by the long-run covariance matrix of the estimated VAR (the spectral density matrix of the variables at frequency zero). The coefficient ranges in columns nine to eleven are those for which the long-run ineffectiveness proposition can not be rejected at the 95% level. The point estimates of the coefficients and their standard errors (in parentheses) implied by long-run ineffectiveness are reported in the last three columns.

Table 10.2: The long-run sterilization of foreign exchange interventions in G-3 countries, overall period (1973:1-1992:12) and two sub-periods (1973:1-1984:12, 1985:1-1992:12).

Country	Period	VAR Estimates			Structural Model Estimates			$\gamma_{mf}=0$ in 95% confidence interval			Estimates imposing $\gamma_{mf}=0$		
		σ_m^2	σ_f^2	cor_{mf}	σ_m^2	σ_f^2	cor_{mf}	λ_{fm}	λ_{mf}	γ_{fm}	λ_{fm}	λ_{mf}	γ_{fm}
Germany	73:1-92:12	72.42	41.77	0.01	67.67	15.64	0.35	>0.2	<-0.06	>-0.47	**0.83 (0.43)**	**-0.27 (0.14)**	1.50 (0.95)
U.S.A.	73:1-92:12	41.90	17.65	-0.22	43.59	7.52	-0.27	<0.0	>-0.09	<1.18	**-0.88 (0.41)**	0.07 (0.08)	-1.55 (1.16)
Japan	73:1-92:12	78.66	58.92	0.12	02.03	22.88	0.02	>-0.6,<0.8	>-0.4,<0.3	>-2.6,<3.4	0.05 (0.26)	0.06 (0.14)	0.11 (1.04)
Germany	73:1-84:12	38.10	38.72	0.13	26.64	16.78	0.63	>0.4	<-0.29	>0.72	**0.65 (0.20)**	**-0.59 (0.20)**	**0.99 (0.27)**
U.S.A.	73:1-84:12	17.93	12.71	-0.00	27.71	5.83	-0.07	>-1.2,<0.4	>-0.2,<0.4	>-3.5,<2.9	-0.28 (0.29)	0.14 (0.13)	-0.32 (1.10)
Japan	73:1-84:12	65.55	59.75	0.10	84.28	25.99	-0.42	<0.4	>-0.25	<0.99	-0.17 (0.26)	0.23 (0.20)	-1.35 (0.87)
Germany	85:1-92:12	101.9	42.56	-0.04	146.1	12.39	0.27	-	-	-	1.06 (1.56)	-0.20 (0.26)	3.20 (6.38)
U.S.A.	85:1-92:12	58.54	21.07	-0.27	68.64	9.72	-0.46	<0.6	>-0.14	<5.43	-1.49 (0.93)	0.11 (0.14)	-3.25 (2.53)
Japan	85:1-92:12	89.55	54.19	0.20	122.0	19.35	0.59	>-0.2	<0.19	>0.53	0.55 (0.46)	-0.09 (0.17)	**3.71 (1.82)**

Key to Table: All results for the second moments are based on VAR's with six lags. σ_i^2 denotes the variance estimate for variable i, cor_{ij} indicates the correlation between variables i and j. Variances and correlations are calculated for the residuals of the unrestricted VAR's and the shocks implied by the long-run covariance matrix of the estimated VAR (the spectral density matrix of the variables at frequency zero). The coefficient ranges in columns nine to eleven are those for which the long-run sterilization proposition can not be rejected at the 95% level. The point estimates of the coefficients and their standard errors are reported in the last three columns.

Table 10.3: The long-run ineffectiveness of foreign exchange intervention policies in EMS countries, second sub-sample (1985:1-1992:12).

Banks, rate	Period	VAR Estimates			Structural Model Estimates			$\gamma_{ef}=0$ in 95% confidence interval			Estimates imposing $\gamma_{ef}=0$		
		σ^2_e	σ^2_f	cor_{ef}	σ^2_e	σ^2_f	cor_{ef}	λ_{ie}	λ_{ef}	γ_{fe}	λ_{ie}	λ_{ef}	γ_{fe}
DEU,FRA	85:1-92:12	114.1	5.45	**0.08**	32.76	9.06	**-0.31**	-	-	-	-0.70 (4.21)	0.01 (0.01)	-1.12 (1.26)
FRA,DEU	85:1-92:12	100.1	5.42	**0.10**	134.9	8.95	0.07	-	-	-	0.23 (9.11)	0.00 (0.03)	1.10 (8.69)
DEU,ITA	85:1-92:12	87.7	10.10	**0.47**	68.97	18.09	0.76	no	no	-	**11.8 (3.31)**	-0.28 (0.23)	**2.88 (1.19)**
ITA,DEU	85:1-92:12	101.8	10.64	**0.51**	97.27	23.19	0.80	>-1.50	>0.09	-	**13.3 (4.67)**	-0.32 (0.43)	**3.37 (1.48)**
DEU,NDL	85:1-92:12	48.31	1.35	**0.20**	26.8	0.82	0.29	-	-	-	3.04 (8.35)	0.00 (0.01)	9.58 (9.20)
NDL,DEU	85:1-92:12	101.8	1.32	**-0.23**	138.2	1.09	-0.73	-	-	-	-73.9 (43.1)	0.01 (0.01)	**-92.3 (46.3)**
DEU,BEL	85:1-92:12	77.22	2.78	**0.23**	68.66	3.39	0.16	-	-	-	3.96 (6.90)	0.00 (0.01)	3.33 (7.01)
BEL,DEU	85:1-92:12	101.7	2.88	**0.05**	155.4	3.52	-0.03	-	-	-	-3.73 (20.7)	0.00 (0.02)	-1.47 (27.7)
DEU,DNK	85:1-92:12	121.4	3.97	**0.42**	02.68	4.43	0.21	-	-	-	-10.2 (12.2)	0.02 (0.01)	4.75 (7.35)
DNK,DEU	85:1-92:12	100.9	3.88	**0.12**	147.4	5.68	-0.09	-	-	-	-5.76 (15.8)	0.01 (0.02)	-2.43 (15.6)
DEU,IRE	85:1-92:12	97.48	11.89	**0.03**	89.43	15.06	0.12	-	-	-	0.77 (2.03)	-0.01 (0.03)	0.71 (2.33)
IRE,DEU	85:1-92:12	102.1	12.16	**0.22**	127.8	14.70	-0.21	-	-	-	-3.76 (5.76)	0.07 (0.06)	-1.79 (5.02)
DEU,GBR	88:1-92:12	185.4	17.81	**-0.29**	40.02	29.12	0.38	-	-	-	2.00 (3.80)	-0.04 (0.03)	1.83 (2.35)
GBR,DEU	85:1-92:12	101.5	21.18	**0.25**	145.3	30.92	0.32	-	-	-	1.01 (2.35)	0.01 (0.10)	1.49 (2.59)

Key to Table: All results for the second moments are based on VAR's with six lags. σ^2_i denotes the variance estimate for variable i, cor_{ij} indicates the correlation between variables i and j. Variances and correlations are calculated for the residuals of the unrestricted VAR's and the shocks implied by the long-run covariance matrix of the estimated VAR (the spectral density matrix of the variables at frequency zero). The coefficient ranges in columns nine to eleven are those for which the long-run independence proposition can not be rejected at the 95% level. The point estimates of the coefficients and their standard errors (in parentheses) implied by long-run independence are reported in the last three columns.

Table 10.4: The long-run sterilization of foreign exchange interventions in EMS countries, two sub-periods (1973:1-1984:12, 1985:1-1992:12).

Country	Period	VAR Estimates			Structural Model Estimates			$\gamma_{mf}=0$ in 95% confidence interval			Estimates imposing $\gamma_{mf}=0$		
		σ^2_m	σ^2_f	cor_{mf}	σ^2_m	σ^2_f	cor_{mf}	λ_{fm}	λ_{mf}	γ_{fm}	λ_{fm}	λ_{mf}	γ_{fm}
Germany	73:1-84:12	38.10	38.72	0.13	26.64	16.78	0.63	>0.40	<-0.29	>0.72	**0.65 (0.20)**	**-0.59 (0.20)**	**0.99 (0.27)**
France	73:1-84:12	104.0	47.41	-0.08	135.9	36.64	-0.70	<-0.20	>0.05	<-0.99	**-1.04 (0.53)**	0.19 (0.11)	**-2.60 (0.86)**
Italy	78:1-84:12	45.80	24.92	0.01	102.1	12.49	-0.08	-	-	-	-0.39 (0.77)	0.12 (0.22)	-0.67 (3.65)
Netherl.	73:1-84:12	57.24	25.83	0.08	39.14	15.87	-0.31	>-0.4,<1.2	>-0.2,<0.1	<0.38	0.45 (0.37)	-0.06 (0.07)	-0.76 (0.52)
Belgium	73:1-84:12	50.57	20.87	0.01	46.59	16.74	0.15	>-0.8,<1.6	>-0.2,<0.1	-	0.12 (0.46)	-0.02 (0.07)	0.41 (0.80)
Denmark	73:1-84:12	491.5	65.56	0.02	286.4	53.52	-0.53	<1.80	>-0.2	-	-1.05 (1.41)	0.02 (0.02)	**-2.82 (1.29)**
Ireland	73:1-84:12	86.52	45.13	0.16	72.01	30.92	0.26	>-0.60	>-0.3,<0.2	-	0.20 (0.38)	0.03 (0.10)	0.62 (0.60)
U.K.	n.a.	n.a.	n.a.	n.a.	n.a.	n.a.	**n.a.**	n.a.	n.a.	n.a.	n.a.	n.a.	n.a.
Germany	85:1-92:12	101.9	42.56	-0.04	146.1	12.39	0.27	-	-	-	1.06 (1.56)	-0.20 (0.26)	3.20 (6.38)
France	85:1-92:12	113.1	50.00	-0.32	30.92	21.65	0.23	>-1.20	<-0.27	>-0.58	-0.32 (0.43)	-0.08 (0.07)	0.33 (0.39)
Italy	85:1-92:12	91.93	21.36	0.06	79.57	16.42	0.48	-	-	-	0.83 (1.13)	-0.03 (0.06)	2.34 (1.57)
Netherl.	85:1-92:12	47.46	72.17	0.11	30.69	33.16	0.63	>0.00	<0.16	>0.31	0.25 (0.15)	-0.43 (0.32)	**0.58 (0.25)**
Belgium	85:1-92:12	76.69	20.96	-0.06	65.55	11.45	0.18	>-0.60	<0.01	-	1.36 (1.03)	-0.12 (0.07)	1.02 (1.81)
Denmark	85:1-92:12	120.7	173.7	0.16	124.4	140.0	0.14	-	-	-	0.35 (0.23)	-0.53 (0.51)	0.12 (0.34)
Ireland	85:1-92:12	96.32	43.51	0.30	87.35	23.56	0.48	>0.40	<0.01	>-0.13	**1.34 (0.56)**	-0.17 (0.14)	1.77 (0.98)
U.K.	88:1-92:12	174.9	32.09	-0.05	138.8	7.99	0.40	-	-	-	0.34 (1.60)	-0.02 (0.05)	6.89 (5.84)

Key to Table: All results for the second moments are based on VAR's with six lags. σ^2_i denotes the variance estimate for variable i, cor_{ij} indicates the correlation between variables i and j. Variances and correlations are calculated for the residuals of the unrestricted VAR's and the shocks implied by the long-run covariance matrix of the estimated VAR (the spectral density matrix of the variables at frequency zero). The coefficient ranges in columns nine to eleven are those for which the long-run sterilization proposition can not be rejected at the 95% level. The point estimates of the coefficients and their standard errors (in parentheses) implied by long-run sterilization are reported in the last three columns.

References

Bordo, M.D., and A.J. Schwartz (1991), "What has Foreign Exchange Market Intervention Since Plaza Agreement Accomplished?" *Open Economies Review,* 2, pp. 39-64.

Catte, P., G. Galli, and S. Rebecchini (1992), "Concerted Intervention and the Dollar: An Analysis of Daily Data," Mimeo.

Dominguez, K.M. (1990), "Market Response to Coordinated Central Bank Intervention," *Carnegie Rochester Conference Series on Public Policy,* 32, pp. 121-163.

Dominguez, K.M. (1992), "Does Central Bank Intervention Increase the Volatility of Foreign Exchange Rates?" Harvard University, Mimeo.

Dominguez, K.M., and J. Frankel (1992), "Does Foreign Exchange Intervention Matter? Disentangling the Portfolio and Expectations Effect for the Mark," University of California at Berkeley, Mimeo.

Dominguez, K.M., and J. Frankel (1993), "Does Foreign Exchange Intervention Matter? The Portfolio Effect," *American Economic Review,* 83, pp. 1356-1369.

Edison, H. (1993), "The Effectiveness of Central Bank Intervention: A Survey of the post-1982 Literature," Division of International Finance, Board of Governors of the Federal Reserve System, Mimeo.

Funabashi, Y. (1988), *Managing the Dollar: From Plaza to the Louvre,* Institute for International Economics, Washington D.C..

Gaiotti, E., P. Giucca, and S. Micossi (1989), "Cooperation in Managing the Dollar (1985-1987): Interventions in Foreign Exchange Markets and Interest Rates," Banca d'Italia, *Discussion Paper,* N° 119.

Ghosh, A.R. (1992), "Is it Signaling? Exchange Intervention and the Dollar-Deutsche mark Rate," *Journal of International Economics,* 32, pp. 201-220.

Hagen, J. von (1989), "Monetary Targeting with Exchange Rate Constraints: The Bundesbank in the 1980s," *Review, Federal Reserve Bank of St. Louis,* September/October.

Herring, R.J., and R. Marston (1977a), *National Monetary Policies and International Financial Markets,* North-Holland Publishers, Amsterdam.

Herring, R.J., and R. Marston (1977b), "Sterilization Policy: the Trade-off Between Monetary Autonomy and Control Over Foreign Exchange Reserves," *European Economic Review.*

Humpage, O.F. (1991), "Central Bank Intervention: Recent Literature, Continuing Controversy," *Economic Review, Federal Reserve Bank of Cleveland,* 27, pp. 12-26.

Jurgensen, P. (Chairman) (1983), "Report of the Working Group on Exchange Market Intervention," Mimeo.

Kaminsky, G.L., and K.K. Lewis (1992), "Does Foreign Exchange Intervention Signal Future Monetary Policy," Division of International Finance, Board of Governors of the Federal Reserve System, Mimeo.

King, R.G., and M.W. Watson (1992), "Testing Long Run Neutrality," NBER, *Working Paper,* N° 4156.

Klein, M., and E. Rosengren (1991), "Foreign Exchange Intervention as a Signal of Monetary Policy," *New England Economic Review,* (May/June), pp. 39-50.

Lewis, K.K. (1992), "Are Foreign Exchange Intervention and Monetary Policy Related and Does It Really Matter," *NBER Discussion Paper,* N° 4377.

Mastropasqua, C., S. Micossi, and R. Rinaldi (1988), "Interventions, Sterilization and Monetary Policy in the European Monetary System Countries, 1979-87," in Giavazzi, F., S. Micossi and M. Miller (eds), *The European Monetary System,* Cambridge University Press, pp. 252-287.

McKinnon, R.I. (1993), "The Rules of the Game: International Money from a Historical Perspective," *Journal of Economic Literature,* 31, pp. 1-44.

Micossi, S. (1985), "The Intervention and Financing Mechanisms of the EMS and the Role of the ECU," *Banca Nazionale del Lavoro Quarterly Review,* 155, pp. 327-345.

Mussa, M. (1981), "The Role of Official Intervention," Group of Thirty, *Occasional Paper,* N° 6, New-York.

Neumann, M.J.M. (1984), "Intervention in the Mark/Dollar Market: the Authorities' Reaction Function," *Journal of International Money and Finance,* 3, pp. 223-239.

Neumann, M.J.M., and J. von Hagen (1991), "Monetary Policy in Germany," in: Fratianni, M., and D. Salvatore (eds), *Handbook of Monetary Economics,* Greenwood Press.

Obstfeld, M. (1983), "Exchange Rates, Inflation and the Sterilization Problem: Germany 1975-1981," *European Economic Review*, 21, pp. 161-189.

Obstfeld, M. (1988), "The Effectiveness of Foreign Exchange Intervention: Recent Experience," *NBER Discussion Paper*, N° 2796.

Obstfeld, M. (1990), "The Effectiveness of Foreign Exchange Intervention: Recent Experience: 1985-1988," in Branson, W., J. Frenkel, and M. Goldstein (eds), *International Policy Coordination and Exchange Rate Fluctuations*, NBER Conference Volume, Chicago University Press, Chicago.

Rogoff, K. (1984), "On the Effects of Sterilized Intervention: An Analysis of Weekly Data," *Journal of Monetary Economics*, 14, pp. 133-150.

Takagi, S. (1991), "Foreign Exchange Market Intervention and Domestic Monetary Control in Japan, 1973-89," *Japan and the World Economy*, 90, pp. 147-180.

Truman, E.M. (1992), "Comments on paper entitled: 'Concerted Intervention and the Dollar: An Analysis of Daily Data'," Mimeo.

Weber, A.A. (1991), "Credibility, Reputation and the European Monetary System," *Economic Policy*, 12, pp. 57-102.

Weber, A.A. (1994a), "Testing Long-run Neutrality: Empirical Evidence From the G7-Countries with Special Emphasis on Germany," *Carnegie Rochester Conference Series*, 41, forthcoming.

Weber, A.A. (1994b), "Foreign Exchange Intervention and International Policy Coordination: Comparing the G-3 and EMS Experience," *CEPR Discussion Paper*, N° 1038.

p 202 :)   *235 - 42*   EU
                                                              USA
⤷ **Discussion**   Japan
_____   Germany
                                                              ES8
                                                              F3 /
CHRISTIAN BORDES   F33

This is a very interesting and stimulating paper dealing with several important issues: the effectiveness of interventions on the exchange market; the coordination of economic policy; the origins of exchange market crises; the nature of the EMS; monetary cooperation inside G3 countries; etc. Until now, these issues have been analysed empirically separately. In my view, the main merit of the paper is to analyse these different topics inside a common unified framework - the methodology proposed by King and Watson (1992) to estimate a simultaneous two equations system. In this respect, this paper marks a major improvement upon the existing literature. However, in my eyes, the attempt is not totally successful. What makes the force of the paper is also its main drawback; the methodology used has its own limits: a two equations system is too narrow to encompass all the issues examined.

I will organise my comments in the following way. First, I will emphasize what is in my opinion the main merit of the paper: I will try to show in what respect the present paper bypasses certain limits of the existing literature. Then, I will turn to what I consider as some inadequacies of the paper.

1 Methodology

1.1 *A general model*
Let us start with the following two equations model.

$$(1) \quad \Delta x_t = \lambda_{xy}\Delta y_t + \sum_{j=1}^{p}\alpha_{xx}^j\Delta x_{t-j} + \sum_{j=1}^{p}\alpha_{xy}^j\Delta y_{t-j} + \varepsilon_t^x$$

$$(2) \quad \Delta y_t = \lambda_{yx}\Delta x_t + \sum_{j=1}^{p}\alpha_{xx}^j\Delta x_{t-j} + \sum_{j=1}^{p}\alpha_{yx}^j\Delta y_{t-j} + \varepsilon_t^y$$

This simultaneous equation system is econometrically unidentified. Therefore, additional restrictions are required in order to identify it. Several restrictions have been used in the existing literature dealing with interventions or with the characteristics of exchange rate regimes.

1.2 *The focus on a single identifying restriction*
Traditionally one has focused on a single identifying restriction. It has been supposed that:

• *one of the two variables is exogeneous in the short-run:* in this case the general model is transformed into the following single equation model:

$$(1a) \quad \Delta x_t = \lambda_{xy}\Delta y_t + \sum_{j=1}^{p}\alpha_{xx}^j\Delta x_{t-j} + \sum_{j=1}^{p}\alpha_{xy}^j\Delta y_{t-j} + \varepsilon_t^x$$

• *one of the two variables is exogeneous in the long run:* in this case one adds to equations (1) and (2) the additional constraint (in the case where y_t is supposed to be the exogeneous variable):

$$\gamma_{yx} = \frac{\alpha_{yx}(L)}{\alpha_{yy}(L)} = 0$$

with:

$$\alpha_{yx}(L) = \lambda_{yx} + \sum_{j=1}^{p} \alpha_{xy}^{j} L^{j}$$

$$\alpha_{yy}(L) = 1 - \sum_{j=1}^{p} \alpha_{yy}^{j} L^{j}$$

• *one (at least) of the two variables is predetermined:* in this case one adds the following contraint $\lambda_{yx} = 0$ and one gets the following recursive two equations system:

(1b) $\quad \Delta x_t = \lambda_{xy} \Delta y_t + \sum_{j=1}^{p} \alpha_{xx}^{j} \Delta x_{t-j} + \sum_{j=1}^{p} \alpha_{xy}^{j} \Delta y_{t-j} + \varepsilon_t^x$

(2b) $\quad \Delta y_t = \sum_{j=1}^{p} \alpha_{xx}^{j} \Delta x_{t-j} + \sum_{j=1}^{p} \alpha_{yx}^{j} \Delta y_{t-j} + \varepsilon_t^y$

If one uses simultaneously $\lambda_{xy} = 0$ and $\lambda_{yx} = 0$, one gets:

(1c) $\quad \Delta x_t = \sum_{j=1}^{p} \alpha_{xx}^{j} \Delta x_{t-j} + \sum_{j=1}^{p} \alpha_{xy}^{j} \Delta y_{t-j} + \varepsilon_t^x$

(2c) $\quad \Delta y_t = \sum_{j=1}^{p} \alpha_{yy}^{j} \Delta x_{t-j} + \sum_{j=1}^{p} \alpha_{yx}^{j} \Delta y_{t-j} + \varepsilon_t^y$

The first two possibilities have been used in the existing literature on the question of intervention whereas the last one has been used in the existing literature on the (symmetric or asymmetric) character of the EMS: one tests the hypothesis of one country dominance by using Granger-type causality tests; this method is rather weak, for example, it does not take into account interdependencies between the error terms.

1.3 *The focus on a wide range of identifying restrictions*

The main originality of Axel Weber's paper is to apply the methodology proposed by King and Watson (1992) to the analysis of all these questions: rather than focusing on a single identifying restriction - as in past studies, one reports results for a wide range of identifying restrictions by iterating each of the four reaction coefficients - λ_{xy}, λ_{yx}, γ_{xy}, and γ_{yx} - within a reasonable range, obtaining estimates each time of the remaining parameters and their standard errors.

Let us consider two countries (the home country and the foreign country) and the following variables: Δe: the change in the exchange rate between the currencies of the two countries; Δf the change in the foreign exchange reserves (or the external component of the monetary base) of the home country; Δm: the change in the money supply of the home country; Δi the change in the interest rate of the home country; Δf^*, Δm^* and Δi^* are similar variables for the foreign country.

Axel Weber's paper can be considered as a systematic application of the procedure proposed by King and Watson to most of the couples of variables which can be determined inside this set of variables either for two of the G3 countries, or for two of the EMS countries.

	INTERVENTIONS			COORDINATION	
	Sterilization	Coordination	Effectiveness		
Δe			■		
Δf	■	■	■		
Δm	■				■
Δi		■		■	
Δf^*					
Δm^*					
Δi^*				■	■

One must have in mind that these variables are simultaneously determined, for example, according to the monetary approach of exchange rate determination. Therefore, one implicit assumption of the paper is that the relationship between two variables can be examined without taking into account the level of the others as well as some supplementary variables -such as economic activity- which are left aside. Indeed, this is a strong hypothesis because, for example, it is generally admitted that developments on exchange markets since the beginning of the eighties can largely be explained by the non-synchronisation of business cycles.

The main conclusions are the following:

1) Concerning the effectiveness of interventions: interventions by G3 countries or by EMS countries have been ineffective in the long run (i.e. they did not significantly reverse the trend of bilateral exchange rates);

2) Concerning the sterilization of interventions: there is a predominant use of sterilized interventions inside the G3 or inside the EMS;

3) Concerning the coordination of interventions: there is evidence in support of significant coordination of interventions between the three largest EMS countries and between the Bundesbank and the Federal Reserve; much less evidence of coordination between these two central banks and the Bank of Japan;

4) Concerning the coordination of monetary policies: monetary policies have not been coordinated, except in the case of France and Germany.

As from now, one must notice that these conclusions are not fundamentally different from the ones which emerged from the existing literature. In some respect, the present study can be considered as a confirmation of the results of past studies using recent developments in econometric techniques.

2 The main limits

2.1 *The effectiveness of exchange-market interventions*
First, Axel Weber makes the commonly accepted assumption according to which central banks « lean with the wind » and resist to the market trend to slow down the evolution of a currency, in one direction or another. However, in some circumstances, central banks decide to « lean with the wind » when the wind leans in the good direction. For example, during the autumn of 1984, the Bundesbank intervened on the exchange market just after the Deutsche mark registered a brief improvement.

Second, in traditional studies the one acceptable yardstick by which interventions are judged is profitability. This criteria is adapted in the present study by considering if there is a reversal in the trend of bilateral exchange rates following the intervention. In any case, a serious difficulty is due to the fact that the results obtained will depend crucially on the length of the time horizon. For instance, interventions in support of the pound prior to IMF negotiations appeared unprofitable (i.e., ineffective) at the time when sterling was sinking, profitable (i.e., effective) during the strong petro-pound of early 1980s, but ineffective again by December 1982. These changes are inconvenient, but surely similar to those faced by any portfolio manager, whose performance is judged not merely by the movement of the securities he has purchased in a particular year or quarter, but by the movement of those he has purchased in earlier periods. In the central bank case, performance has to be judged not merely when the intervention is underlaken (or during the sixth following months as in the present study) but in all subsequent periods, so long as there is an outstanding position.

2.2 *The limits inherent to the use of a « bivariate » model*
I do not think that a bivariate model is an appropriate framework to analyze all the questions examined in the paper. I will illustrate this point with some examples.

- First, let us consider the question of the effectiveness of interventions on the DM/dollar exchange rate. Axel Weber analyses this question with two bivariate models which are estimated separately:

1) one for Germany:

$$(1G) \quad \Delta\left[\frac{\$}{DM}\right]_t = \lambda_{xy}\Delta f_t^G + \sum_{j=1}^{p}\alpha_{xx}^j\Delta\left[\frac{\$}{DM}\right]_t + \sum_{j=1}^{p}\alpha_{xy}^j\Delta f_{t-j}^G + \varepsilon_t^x$$

$$(2G) \quad \Delta f_t = \lambda_{yx}\Delta\left[\frac{\$}{DM}\right]_t + \sum_{j=1}^{p}\alpha_{yy}^j\Delta f_{t-j} + \sum_{j=1}^{p}\alpha_{yx}^j\Delta\left[\frac{\$}{DM}\right]_{t-j} + \varepsilon_t^y$$

2) one for the US:

$$(1US) \quad \Delta\left[\frac{DM}{\$}\right]_t = \lambda_{xy}\Delta f_t^{US} + \sum_{j=1}^{p}\alpha_{xx}^j\Delta\left[\frac{DM}{\$}\right]_t + \sum_{j=1}^{p}\alpha_{xy}^j\Delta f_{t-j}^{US} + \varepsilon_t^x$$

$$(2US) \quad \Delta f_t^{US} = \lambda_{yx}\Delta\left[\frac{DM}{\$}\right]_t + \sum_{j=1}^{p}\alpha_{yy}^j\Delta f_{t-j}^{US} + \sum_{j=1}^{p}\alpha_{yx}^j\Delta\left[\frac{DM}{US}\right]_{t-j} + \varepsilon_t^y$$

I am a bit puzzled by this procedure, all the more so that one of the conclusions of the paper is that the Bundesbank and the Fed coordinate their interventions. Is it possible to analyse the effectiveness of interventions on the $ - DM market leaving aside either the Fed - as in the first model - or the Bundesbank - as in the second model? I think a trivariate system - with one equation for the exchange rate and the two other ones relative to the amount of foreign reserves in each country - would be more appropriate (while being conscious of the difficulties faced to implement such a procedure).

I will take the question of the « symmetric » or « asymmetric » character of the EMS as a second example of the limit of the bivariate model. Once more, I think that a bivariate model is not appropriate to examine the relationships between the interest rates of the EMS member countries and to evaluate its symmetrical or asymmetrical nature. Indeed, such an analysis cannot be made by ignoring completely the relationships existing between, for example, these rates and the interest rates in the rest of the world. The test of the hypothesis of German dominance must be implemented with trivariate models. This is a major conclusion of a controversy which took place in a series of papers recently published in the *Journal of Money, Credit and Banking* (see Bordes, et al. (1994)). The studies using the trivariate autoregressive model lead to divergent conclusions from the works using the bivariate autoregressive model. More precisely, they reject the hypothesis of German dominance which is not rejected in the context of bivariate systems.

2.3 *The origin of exchange crisis in the EMS*

According to Axel Weber, one of the main implications of his empirical results is relative to the deficiencies of all managed exchange rate systems; such systems allow each participating central bank to choose its particular trade-off between monetary autonomy and exchange rate fixity. In the case of the EMS the rules of the game would have been violated by the Bundesbank and by other central banks. Therefore, the main reason of the EMS crisis would have been the insufficient coordination of monetary policies. However, this implication cannot be totally accepted on the basis of the results proposed by the paper. It appears clearly that the Bundesbank and the Banque de France have coordinated their policies. Therefore, it is difficult to reconcile the main results of the paper with the 1993 crisis of the EMS.

References

Bordes, C., E. Girardin, and V. Marimoutou (1994), "Has the EMS become asymmetric?" presented at the *Society of Economic Dynamics and Control, Annual Meeting*, University of California, Los Angeles, July.

Humpage, O.F. (1991), "Central-Bank Intervention: Recent Literature, Continuing Controversy," *Economic Review, Federal Reserve Bank of Cleveland*, Quarter 2, pp. 12-26.

Mayer, H., and H. Taguchi (1983), "Official Intervention in the Exchange Markets: Stabilising or Destabilising?" *BIS Economic Papers*, N° 6, March.

Exchange Rate Stability and European Construction

$243 - 49$

EU
$F33$
$F31$
$F36$

1 Introduction

My presentation is devoted less to technical issues than to a general analysis of progress towards exchange rate stability in the European Union and of the functioning of the EMS since the fluctuation bands were enlarged from 2.25% to 2.50%. It is designed to stimulate a general discussion on monetary union issues at the end of this colloquium. The topic I would like to discuss is based on a reasonably optimistic view of the present monetary situation and of exchange rate stability among the countries participating in the ERM and, more generally, among the EMS countries.

In this respect, there are two observations to be made:

- the Common Market was built up on the principle of exchange rate stability and the various mechanisms of the European Union, such as the single market and the Community budget, cannot work properly unless this stability is a reality.

- the fact that, in the end, exchange rate stability was not endangered by the widening of the fluctuation bands in August 1993. Despite such a profound change, the EMS has proven its robustness, even without the support of the fundamental rule applied since the beginning that defines a 2.25% margin for exchange rate fluctuations. This proves that the EMS is not a throwback to the past, an anachronistic construction, an artificial mechanism or an abnormal institution. On the contrary, it is one of the fundamental elements of the Economic Union.

2 Exchange rate stability is a prerequisite for European construction

The goal of exchange rate stability, which will definitively be achieved with monetary union, has been a permanent feature of European construction throughout four decades of monetary history. In 1957, the Treaty of Rome set the fixity of currency parities as a fundamental objective and Article 107 qualified the exchange rate policy of each Member State as a « matter of common interest ».

This principle of exchange rate stability was obvious as the time, but the matter was important enough to be explicitly spelled out in the Treaty. At the end of the sixties, the Barre Plan and the Werner Report called for Economic and monetary Union to be achieved by 1980. The creation of the « Snake » was in line with this aim and was designed to limit the impact of the floating rates resulting from the collapse of the Bretton-Woods system.

About 15 years after the passing of the deadline for monetary union set by the Werner Report, it is interesting to analyze why it was not met.

I see three reasons :

- the target was very ambitious, given the prevailing situation in Europe at the time,

- economic integration was certainly less advanced than it is now,

- the two oil shocks and the various ways the different countries dealt with them created a strongly adverse environment.

The EMS created in 1979 built on the experience of the « Snake » and anticipated major improvements in inflation, competitiveness and exchange rate stability.

My personal view is that these improvements were not fundamentally jeopardized by the 1992-1993 crisis nor by the widening of the bands in August 1993. On the contrary, the latter move was accompanied by a strong confirmation that the parities were appropriate. The widening created a two-way risk for market operators and helped to discourage speculation. This made it possible for the majority of the European countries to continue with their prudent and gradual monetary policies.

Today, as in the past, exchange rate stability remains a key element of European construction. I see two main reasons for this:

2.1 *Trade between the European countries is highly integrated*
The Member States of the European Union have an obvious interest in maintaining exchange rate stability because their economies are already

largely open to foreign trade and highly integrated in the single European market.

The degree of openness is measured by the ratio of foreign trade to GDP. This ratio ranges from 20% to 25% in France, Germany, the UK and Italy. In some smaller European countries it exceeds 50%, with ratios of 50% in the Netherlands, 58% in Ireland and 68% in Belgium. By comparison the same ratio is only 9% in Japan and 11% in the United States. The foreign trade of European countries is also highly concentrated on the European Union: 2/3 of the total in France in 1992 by comparison to only 30% in the late fifties; 50% in Germany by comparison to 1/3 in the late fifties.

In 1992, intra-European trade was equivalent to 40% of GDP in Belgium, 15% in France, 13% in Germany and 9% in Italy.

This means that exchange rate fluctuations, especially those of European currencies, have a strong impact not only on the trade balance of the Member States but also on their GDP itself.

2.2 *These countries are competing with each other*
As well as being higly integrated, the economies inside the European Union are also locked in keen competition against each other.

Intra-Union trade mainly involves industrial goods, such as machines and automobiles, for which the competition is very severe.

Industrial products represent 2/3 of overall intra-Union trade. By contrast, the Union's trade with non-European countries mainly involves non-manufactured products for which the competition among the European countries is less intense.

In services, and in the banking and financial industry in particular, the competition among the main companies and financial centres is also very intense.

The keen competition in the past was made even more intense by recent developments in the institutional framework, and especially the implementation of the single market for financial services in January 1993, which abolished borders and lifted technical and regulatory obstacles. Furthermore, some steps were taken to harmonize the tax system.

The fact that Member States no longer have any significant means to protect themselves from competition coming from the other Member States makes exchange rate instability unacceptable because it would create a totally artificial segmentation of the single market.

The single market is the result of an ambitious process of legal and regulatory harmonization aimed at abolishing, or at least reducing, the old invisible barriers. It is inconceivable that exchange rates, which are a basic element of price formation and which were fairly stable throughout the period of preparation for the single market, should now be left to float freely. If they were, the result would be the creation of a new set of artificial barriers.

European companies needed a unified market to expand. When the single market was planned an organized, the EMS was stable. We must ensure that this situation continues today and in the future. Otherwise, the single market would be in great danger and the whole European edifice would be under threat as the common agricultural policy, the Community budget and the other European institutions could not work properly with floating exchange rates.

To conclude these macroeconomic considerations, I would like to stress that economic integration in Europe is much deeper and very different from that prevailing in North America, which is frequently cited as an example of large trade flows taking place among countries with floating exchange rates. In fact, the economies of the USA, Canada and Mexico are largely complementary and they rarely compete on the same products as is the case in Europe. In such a situation, floating exchange rates are certainly less destabilizing and more acceptable. However, after the NAFTA treaty was signed, the three member countries started to work towards a more orderly arrangement in the monetary field.

This proves that the development of a large integrated market cannot be envisaged without a certain degree of monetary organization. In Europe, we have been convinced of this from the beginning.

3 Exchange rate stability in Europe after the widening of the ERM bands

Despite the widening of the fluctuation margins in August 1993, exchange rate stability has been maintained inside the ERM.

In theory, the decision to widen the fluctuation bands from 2.25% to 15% could have changed the direction of monetary policies. Even though the parities were left unchanged, the member countries could have used the room for manoeuvre allowed by the agreement to implement a less vigilant monetary policy.

Things turned out differently in the end, as none of the ERM countries engaged in a counter-productive round of competitive devaluation.

With the appropriateness of the parities reaffirmed, the bands appeared more as a move to fight off speculative attacks than as a reorientation of macro-economic policies.

Finally, the monetary credibility of the ERM has largely been maintained and probably even reinforced.

3.1 *Short-term interest rate policy*

The gradual reduction of interest rates in all the ERM countries helped to ease monetary constraints without jeopardizing exchange rate stability.

Rather than commenting on the downwards trend of interest rates in Germany and the other ERM countries, I will focus on only a few points:

The pace of reduction turned out to be quite rapid, with the call money rate being cut by 75 basis points during the second half of 1993 and by a further 120 basis points in the first half of 1994.

All in all, the drop was nearly two full percentage points in one year. The reduction of the 3-month PIBOR also illustrates the rapid decline in French short-term rates. It fell 12% in January 1993 to 7.5% in the middle of 1993 and then to 6.20% at the end of 1993. It now stands at 5.50%.

The present level of short-term rates does not seem to be an obstacle to investment in France. The large majority of businessmen feel that interest rates are no longer a constraint on investment (see Banque de France, *Monthly Bulletin,* April 1994, p. 157). Furthermore, the trend in credit is negative due to a low demand for funds from the leading companies, which currently appear to have very large cash holdings.

In the U.K., the rapid decline of interest rates decided in September 1992, after the pound left the ERM, ended in 1993 and the Bank of England's interest rate policy has been cautious since then. The spread between UK and French short-term rates was about 5 percentage points in January 1993. It has disappeared today.

In Italy, the dicount rate was more or less cut in half from 15% in october 1992 to 7% today.

3.2 *Long-term rates*

Monetary policy in Europe since August 1993 has helped maintain and even strengthen the global credibility of our currencies. After the widening of the fluctuation bands, long term interest rates declined continuously until February 1994, when the Fed started to raise its own short-term rates. In January 1994, long-term rates in France and Germany had reached a historic low of 5.5%, which was the lowest yield in France in thirteen years. Continental European countries were unable to prevent a sharp rebound in their long-term rates when the market deteriorated after February 1994. However, a comparison with some floating-rate countries, like the UK, Sweden and Canada, shows that the impact of the bond market crisis was much less pronounced in the countries with a more permanent commitment to monetary stability, like Germany, the Netherlands or France.

3.3 *Exchange rates*
Interest rate reductions in the ERM have been made in such a way that the discrepancies between the stated parities and actual exchange rates in the ERM countries have been slight. The present grid of exchange rate parities inside the ERM seems economically sound. The devaluations or depreciations in 1992 and 1993, especially in the case of the pound, the peseta and the escudo, offset the divergent trends in prices and costs between 1987 and 1992. There are no signs that the depreciation of these currencies was excessive. Exchange rate movements merely restored the competitiveness pattern established 6 years earlier. Only the lira seems to be under-valued in comparison to the 1986-1987 parities. But in my view, this appears to be more the result of market expectations than any deliberate policy by the Italian authorities, as real interest rates in Italy have been kept rather high and currently stand at about 3.5%. All in all, the grid of exchange rate parities inside the ERM has proven to be satisfactory and there has been only limited volatility of exchange rates despite the widening of the fluctuation margins. To be sure, a positive assessment of this period is fully warranted.

3.4 *Prospects for the future*
Foreign exchange rates are always difficult to forecast and central banks are traditionally very cautious in this area. However, one can express a reasonably positive opinion about the future:
   - Price stability has been more or less achieved, or is about to be achieved, in most countries.
   - Eight currencies and nine countries continue to manage their exchange rate carefully in the ERM.
   - Economic integration is firmly established and economic convergence has come a long way among the ERM countries.

- Economic disparities remain limited in most cases.

- The recovery appears to be well under way in continental Europe, and this will allow more flexibility for the conduct of macroeconomic policies and for further economic integration in Europe.

- Finally, technical work on Stage II is proceeding actively and the recent creation of the EMI will certainly give it more impetus. No doubt the technical preparations for Stage III will be made on schedule.

I should like to conclude with the idea that exchange rate stability is still a reality in Europe despite the succession of crises in 1992 and 1993. In the end, the widening of the margins has given the system more flexibility, but it did not lead to freely floating rates, as was certainly possible from a technical point of view. The ERM continues to operate in a more flexible mode but it still produces definite results in terms of stability. Thus, the process of monetary union remains on track and I should think that its achievement is more a political question than a technical one. Monetary integration does not precede economic integration. It parallels it and underpins it.

Index of names